THE ASCENTS OF JAMES
History and Theology of a Jewish-Christian Community

SOCIETY
OF BIBLICAL
LITERATURE

DISSERTATION SERIES
J. J. M. Roberts, Old Testament Editor
Charles Talbert, New Testament Editor

Number 112

THE ASCENTS OF JAMES
History and Theology of a Jewish-Christian Community

by
Robert E. Van Voorst

Robert E. Van Voorst

THE ASCENTS OF JAMES
History and Theology
of a Jewish-Christian Community

Scholars Press
Atlanta, Georgia

BS
2880
.A872
v36
1989

THE ASCENTS OF JAMES

Robert E. Van Voorst

Ph.D., 1988
Union Theological Seminary
(New York)

Advisor:
J. Louis Martyn

Grateful acknowledgment is given to Glenn A. Koch for permission
to reprint his translation of Epiphanius' *Panarion* 30.16.6-9.

Library of Congress Cataloging in Publication Data

Van Voorst, Robert E.
    The Ascents of James ; History and Theology of a Jewish-
Christian Community / Robert E. Van Voorst.
        p. cm -- (Dissertation series / Society of Biblical
    Literature : no. 112)
        Translations of the Latin and Syriac versions of the Ascents of
    James. English rendition of the passages from Book 1 of the Latin
    and Syriac versions of the Pseudo-Clementine Recognitions which in
    the translator's view reflect the lost original of the Ascents of
    James.
        Bibliography: p.
        ISBN 1-55540-293-3 (alk. paper). -- ISBN 1-55540-294-1 (pbk. :
    alk. paper)
        1. Ascents of James--Commentaries. 2. Recognitions (Pseudo
    -Clementine)--Commentaries. I. Recognitions (Pseudo-Clementine).
    Book 1. English. Selection. 1989. II. Title. III. Series:
    Dissertation series (Society of Biblical Literature) ; no. 112.
    BS2880.A87V36 1989
    229'.92--dc   88-31163
                                                         CIP

Printed in the United States of America
on acid-free paper

To Mary

Yahweh gives the childless woman a home,
making her the joyous mother of children.
(Psalm 113:8)

CONTENTS

PREFACE   ix

ABBREVIATIONS   xi

TABLES   xi

I.   THE HISTORY OF RESEARCH
     INTO *RECOGNITIONS* 1.33-71   1
     Introduction   1
     Early Research into the Pseudo-Clementines   3
     F. C. Baur and the Tübingen School   6
     Opponents of the Tübingen School   11
     Modern Opponents of Source Criticism   17
     Recent Proponents of Source Criticism   19
     Summary of the History of Research   26
     Plan of the Present Work   26

II. ISOLATION AND IDENTIFICATION
     OF THE SOURCE   29
     Introduction   29
     Isolation of the Source   30
     The Unity of the Source   41
     General Opposition to Source Criticism   42
     Identification of the Source   43
     Conclusion   46

III. TRANSLATIONS OF
     THE ASCENTS OF JAMES   47
     Introduction   47
     Translations of *The Ascents of James*   48

IV. A COMMENTARY ON
 THE ASCENTS OF JAMES   77
 Introduction   77
 Provenance   78
 Authorship   78
 Date   79
 Occasion   80
 Notes to *R* 1.33.3 - 1.44.3   81
 Comment on *R* 1.33.3 - 1.44.3   115
 Notes to *R* 1.55 - 65   118
 Comment on *R* 1.55 - 65   144
 Notes to *R* 1.66 - 71   145
 Comment on *R* 1.66 - 71   160

V. MAJOR ISSUES IN THE INTERPRETATION OF
 THE ASCENTS OF JAMES   163
 The Christology of *The Ascents of James*   163
 The Historicity of *The Ascents of James*   170
 The Community of *The Ascents of James*   174
 Summary and Conclusion   180

BIBLIOGRAPHY   181

INDEX OF PASSAGES   193

PREFACE

This study is an examination of *The Ascents of James*, a source of the Pseudo-Clementine *Recognitions*. It was originally submitted as a Ph.D. dissertation to the faculty of Union Theological Seminary in New York City under the title "*The Ascents of James*: History and Theology of a Jewish-Christian Community as Reflected in the Pseudo-Clementine *Recognitions* 1.33-71."

Research into *The Ascents of James* began in the last century and still continues today. It has been limited, however, in method and scope. This study provides a full analysis of this document, including several items lacking in previous research: a complete history of research; a thorough isolation of the source; a fresh translation of its Latin version and the first translation of the Syriac version; a complete commentary; finally, a rather full exploration of the relationship of this document to other forms of first and second-century Christianity. By this analysis of a fascinating Jewish-Christian document, I hope to contribute to our knowledge of Jewish Christianity in the second century. I also hope to contribute in a lesser way to our understanding of the relationship of Jewish Christianity to the Great Church, to early Judaism, and to the New Testament.

I should like to thank the many people who contributed to my moral and financial support during my graduate study at Union. My parents, Robert and Donna Van Voorst, and parents-in-law, James and Genevieve Bos, gave constant support. Robert A. Coughenour and the John and Mattie Osterhaven Fund provided helpful grants as I began my program. Union Seminary furnished a liberal fellowship throughout my doctoral study. The consistory and congregation of the Rochester Reformed Church, Accord, New York, which I served as pastor during my study, enabled me to make the ministry of biblical scholarship a part of my pastoral ministry.

Thanks are also owed to the members of my dissertation committee for their careful reading and helpful comments: J. Louis Martyn, Raymond Brown and Richard Norris, of Union Theological Seminary; and David Marcus of the Jewish Theological Seminary of America. Professsor Marcus generously provided me with instruction in Syriac.

In several courses, Professor Norris gave excellent instruction in Patristics and Gnosticism. Professor Brown has taught me much about both biblical scholarship and its relationship to the church. Professor (now Emeritus) Martyn graciously served as my dissertation director. This study began as a paper in his doctoral seminar on Jewish Christianity. His careful reading and helpful, encouraging advice have made my task more enjoyable and the result more sound. All these have helped to improve this work by making valuable suggestions for its revision, but any deficiencies that remain are solely my own.

Other thanks go to Nancy Ondra, who skillfully typed the first draft; to Robert Gram, who read and critiqued two chapters of the first draft; to Barry and Deborah Medenbach, who generously allowed me the use of their computer; to Charles Talbert, New Testament editor for the Society of Biblical Literature Dissertation Series, and his committee of peer reviewers for selecting this volume for the series; and to John Hiemstra, Executive Minister of the Synod of New York, Reformed Church in America, who helped me considerably in using the Synod's desk-top publishing equipment to produce the camera-ready copy of this book for the publisher.

Finally, the members of my family deserve my thanks. My son Richard twice waited patiently for his father to finish this project, first as a dissertation and then as a book. Son Nicholas had the good sense to be born after the dissertation was completed. The person to whom most thanks are due is my wife, Mary. Her constant encouragement and assistance made my doctoral study possible.

ROBERT E. VAN VOORST

Department of Religion
Lycoming College
Williamsport, PA 17701

ABBREVIATIONS

AJ - Ascents of James
Cont - Contestatio
EpCl - Epistula Clementis
EpPt - Epistula Petri
G - Grundschrift
H - Homilies
KerygmaP - Κηρυγμα Πετρου
KerygmataP - Κηρυγματα Πετρου
L - Latin
PP - Περιοδοι Πετρου
PsCl - Pseudo-Clementine (adjective), the Pseudo-Clementines
R - Recognitions
S - Syriac

All other abbreviations, together with the rules of style followed here, can be found in the "Instructions for Contributors," *Journal of Biblical Literature* 107 (1988) 579-96.

TABLES

1. Sources of *R* 1.33-71 in the History of Research   25
2. Major Aporias between the Source in *R* 1
    and the Remainder of PsCl   39
3. NT Lists of the Twelve and their Order in the *AJ*   121

CHAPTER ONE

THE HISTORY OF RESEARCH INTO
RECOGNITIONS 1.33-71

Introduction

In this study of *The Ascents of James* we will be dealing with the
Pseudo-Clementine literature. As this literature has not been a major
concern of most New Testament scholars or church historians since
the nineteenth century, we offer a brief overview of the Clementine
corpus and the issue of its sources.

The Pseudo-Clementines (hereafter PsCl) contain two lengthy
treatises of approximately equal size: the *Recognitions* (*R*) in ten
books, and the *Homilies* (*H*) in twenty "sermons." Three short documents are associated with *H*: the *Epistle of Peter to James* (*EpPt*) with
its *Contestation* (*Cont*), and the *Epistle of Clement to James* (*EpCl*).
H and its associated documents survive in their original Greek. The
Greek of *R* is now lost, but *R* survives in a Latin translation by Rufinus
of Aquila (d. 410). A Syriac version of *R* 1-3 and *H* 10-17 is also extant
in two manuscripts, one from 411 and the other from the ninth century.

The *Recognitions* purports to be the the first-person story of Clement, presbyter-bishop of Rome at the end of the first century. This
Clement is known to us from extra-NT writings, in particular the letter
to the Corinthians attributed to him, which is now known as *I Clement*
and dated at AD 96. In *R*, Clement is a seeker after truth, in particular
about the fate of the soul after death. After going from one philosophi-
cal school to another, he hears the gospel and journeys to Caesarea.
There he learns from Peter of the True Prophet, believes and is
baptized. He then accompanies Peter on his missionary travels and

1

assists him in his encounters with Simon the magician. Meanwhile, back in Rome, the members of Clement's family are separated from each other by dreams, shipwrecks and other hardships. Clement's father, mother, two brothers and Clement himself then search for each other. The several mutual identifications and reunions of the family members, who in the end all receive baptism, give the name "recognitions" to this document. *R* was probably written ca. 350 in Syria or Palestine by an orthodox Catholic.

The *Homilies* shares this narrative framework. Long passages in *H* are parallel to *R*, many with word-for-word similarity. Some differences also appear. *R* has only one debate with Simon, at Caesarea; *H* has two, at Caesarea and Laodicea. *H* contains a dispute between Clement and Appion which is lacking in *R*, but much of the content of this dispute is found in other contexts of *R*. While their titles seem to imply that the *Recognitions* are largely composed of the recognition-romance, and the *Homilies* of preaching, in fact both are largely didactic treatises placed in the framework of the recognition-romance. As J. A. Fitzmyer has aptly remarked, "There is as much homiletic material in the *Recognitions* as there is recognition in the *Homilies*."[1] *H* was written in the early fourth century by an Arian Christian, probably in Syria.

The three other documents of PsCl can be summarized briefly. The *Epistle of Peter to James* urges that the books of Peter's preachings be kept from those who could misuse them. Only those who have been tested and found faithful to Peter's "lawful preaching" are to be entrusted with his books. The *Contestation* (or *Attestation*; Διαμαρ-τυρια) contains the specifications for this testing, and a solemn oath to be sworn by those who receive the books. The *Epistle of Clement to James* tells how Peter, before his martyrdom, installed Clement as his successor as bishop of Rome.

In view of the notable similarities between *R* and *H*, what might their literary relationship be? Most modern scholars hold that both drew on a common source, the so-called "Basic Writing" (known by the German *Grundschrift*, hereafter *G*). This *G* was a Jewish-Christian work written in Syria in the third century, but is now lost. *G* itself was made up of several older sources, the chief of which are: (1) The

---

1 Fitzmyer, "The Qumran Scrolls, the Ebionites, and Their Literature," *TS* 16 (1955) 346-7. This statement is somewhat exaggerated, but does point up the shortcomings of the titles "Recognitions" and "Homilies."

recognition-romance of Clement; (2) The sermons of Peter during his missionary travels, entitled the "Preachings of Peter" (Κηρυγματα Πετρου, *KerygmataP*); (3) The narratives of the encounters of Peter with Simon the magician; and (4) The dialogues of Peter with Appion.

The present study will seek to determine if *G* used another source, *The Ascents of James* (Αναβαθμοι Ιακωβου, *AJ*). The *AJ* is a history of the people of God from Abraham to the earliest church. It presents Jesus as the Prophet like Moses, features a debate between the twelve apostles and the representatives of the Jews, and has as its climax a speech of James the bishop in the temple. Important in the identification of this source will be the witness of Epiphanius in his *Panarion* to an Αναβαθμοι Ιακωβου of which he knows.

Early Research into the Pseudo-Clementines

The history of research into the sources of *R* 1.33-71 is best understood by beginning with the earliest research into the PsCl corpus.[2]

Research into the PsCl began with the publication of the first edition of *R* in 1504 by J. Lefevre d'Etaples (Faber Stapulensis, Jacobus Faber).[3] The next edition, one more influential than the first, was by

---

2 For the recent histories of research on PsCl as a whole, see especially G. Strecker, *Das Judenchristentum in den Pseudoklementinen* (TU 70,2; 2d ed.; Berlin: Akadamie, 1981) 1-34. The most recent is also the most exhaustive, especially in matters of source criticism: F. S. Jones, "The Pseudo-Clementines: A History of Research," *SecCent* 2 (1982) 1-33, 63-96. The period of research before F. C. Baur is examined best by A. Schliemann, *Die Clementinen nebst den verwandten Schriften und der Ebionitismus* (Hamburg: Perthes, 1844) 17-41; G. Uhlhorn, *Die Homilien und Recognitionen des Clemens Romanus nach ihrem Ursprung und Inhalt dargestellt* (Göttingen: Dieterich, 1854) 1-12; and J. Lehmann, *Die Homilien und Recognitionen des clementinischen Schriften mit besonderer Rücksicht auf ihr literarisches Verhältniss* (Gotha: Perthes, 1869) 1-12. Due to the unavailability of the earliest books, I am especially indebted to these three surveys for research up to Neander.

3 *Pro piorum recreatione et in hoc opere contenta: . . . Epistola Clementis. Recognitiones Petri . . .* (Basel: Stephanus).

J. Sichard (Sichardus), *Divi Clementis Recognitionum libri X. ad Jacobum fratrem Domini Rufino Torano Aquil. interprete.*[4] For the next one hundred and fifty years, church historians and dogmaticians touched upon *R* in the course of larger surveys, but never gave it independent examination. Doubts arose over its authenticity, especially after J. Calvin sharply argued its pseudonymity.[5] The authenticity of *R* was maintained against Calvin and other Protestants by the Roman Catholic historian L. G. Venradius in the third edition of *R*.[6]

But doubts about the authorship of *R* were to grow. In 1588, C. Baronio (Baronius), a leading Roman Catholic historian, argued that *R* had been so corrupted by Ebionites that Clement's authentic writing was almost unrecognizable.[7] G. Arnold accepted the authenticity of *R*, but pointed in his preface to substantial reasons for doubt.[8] Others from 1700 to 1750 also posited substantial reasons for doubt.[9] After 1750 the movement to deny authenticity was so strong that Lutheran, Reformed and Roman Catholic scholars were nearly unanimous for pseudonymity.

In the meantime, research into *H* had begun, and historical scholarship soon gave its full attention to *H*, neglecting *R*. This preference for *H* lasted through much of the period of the "Tübingen School" (ca. 1840-1870), and had a negative impact on research into the sources of Book One of *R*. As Lehmann relates, the same fate befell *H* as *R* -

---

4   Basel: Stephanus, 1526; reprinted 1536, 1541, and 1568.

5   Calvin, *The Acts of the Apostles* (2 vols.; Edinburgh: Oliver & Boyd, 1965; 1st Latin and French editions, 1552) 1.19: "Satan directed all his ingenuity to the end that nothing [beyond the canonical Acts] about the things done by the apostles might remain extant, except what was defiled with lies, so as to render suspect everything said by them . . . For he incited crazy men or cunning mockers to spread obnoxious tales with suppositious names . . . We must pass the same judgment about all that farrago which is found in the *Recognitions* and *Homilies* of Clement."

6   Venradius, *Clementina h.e. Clementis Opera cum nova praefatione de veris falsisque Clementis Scriptis* (Cologne: Friess, 1570).

7   Baronio, *Annales ecclesiastici* (Frankfurt: Schonwetter; in the 1614 edition, p. 144).

8   Arnold, *Das heiligen Clementis von Rom Recognitiones . . . Nunmehr ins Teusche übersetzt* (Berlin: Rudiger, 1702).

9   Uhlhorn, *Homilien*, 3-4, gives a list.

when it was recognized as a pseudonymous, "heretical" work, it was treated as virtually worthless by most historians.[10] Where a source-critical issue was raised on the relationship of *H* to *R*, historians in this period commonly assigned the whole PsCl corpus to one author or editor.

Two noteworthy scholars, H. Dodwell and J. L. von Mosheim, went against the mainstream of Clementine scholarship. Already in 1689, Dodwell viewed the *KerygmaP* as the source of first *R* and later *H*. This *KerygmaP* was an Ebionite work from the second century.[11] Well did Lehmann remark that, although few of Dodwell's source-critical and historical positions on PsCl have endured, "So bleibt es also Dodwells Ruhm, dass er zuerst die literar-historische Frage nach dem Verhältniss der verschiedene, so verwandten clementinischen Schriften, besonders der Recognitionen und Homilien, berührt."[12] While others devalued the Clementines because of their pseudonymity, Mosheim argued in 1733 that despite their pseudonymity, they are an important witness to early church history.[13] In his *Institutes of Ecclesiastical History* he said of *R*, "A careful perusal of them will assist a person much in gaining a knowledge of the state of the ancient Christian church."[14]

J. A. W. Neander was the first historian to give *H* a sustained and independent treatment. Neander made a thorough examination of the doctrinal teachings of in a lengthy "Beilage" to his *Genetische Entwicklung der vornehmsten gnostischen Systeme*,[15] and characterized *H* as a form of gnostic Ebionism. He dated it at ca. 200, but held that many of its doctrines were derived from the first century. Like most of his contemporaries, Neander dealt almost exclusively with *H*, neglecting *R*. This is borne out by his misreading of Epiphanius' reference to the *AJ* which a passing knowledge of *R* 1 would have corrected: "From this [Ebionite] sect proceeds a book under the name of Jacob, $\alpha\nu\alpha\beta\alpha\theta\mu\omicron\iota$

---

10 Lehmann, *Schriften*, 4-5.
11 Dodwell, *Dissertationes in Irenaeum* (Oxford: Sheldonian Theatre); cf. dissertation VI, "De aliis Irenaei scriptis," section X.
12 Lehmann, *Schriften*, 7.
13 Mosheim, *Disseration de turbata per recentiores Platonicos ecclesia.* Published in R. Cudworth, *Systeme Intellectuale huius Universi* (Jena: Meyer, 1733).
14 (2 vols; 2d ed. London: Longmans, 1850) 1.97; 1st German ed., 1737.
15 Berlin: Dummler, 1818.

Ιακωβου, Steps of Jacob (probably intended to denote the steps of initiation with reference to the true Gnosis), in which the patriarch is introduced as discoursing against the sacrificial and temple worship."[16] Despite this misunderstanding of the meaning of *AJ* and misidentification of its main character, the work of Neander brought research into PsCl to its highest point in three centuries. From this point we enter a new period of research, that of F. C. Baur and his followers.

F. C. Baur and the Tübingen School

In 1831 F. C. Baur published "Die Christuspartei in der korinthischen Gemeinde, der Gegensatz des petrinischen und paulinischen Christentums in der ältesten Kirche, der Apostel Petrus in Rom."[17] In this seminal essay, Baur argued for a basic split in NT times between Petrine (Jewish) and Pauline (Gentile) Christianity. This split did not heal with the death of Paul, but continued to the end of the second century, when the Great Church emerged from the growing fusion of the two previously irreconcilable enemies. *H* is the primary witness at the end of the second century to a continuing hostility of some parts of Jewish Christianity to Paulinism.[18]

With this essay, Baur laid down three basic perspectives which were to endure throughout his career. First, he "enunciated . . . those views which were to form the basis of that total perspective of the early church which may broadly be called the Tübingen perspective."[19] This perspective interpreted every piece of early Christian literature in

---

16 Neander, *General History of the Christian Religion and Church* (2 vols.; Boston: Crocker & Brewster, 1872) 1.352; German original, Hamburg: Perthes, 1825.

17 *Tübinger Zeitschrift für Theologie*, 1831, 61-206; also published in K. Scholder, ed., *F. C. Baur, Ausgewählte Werke in Einzelausgaben* (6 vols.; Stuttgart: Fromann, 1963) 1.1-146.

18 Ibid., 116 (cited from the *Zeitschrift*).

19 H. Harris, *The Tübingen School* (Oxford: Clarendon, 1975) 181.

terms of the split between Petrine and Pauline Christianity, using PsCl as a key.[20]

Second, and more important for our research, this essay laid down Baur's life-long perspective on PsCl. "Christuspartei" dealt mainly with *H*, occasionally touched upon *EpPt* and *Cont*, but left *R* completely out of view. This led Baur into a misstatement when he argued, "Es ist nur eine einzige Stelle in den Clementinen, in welcher die Beschneidung erwähnt wird und zwar in der den Homilien voranstehenden Contestatio pro iis, qui librum accipiunt."[21] Here Baur ignored *R* 1.33.5, which exalts circumcision as "the proof and sign of purity." This error is continued through the third edition of his *Kirchengeschichte der drei ersten Jahrhunderte:* "Even the pseudo-Clementine writings do not mention circumcision as an essential article of Judaism."[22] More importantly, Baur never entered into the source-critical questions which were to become an essential element of research in PsCl by members of the Tübingen School and others. Commenting on the labors of Hilgenfeld, Ritschl and Uhlhorn, Baur said, "The relationship of these writings [*H* and *R*] to each other and to an older work, a monument of the Petrine party, the *Kerygmata Petrou*, has lately been the subject of very thorough and elaborate discussion, in which, however, the results of different scholars travel widely apart."[23] Baur was sharply criticized for refusing to enter into the source-critical question, or even to admit its importance for continuing research.[24]

---

20 The importance of PsCl to the Tübingen School is best shown by the opening sentence of A. Hilgenfeld's *Die clementinischen Recognitionen und Homilien* (Jena: Schreiber, 1848, 1): "Es giebt kaum eine Schrift, welche für die Geschichte des Urchristentums von solcher Bedeutung wäre und bereits unter den Händen der bedeutendsten Kritiker gläzendere Aufschlüsse über die älteste Geschichte der christlichen Kirche gegeben hätte, als die unter dem Names des römischen Clemens verfassten *Recognitionen* und *Homilien.*"

21 Baur, "Christuspartei," 195.

22 Quoted from the English translation of this book, *The Church History of the First Three Centuries* (London: Williams & Norgate, 1878) 106.

23 Ibid., 190.

24 E.g., Uhlhorn, *Homilien*, 16.

Third, Baur increasingly linked the Ebionites of PsCl with the opponents of Paul, even those of his own time. His 1831 essay largely confined them to the second century, but later works were to associate them closely with the first century. In an 1838 essay he stated, "Alle diese Judenchristen der altesten Zeit einen mehr oder minder ebionitischen Character an sich tragen."[25] Baur's position is summed up well in his statement on Paul: "The open and outspoken hatred with which the Ebionites regarded him is the extreme point reached by that Jewish Christian opposition to him of which we see the beginnings in his own epistles. The Ebionites are generally regarded as mere heretics, *but their connection with the original Jewish Christianity is unmistakable.*"[26]

In summary, it can readily be seen that Baur's work on PsCl was a marked departure from earlier work. More importantly, it set the agenda for much subsequent research into this literature and the NT. A split between Jewish Christianity and Gentile Christianity has continued to be debated until the present. Baur's lack of interest in the source criticism of PsCl spurred on some of his students to this task. Finally, his view that the opponents of Paul and the Ebionites form one Jewish-Christian movement in the early church would also have a great impact on scholarship.

Baur's research into early Christianity was quickly taken up by his students and followers, thus giving rise to the "Tübingen School." Important for the history of research into Book One of *R* are Hilgenfeld, Köstlin and Ritschl.

---

25 Baur, "Über den Ursprung des Episcopats in der christlichen Kirche," *Tübinger Zeitschrift für Theologie*, 1838, 123.

26 Baur, *History*, 89-90; emphasis mine.

A. B. C. Hilgenfeld's interest in PsCl was reflected in three publications.[27] Hilgenfeld opened up the issue of the literary sources of the Clementine corpus. According to his reconstruction, the Grundschrift[28] of PsCl is embedded in R 1-3, and can be identified as the KerygmaP. R 1.27-72 is an especially notable part of this source and contains its "chief contents." This G was written in Rome soon after the fall of Jerusalem in AD 70. He also demarcated 1.44-54 from R 1.27-72 as a recapitulation by the redactor of R of the christology of the KerygmaP.[29] Hilgenfeld's work would prove to be a long stride forward in research into PsCl. In opening the question of their sources, he was the first to deny the unity of R, which would no longer be taken for granted. Hilgenfeld saw in R 1 the earliest source of the PsCl corpus, thus beginning the search for a discrete literary source in R 1.27-72.

K. R. Köstlin wrote a lengthy review of Hilgenfeld's book in the Allgemeine Literature-Zeitung (Halle) in 1849.[30] He disagreed with Hilgenfeld on the existence of a KerygmaP source in R 1-3. Instead, he upheld the unity of R 1-7, with one exception: "Ich glaube . . . dass sie [the Periodoi Petrou or "Journeys of Peter"] allerdings in Buch 1 mit einer ebionitischen 'Grundschrift' sich berühren mögen, nämlich mit den ebionitischen πραξεις αποστολων in welchen nach Epiphanius 30,16 besonders von den αναβαθμοι und υφηγησεις Ιακωβου gegen Tempel und Opfer die Rede war (wie Recogn. 1,36-71)."[31] This short description was to prove highly important in further research into Book One of R. Köstlin thus became the first researcher to identify a part of R 1 with the Ascents of James known from Epiphanius.

---

27 His first publication on PsCl, Recognitionen (see footnote 20 above) is also the most important for our purposes. He followed this up with "Über die Composition den klementinischen Recognitionen," Theologische Jahrbücher, 1850, 63-93, and "Der Ursprung der pseudoclementinische Recognitionen und Homilien, nach dem neuesten Stand den Untersuchung," Theologische Jahrbücher, 1854, 483-535.

28 It should be noted that in Hilgenfeld's view this term does not refer, as in later research, to a common source of R and H, but only of R.

29 Hilgenfeld, Recognitionen, 52-99.

30 "Die clementinischen Recognitionen und Homilien," in Nrs. 73-77, cols. 577-8, 585-608, 612-6.

31 Ibid., cols. 603-4.

A. Ritschl was at first a convinced member of the Tübingen School. After his break with Baur he wrote *Die Entstehung der altkatholischen Kirche*.[32] In its first edition he devoted a good deal of attention to PsCl, and in general followed Hilgenfeld's analysis, with some reference to the labors of Köstlin.[33] In the second edition, much of his treatment of PsCl was eliminated, but still preserved is a reference to the *AJ* as a source of R 1.[34] Ritschl's continuing acceptance of an *AJ* source in R 1 is all the more remarkable because of his growing skepticism about the value of the PsCl literature for an understanding of the early church. Nevertheless, his treatment of R 1 did not advance research into it.

Those who came after the Tübingen School carried on much subsequent research into PsCl, especially in source criticism. To be considered here are three scholars who, while not properly called members of the Tübingen School, carried on its work: Lehmann, Lipsius and Langen.

J. Lehmann attempted to mediate between the source-critical positions of Hilgenfeld and his opponent G. Uhlhorn. He argued that R 1-3, which he held as the *KerygmaP*, was written first. Lehmann noted the special character of R 1.27-72: it is "ein Abschnitt, der in unsern Homilien sich nicht findet, nämlich als entsprechender Parallelabschnitt."[35] He repeated Hilgenfeld's description of it as the "chief content" of the *KerygmaP*.[36] Although he knew of Köstlin's identification of R 1.27-72 as the *AJ*, Lehmann did not pick up this source-critical issue.

R. A. Lipsius followed Hilgenfeld in the reconstruction of the sources of the PsCl corpus.[37] He renamed the *KerygmaP* the *KerygmataP*, ending for most further research its connection with the *KerygmaP* known to Clement of Alexandria. Against Hilgenfeld, Lipsius held that 1.44-71 was the oldest part of R, and went behind the

---

32 Bonn: Marcus, 1851; 2nd ed., 1857.

33 Ibid., 196-215.

34 Ibid., 264.

35 Lehmann, *Schriften*, 35.

36 Ibid., 105; cf. other references to 1.27-72 on pp. 69 and 72.

37 Lipsius, *Die Quellen der römischen Petrus-Sage kritisch untersucht* (Kiel: Schwers, 1872).

KerygmataP to an older *Praxeis Petrou* (*Acts of Peter*, an apocryphal work partially preserved by citation in other apocryphal literature). Lipsius labelled *R* 1.27-43 a "religionsgeschichtliche Einleitung" to 1.44-71. It is not a part of the source, but ". . . wurde wahrscheinlich erst in den Kerygmen hinzugefügt." As for 1.44-71, Lipsius related it to traditions about James, acknowledging, "Offenbar liegt dieser Darstellung die bekannte Erzählung von dem Tode des Jacobus . . . zu Grunde."[38] However, he did not see the *AJ* or its traditions as the source of 1.44-71, nor did he find any connection between the *AJ* and 1.27-43.[39]

J. Langen assigned most of *R* to the *KerygmaP* (note the reversion to the singular), and identified this with *G*. Written in Rome shortly after 135, its purpose was to persuade Jewish Christians to accept Roman primacy. Langen was the first of only a few to claim that this was not a Jewish-Christian document.[40] He only once raised the issue of older sources behind the *KerygmaP*, noting that parts of *R* 1 could go back to older sources; but he was not as sure as Uhlhorn.[41] In his chapter on *R*, Langen treated 1.27-72 as one part of the whole of *R*. Because it showed the *Tendenzen* of *R*, 1.27-72 was not drawn from any special source.

Opponents of the Tübingen School

The perspective of Baur and his followers on early Christianity and PsCl did not go unchallenged. Opposition to their views arose almost immediately in Germany and later in England. Four scholars are important at this juncture: Uhlhorn,[42] Salmon, Hort and Lightfoot.

---

38 Ibid., 27.
39 Cf. also Lipsius's *Die apokryphen Apostelgeschichten und Apostellegenden* (2 vols.; Braunschweig: Schwetschke, 1887; reprinted, Amsterdam: APA-Philo, 1976) 2.244-5, where he disputes Köstlin's identification of *R* 1.27-71 with the *AJ*.
40 Langen, *Die Klemensromane* (Gotha: Perthes, 1890) 105-56.
41 Ibid., 130, n.1.
42 While Strecker, *Judenchristentum*, 6-7, seems to include Uhlhorn as a follower of the Tübingen School, he is properly considered its opponent. For a description of Uhlhorn's strong opposition to the Tübingen School, see Harris, *School*, 239-42.

In 1854 G. Uhlhorn published *Die Homilien und Recognitionen des Clemens Romanus nach ihre Ursprung und Inhalt dargestellt.*[43] Against Hilgenfeld, who saw *R* 1.27-72 as a key part of the *KerygmaP*, Uhlhorn argued that *R* 1.27-74 was added by the editor of *R* from the *AJ*. Uhlhorn was the first to use an analysis of incongruities in the text to isolate this source, noting several between *R* 1.1-26 and 1.27-74. He identified the *Anabathmoi* of this source's title as "das mehrmalige Hinaufsteigen des Jakobus zu Reden."[44] He did not explicitly date this source, but saw it as earlier than *G* (ca. 150). Uhlhorn later changed his mind, claiming that 1.27-71 belongs to *G*, not to an older source.[45]

In 1877 G. Salmon contributed a lengthy article, "The Clementine Literature," to the *Dictionary of Christian Biography.*[46] Of *R* 1, he said, "The story of Clement has been added to an older document. It has been conjectured that this document was an Ebionite work, Αναβαθ—μοι Ιακωβου . . . But this conjecture encounters the difficulty that the author himself indicates a different source for this part of his work."[47] As the indication of this different source, Salmon pointed to the books listed in *R* 3.75, the "Table of Contents" of *R* that he (and most others of his day) considered genuine: "One of the books [listed in *R* 3.75] is described as treating of the Apostles' disputation at the temple; and therefore it seems needless to look for the original of this part in the 'Ascents of James.'"[48]

---

43 Göttingen: Dieterich.
44 Ibid., 365-6.
45 *RE* 4.171-9, especially 177-8.
46 Ed. W. Smith and H. Wace (London: Murray, 1877) 1.567-78.
47 Ibid., 568.
48 Ibid., 569. A more non-committal attitude to the *AJ* was taken by C. Bigg ("The Clementine Homilies," *Studia Biblica et Ecclesiastica* [2 vols.; Oxford: Clarendon, 1890] 2.157-93), who argued that the editor of *R* inserted "a long historical episode" into Book One, which "some have regarded as drawn from the *Ascents of James*" (183-4).

In a volume of posthumously published lectures, F. J. A. Hort agreed with recent German scholarship in identifying the *AJ* as the earliest source behind *R* 1. He commented on its title: "The αναβαθμοι meant [in recent scholarship] are the steps of the temple; whereas Epiphanius seems to me to understand the word figuratively, as it were steps in teaching, instructions; but it is not at all clear that he had even seen the book himself, so that he may easily have misunderstood the title." Hort added that the contents of the *AJ* "were either largely or wholly fictitious."[49]

This treatment was expanded in another posthumous work, *Notes Introductory to the Study of the Clementine Recognitions.*[50] Hort repeated his earlier conclusion that the *AJ* is a source of *R* 1. *R* 1.66-71 is "unlike anything else in Recognitions or Homilies."[51] In his appendixed "Comparative Analysis of Hom. I-III and Rec. I-III," Hort noted that *R* 1.22a-74 (within which 44b-54 are a "digression") has no parallel in *H*.[52] He never gave an exact statement of the range of the *AJ* source, but it is evident that he had in mind at least *R* 1.66-71.[53] In conclusion, Hort's treatment of an *AJ* source in *R* 1 is cautious but positive.

J. B. Lightfoot was, like Hort, an opponent of Baur, and skeptical about source criticism of PsCl. But he did accept the *AJ* as a source of

49 *Judaistic Christianity*, ed. J. O. F. Murray (London: Macmillan, 1894) 152.; cf. also p. 201.

50 Ed. J. O. F. Murray (London: Macmillan, 1901).

51 Ibid., 115.

52 Ibid., 146-51.

53 *Notes*, 115-9. Jones, "History," 25, seems to follow the heading in the table of contents (p. x) in *Notes* when he states that Hort saw a source in 1.70-73. But the table of contents was written by the editor, Murray, and it is likely that on this point Murray misread Hort's meaning.

R 1.54-71, and interpreted αναβαθμοι as "ascents up the temple stairs."[54]

The Beginning of Modern Source Criticism

The modern period sees the commencement of truly scientific source criticism of PsCl. It begins with the labors of one who was to set much of the agenda for modern research, Hans Waitz.

Waitz issued his *Die Pseudoklementinen Homilien und Rekognitionen: Eine quellenkritische Untersuchung* in 1904.[55] He saw the *KerygmataP* as written by a Jewish-Christian gnostic soon after 135. Its contents, minus the fourth and seventh books, are the ten books listed in *R* 3.75.[56] The next source is *G*, a mainly Catholic work written in Rome ca. 220-230.[57] Waitz wrote several articles over the next three decades defending his views against criticism.[58]

Waitz treated *R* 1.27-42 as a part of the *KerygmataP*'s "Book of the True Prophet" (following *R* 3.75). He gave most of his attention to 1.54-71. In this section he found two literary units, 1.54-65 and 66-71. *R* 1.54-65 is a part of the "seventh book" of the *KerygmataP* (*R* 3.75), which along with the "fourth book" was added by the *G* author to the

---

54 Lightfoot, *The Epistle of St. Paul to the Galatians* (London: Macmillan, 1865) 330, n. 2; cf. also 276, 291.

55 Leipzig: Hinrichs.

56 Ibid., 88-113.

57 Waitz later altered this position, which is characteristic of older research, to a Syrian, Jewish-Christian provenance; cf. "Die Lösung des pseudoclementinischen Problems?" *ZKG* 59 (1940) 340.

58 "Die Pseudoklementinen und ihre Quellenschriften," *ZNW* 28 (1929) 241-72 (against Heintze and Schmidt); "Pseudoklementinische Probleme," *ZKG* 50 (1931) 186-94 (a highly critical review of Cullman); "Neues zur Text- und Literatur-Kritik den Pseudoklementinen," *ZKG* 52 (1933) 305-18 (against Schwartz); and "Lösung," (against Rehm). These articles played an important role in maintaining Waitz's source-critical labors as one of the most important of recent times.

original *KerygmataP*.[59] It originated in an apocryphal writing that had reference to Thomas. Waitz denied that 1.66-71 can be identified as the *AJ* mentioned by Epiphanius. He approvingly quoted Hort's statements on the different understanding of $\alpha\nu\alpha\beta\alpha\theta\mu\omega$ in Epiphanius and *R* 1 (not mentioning, however, that in spite of this difference, Hort did identify this section with the *AJ*). Also, he argued that the *AJ* known to Epiphanius is syncretistic and anti-Pauline, but that *R* 1.54-71 is not. Although 1.54-65 and 1.66-71 stem from two different sources, Waitz held that they form in *R* 1 a literary unit which has no trace in *H*.[60] In a comparison of *R* 1.54-71 with the *KerygmataP*, he listed six differences between them.[61]

In a critical review of Waitz's Homilien,[62] W. Bousset sharply disagreed with Waitz that 1.27-71 was added by *G*. "G ist ein viel zu geschickter Arbeiter, als dass ihm derartige Unstimmigkeiten zuzutrauen wären." Instead, *R* 1.27-71 was added by the Recognitionist to his work.[63] Bousset differed with Waitz when he argued that all of 1.27-71, with the exception of 1.44-52 and other shorter interpolations, is an "einheitliche und zusammengehörige Stuck."[64] Moreover, he did not hesitate to identify this section with the *AJ* and to call it Jewish-Christian.[65]

---

59 Waitz, *Homilien*, 109-10.
60 Ibid., 167-9.
61 These differences, found on pp. 109-10, are: (1) 1.71 refers to Peter in the third person; (2) 1.54-71 is not "judaistisch" or (3) anti-Pauline, or (4) "nomistisch"; (5) John the Baptist is positively valued as a prophet in 1.54-71, negatively in the *KerygmataP* ; (6) 1.54-71 deals with the theme of whether Jesus is the Christ, which differs from the *KerygmataP*'s presentation of him as the True Prophet.
62 *Göttingische gelehrten Anzeigen* 167 (1905) 425-47.
63 Ibid., 426-7.
64 Ibid., 437.
65 Ibid., 427.

At nearly the same time as Waitz's book, H. U. Meyboom issued a two-volume study of PsCl.[66] He saw two literary units in *R* 1.27-71: a history of salvation from the creation to Christ (1.27-41), and the debate between Judaism and Christianity (1.42-71). Both these units "are of a very particular nature," and "It is not unlikely that they have been drawn from a lost writing."[67] Like Waitz, he cited Hort's notation of differing meanings of ἀναβαθμοι in Epiphanius and *R* 1, arguing that this makes Hort's identification of 1.66-71 as the *AJ* problematic. Meyboom repeated the words of Uhlhorn when he concluded about the identification of *R* 1.53-71 as the *AJ*, "We remain here groping in the dark and must be dealing with a 'conjecture' which may at most be qualified as 'not too bold.'"[68] Thus, while he did note the distinctiveness of 1.27-71, Meyboom was non-committal toward the identification of 1.53-71 as the *AJ*.

In 1930 appeared the Licentiatsdissertation of O. Cullmann, *Le Problème littéraire et historique du Roman Pseudo-Clémentin*.[69] Cullmann returned to the Tübingen School's view of the Clementines as a key text for understanding early Christian history. In this respect it is proper for Strecker to describe him (along with Thomas and Schoeps, to be considered below) as a "neo-Tübinger."[70] Cullmann assigned *R* 1.27-72 to "Book One" of the "Table of Contents."[71] He traced *R* 1.54-71 to "Book Seven," taking issue with Waitz by arguing that it is an integral part of *KerygmataP*.[72] It is uncertain from his treatment where Cullmann would assign *R* 1.43-53. But in a later work he assigned 1.43 to the *KerygmataP*, and Cullmann probably under-

---

66 *De Clemens-Roman* (Groningen: Wolters, 1902, 1904).

67 Ibid., 2.71. (Quotations from Meyboom are in my translation.) Despite this "very particular nature," Meyboom in his first volume sets 1.27-74 in parallel columns with *H* 2.42 - 3.20, thus becoming the only researcher into PsCl to imply that *R* 1.27-71 has parallel treatment in *H*.

68 Ibid., 2.74; quoting Uhlhorn, *Homilien*, 367.

69 (Etudes d'Histoire et de Philosophe religieuses 23; Paris: Alcan). Cullmann summarized this work in *RHPR* 10 (1930) 471-6.

70 Strecker, *Judenchristentum*, 20. In other respects, Cullmann's theological outlook, which is summed up in the term "Die heilsgeschichtliche Schule," is very different from the Tübingen School.

71 Cullmann, *Probleme*, 82, especially n. 3.

72 Ibid., 90.

stood all of R 1.27-71 to originate there.[73] In placing 1.27-71 in the *KerygmataP* and refusing to consider whether the *AJ* is its source, Cullmann is a dissenting voice in the search for an *AJ* source in R 1.

In his *Le Mouvement baptiste en Palestine et Syrie*,[74] J. Thomas took a step back toward the earlier recognition of an *AJ* source. He saw a "particular document" in 1.27-72, and noted Bousset's identification of it as the *AJ*. While he did not fully endorse this identification, Thomas did admit, "En tous cas, nous sommes pour le moins en présence d'un document proche, par son contenu, de ces Anabathmoi."[75] This document incorporated by the Recognitionist, "Peut-être les Anabathmoi de Jacque, pourrait refléter une autre nuance baptiste [than the rest of R], assez modérée et plus primitive." That the Ebionism of this source is "assez modéré et non encore teinté d'elchasaïsme" led Thomas to suggest a date for it at the end of the first century or the first half of the second.[76]

Modern Opponents of Source Criticism

Not all twentieth-century research supported the source-criticism of the PsCl or gave them an important role in early Christian history. A line of scholars quite skeptical of source criticism had an impact on research into R 1. The most significant are Chapman, Schwartz, Rehm and Irmscher.

J. Chapman expressed strong opposition to contemporary source criticism of PsCl and the consensus that they are in largely Jewish-Christian.[77] He quoted with approval A. C. Headlam's conclusion on PsCl: "They are all products of one design and plan, coming from one writer or group of writers, and we have no need to inquire about older sources, which in all probability did not exist."[78] He rejected Waitz's restoration of the *KerygmataP* and *PP*, and he labelled the "Table of Contents" (R 3.75) "merely a part of the gigantic fraud." This fraud has deceived both ordinary readers and source critics: "The author of these

---

73 *Christology of the New Testament* (rev. ed.; Philadelphia: Westminster, 1963).
74 Universitas Catholica Lovaniensis Dissertationes, Series 2, 28; Gembloux: Duculot.
75 Ibid., 119-20.
76 Ibid., 120.
77 "On the State of the Clementines," *ZNW* 7 (1908) 21-34, 147-59.
78 Ibid., 147; quoting Headlam, "The Clementine Literature," *JTS* 3 (1902) 49-50.

documents was a clever man, for he has imposed on a good many modern critics as well as upon many of the ancients." On the provenance of PsCl, he said, "There is no trace of Judaeo-Christianity" in them."[79]

Like Chapman, E. Schwartz in his essay, "Unzeitgemässe Beobachtungen zu den Clementinen,"[80] denied the Jewish-Christian provenance of PsCl. He opposed much of the source criticism of them, especially the work of Hilgenfeld and Waitz. Schwartz advanced several "untimely observations" on source criticism, indicating that he knew he was swimming against a strong stream. He labeled the *KerygmataP* a "fiction" invented by *H*, and the "Table of Contents" of *R* 3.75 "ein πλασμα ist von Anfang bis zu Ende."[81] Schwartz held similar views on an *AJ* source in *R* 1. Of Epiphanius' knowledge of Ebionite documents, he said, "Sonst hatte er nur Berichte, ausser dem über die Clementinen einen über apokryphe Apostelakten [30, 16. 23] und die 'Stufenleiter des Iakobus', die schon aus sprachlichen Gründen nicht auf recogn. I, 69 bezogen werden darf."[82] Schwartz did not elaborate on these "sprachlichen Gründen," from which he argued that *R* 1.69 is not the *AJ*.

In a comprehensive article, "Zur Entstehung der pseudoclementinischen Schriften,"[83] B. Rehm argued that source criticism behind *G* is fruitless. He held that *R* 1.27-74 was written by the Recognitionist on the basis of the OT, Acts 5 and 9, and possibly another source, perhaps Hegesippus.[84] But Rehm did not attempt further identification of this source beyond suggesting that it was drawn from Hegesippus. He gave *R* 1.27-74 a unity that would be at best difficult if the Recognitionist is working here with several sources. Viewed in the light of Rehm's strong skepticism of source criticism of PsCl, his

---

79 Ibid., 147-9.
80 *ZNW* 31 (1932) 151-99.
81 Ibid., 181.
82 Ibid., 189, n. 2.
83 *ZNW* 37 (1938) 77-184. See also Rehm's "Clemens Romanus II (PsClementinen)," *RAC* 3.197-206.
84 Rehm, "Entstehung," 146, 162.

endorsement of a source behind *R* 1.27-74, hesitant though it is, is significant.[85]

J. Irmscher followed Rehm in positing only a *G* source for *R* and *H*. He denied Waitz's restored *KerygmataP* and *PP*. Irmscher placed *G* in Syria and dated it ca 300-350.[86]

Recent Proponents of Source Criticism

A renewed impetus for the study of the sources of PsCl was given in 1949 by the publication of H. J. Schoeps's *Theologie und Geschichte des Judenchristentums*.[87] The "Judenchristentum" of this book is equated with Ebionism, and Schoeps here was largely concerned with PsCl and their sources. With Schoeps's several works on Jewish Christianity comes a strong recrudescence of some of the perspectives of the Tübingen School.

Schoeps held that one of the sources of the *KerygmataP* is an "Ebionite Acts of the Apostles" mentioned by Epiphanius (*Pan* 30.16). This document underlies *R* 1.27-71. The final part of this "Acts" is the source of *R* 1.66-71, and was probably entitled Αναβαθμοι Ιακωβου.[88] Schoeps placed a premium on the historicity of this source's portrayal of the early church. He even argued that the Stephen of canonical Acts is an *Ersatzfigur* for James, whose speech in the temple was the true occasion for the beginning of the persecution of the church.[89]

In his later *Jewish Christianity: Factional Disputes in the Early Church*,[90] Schoeps reconsidered two of these positions. First, he

85 Fitzmyer, "Scrolls," 349, also expresses doubt on the source criticism of PsCl, citing Rehm. But he does employ it in his analysis of the relationship of Qumran and the Ebionites as he compares the key features of Qumran with *KerygmataP* (pp. 350-371).

86 "The Pseudo-Clementines," in E. Hennecke, *New Testament Apocrypha*, ed. W. Schneemelcher (2 vols.; Philadelphia: Westminster, 1963-64) 2.53-54.

87 Tübingen: Mohr.

88 Ibid., 383, 406.

89 This interpretation of 1.27-71 is also found in Schoeps's "Die Urgeschichte nach den Pseudoklementinen," *Aus frühchristlicher Zeit* (Tübingen: Mohr, 1950) 1-37.

90 Philadelphia: Fortress, 1969; German original, *Das Judenchristentum* (Berne: Francke, 1964).

seemed to accept Strecker's delineation of the *AJ* source, but still restricted it to *R* 1.66-71.[91] Second, he retreated slightly from his earlier claim that Stephen is an *Ersatzfigur* in Acts.[92] But Schoeps continued to defend the historical value of several other key elements: the primacy of James; the dispute between the twelve apostles and the Jewish sects; the persecution led by Paul that broke out upon the speech of James in the temple; and the flight to Pella.[93]

In 1958 G. Strecker published his dissertation, *Das Judenchristentum in den Pseudoklementinen*.[94] His aim was to discern the historical development of Jewish Christianity in PsCl, and his study is the most thorough and careful source-critical analysis of the entire PsCl corpus to date. Strecker put forth cogent reasons to show that the "Table of Contents" in *R* 3.75 is indeed fictitious and cannot be used as a basis for reconstructing the *KerygmataP* (or, although Strecker did not say so, for denying an *AJ* source in *R* 1). Instead, using the contents of the *EpPt* and *Cont* as a key, he isolated the *KerygmataP* from *R* and *H*. Claiming it is gnostic Jewish Christian rather than Ebionite, Strecker located the work in Syria and dated it ca. 200.[95]

Another source behind *G* is the *AJ*. This source is found in *R* 1.33-71, minus one large interpolation in 1.44.4-1.53.3, and many smaller ones throughout. Jesus the Prophet like Moses is its main christological figure, and it stems from a law-observant, anti-Pauline community. After a comparison of *R* 1.33-71 with the *AJ* mentioned

---

91 Ibid., 38-46. The same position on Strecker's source criticism is found in Schoeps's review of Strecker, "Das Judenchristentum in den Pseudoklementinen," *ZRGG* 11 (1959) 72-7.

92 Ibid., 43, especially n. 5.

93 Ibid., 39-46.

94 TU 70; Berlin: Akadamie.

95 Ibid., 137-220.

by Epiphanius, Strecker concluded with several researchers that they are related, but that differences between the two indicate that they are not the same document. Strecker solved the problem by positing a common archetype, which he labelled "*AJ*." The *AJ* known to Epiphanius is "*AJ* I," that in *R* 1 is "*AJ* II." The source of *R* 1.33-71 was written in Pella between 150-200 in a Jewish-Christian community that saw itself as the heir of the earliest church of Jerusalem.[96]

Strecker's research on PsCl has been the benchmark for all later study. While he published two subsequent studies on Jewish Christianity and PsCl,[97] he has not altered his basic positions on the *AJ* source. Researchers who followed Strecker either built on or tried to dismantle the foundation he laid. These scholars bring us up to the present: Brown, Martyn, Stötzel, Lüdemann, and Wehnert.

In his tradition-critical study, "James,"[98] S. K. Brown analyzed the James tradition in the *KerygmataP* and the *AJ*. He affirmed the limits of the *AJ* as laid down by Strecker, and added evidence of his own why *R* 1.33-71 cannot be identified as part of the *KerygmataP*.[99] The *AJ* does indeed show an interest in James, especially his primacy, and this passes beyond the limits of "Catholic-oriented writers" such as Clement of Rome and Eusebius. However, "There is nothing to suggest that the *AJ* II's portrayal of James should be characterized as specifically Jewish or Jewish Christian in orientation and origin." Instead, its author is "a Gentile Christian who, in the wake of Jewish disillusionment with [Judaism] when Jerusalem fell for the second time in less

---

96 Ibid., 221-54.

97 The first was in an appendix to the second edition of W. Bauer's *Rechtgläubigkeit und Ketzerei im ältesten Christentum* (Tübingen: Mohr, 1964), English translation *Orthodoxy and Heresy in Earliest Christianity*, ed. R. A. Kraft and G. Krodel (Philadelphia: Fortress, 1971) entitled "On the Problem of Jewish Christianity." The second is in the second edition of his *Judenchristentum*, which updates his treatment of the *AJ* with six pages of endnotes.

98 Subtitled "A Religio-historical Study of the Relations between Jewish, Gnostic, and Catholic Christianity in the Early Period through an Investigation of the Traditions about James the Lord's Brother" (Ph.D. dissertation, Brown University; Ann Arbor: University Microfilms, 1972).

99 Ibid., 194-201.

than sixty years, wrote a conciliatory tract in which he sought to minimize the differences between the beliefs of Jews and Christians, thus intending to make Christianity attractive to the Jewish audience."[100]

J. L. Martyn, in his essay, "Clementine Recognitions 1, 33-71, Jewish Christianity, and the Fourth Gospel,"[101] probed the relationship of R 1.33-71 and the Fourth Gospel. He accepted Strecker's isolation of this source, its identification as the AJ, and Strecker's conclusions on provenance and date. Martyn's contribution to the study of the AJ is his hypothesis that a common oral tradition on the trial of Jewish Christians as mesithim (religious seducers) before Jewish religious courts may underlie parts of the Fourth Gospel and the AJ. Its use in the AJ is not that of a present situation of such a trial, or a repeated situation in the past or present (a Sitz im Leben). Rather, it is "a piece of tradition, available to this littérateur who wished to employ it for the sake of its literary potential."[102] This tradition, Martyn argued, is employed in R 1.62.2-8, the "trial" of public debate between Peter and James and the Jewish religious authorities.[103]

A. Stötzel, in a general overview of the AJ source, held that it reflects the history and theology of a Jewish-Christian group between AD 70 and 135. The main points of controversy for the AJ were the separation from Judaism, the nature of the mission to the Gentiles, and the debate about Paul and his law-free gospel.[104]

In his tradition-critical study of anti-Paulinism in early Christianity, G. Lüdemann analyzed PsCl.[105] He divided R 1.33-71 into two units: (1) 1.33-65, a history of salvation from Abraham to the founding of the

---

100 Ibid., 278-85.

101 God's Christ and His People: Studies in Honour of Nils Alstrup Dahl (ed. J. Jervell and W. Meeks; Oslo: Universitetsforlaget, 1977) 265-95; reprinted in a less technical form in Martyn, The Gospel of John in Christian History (New York: Paulist, 1978) 55-89.

102 Ibid., 290.

103 Ibid., 278-85

104 A. Stötzel, "Die Darstellung der ältesten Kirchengeschichte nach den Pseudo-Clementinen," VigChr 36 (1982) 24-37. Stötzel claims to follow Schoeps in assigning H 17.13-19 to the AJ; but Schoeps only reckons it to the Ebionite Acts, not to the AJ (Schoeps, Theologie, 383-4).

105 Paulus, der Heidenapostel, vol. 2: Antipaulinismus im frühen Christentum (FRLANT 130; Göttingen: Vandenhoeck & Ruprecht, 1983) 228-57.

church; (2) 1.66-71, the account of James in the temple. Aside from the large interpolation in *R* 1.44.3-1.53, Lüdemann also insisted on the secondary character of 1.55-65, the dispute of the twelve apostles with the Jewish sects in the temple. He argued that 1.55-65 is not a part of the *AJ*, but was added by the author of *R* and/or *G*.[106] He then examined the relationship of the *AJ* of Epiphanius and *R* 1.33-71 and reversed the relationship argued by all previous researchers: The *AJ* is dependent upon the traditions found in *R* 1.66-71, not *vice-versa*. Only *R* 1.66-71 is related to the *AJ*. Since 1.33-71 is a "doublet" of 1.66-71, it is redactional as well: "Da die Rede des Petrus (und der anderen Apostel) in I 33f und die Rede des Jakobus in I 66ff Dublettencharakter haben, halte ich es für plausibel, daß der Redaktor aus der von ihm benutzten, in I 66ff besonders sichtbar werdenden Tradition Material entnommen hat und dem Petrus (und den anderen Aposteln) in den Mund gelegt hat." Lüdemann also named *R* 1.33-71 the "R I-Quelle."[107]

Finally, J. Wehnert has advocated an analysis of language and literary style in PsCl and their sources over the more established analysis of content. In "Literarkritik und Sprachanalyse: Kritische Anmerkungen zum gegenwartigen Stand der Pseudoklementinen-Forschung,"[108] he compared the language of the *KerygmataP*'s commonly-accepted introductory documents, the *EpPt* and *Cont*, with the sections of it in *R* and *H* isolated by Strecker and others. Wehnert concluded that these documents show no relationship to the material in *R* and *H* commonly assigned to *KerygmataP*, and therefore this

---

106 Ibid., 237-40.
107 Ibid., 242.
108 *ZNW* 74 (1983) 268-301. Wehnert's method and his conclusion on the *KerygmataP* were largely anticipated by J. Rius-Camps, "Las Pseudoclementinas: Bases Filológicas para una Nueva Interpretación," *Revista Catalana de Theologia* 1 (1976) 79-158. Wehnert could make use of the forthcoming concordance to PsCl, the publication of which may encourage the kind of research method he has employed. For a report on the plans for this concordance, see *VigChr* 37 (1983) 413-5.

source does not exist. Wehnert did not apply his method to *R* 1, nor deal with an *AJ* source.

Other modern scholars who have not done source-critical analysis of *R* 1 have accepted the presence of an *AJ*. They should be mentioned here because they contribute to the consensus relating *R* 1.33-71 to the *AJ*. A. F. J. Klijn and G. J. Reinink approvingly noted the consensus that related *R* 1.33-71 to the *AJ*.[109] M. Simon also concurred that *R* 1.33-71 is to be identified as the *AJ*.[110] Although he did not explicitly mention *R* 1, F. F. Bruce argued that the part of the Ebionite *Acts of the Apostles* which dealt with the ascents of James to the temple for debate is "largely incorporated" in PsCl.[111] A. Lindemann, in his study of the traditions about Paul, accepts Strecker's source analysis of *R* 1,[112] as does O. Skarsaune in his study of Justin.[113] Finally, W. H. Harter stated that "it is probable" that *R* 1.33-71 is the *AJ* mentioned by Epiphanius.[114]

Our history of research has shown that many different proposals have been made since 1849 on the existence and scope of a source in *R* 1. We can restate in tabular form the more important proposals. (See table on the next page.)

---

109 *Patristic Evidence for Jewish-Christian Sects* (NovTSup 36; Leiden: Brill, 1973) 71.
110 "La Migration á Pella: Légende ou Réalité?" *RSR* 60 (1972) 49.
111 *Peter, Stephen, James, and John* (Grand Rapids: Eerdmans, 1980) 116-7.
112 *Paulus im ältesten Christentum* (BHT 58; Tübingen: Mohr, 1979) 104, 108-9.
113 *The Proof from Prophecy* (NovTSup 56; Leiden: Brill, 1987) 252-3.
114 "The Causes and Course of the Jewish Revolt against Rome, 66-74 C.E., in Recent Scholarship" (Ph.D. dissertation, Union Theological Seminary [New York]; Ann Arbor: University Microfilms, 1984) 114-5.

Table 1

Sources of *R* 1.33-71 in the History of Research

Date	Researcher	Main Contents	Name(s)
1849	Hilgenfeld	1.27-43, 55-72	*KerygmaP*
1849	Köstlin	1.36-71	*AJ*
1845	Uhlhorn	1.27-74	*AJ, G*
1865	Lightfoot	1.54-71	*AJ*
1869	Lehmann	1.27-72	*KerygmaP*
1872	Lipsius	1.27-43 - 1.44-71 -	(unknown) *Praxeis Petrou*
1901	Hort	1.66-71; perhaps also 22-44a, 55-74	*AJ*
1904	Waitz	1.27-71	*KerygmataP*
1905	Boussett	1.27-43, 53-71	*AJ*
1930	Cullmann	1.27-42, 54-71	*KerygmataP*
1935	Thomas	1.27-72	Perhaps *AJ*
1949	Schoeps	1.27-71 - 1.66-71 -	Ebion. *Acts* *AJ*
1958	Strecker	1.33-44.2, 53.4-62, 64-71	*AJ*
1972	Brown	1.33-44, 53.4b-62, 64-71	*AJ*
1980	Lüdemann	1.33-71 - 1.66-71 -	(*R* 1 Source) *AJ*
1982	Stötzel	1.33-44.2, 53.4-62, 64-71; *H* 17.13-19 -	*AJ*

Summary of the History of Research

We now tie together the threads of our findings. First, the presence of an *AJ* source in *R* 1 has been debated from the beginning of source criticism into PsCl through the modern period. Second, those who discern an *AJ* source differ on its limits. Does it underlie *R* 1.22-71, as was thought in much nineteenth century research (and Schoeps), or 1.33-71, as in the recent consensus, or only 1.54/66 - 71/72, as some from Hort to Lüdemann have argued? Third, the study of the relationship of the Clementines and their sources to the early history of Christianity has been a continuing legacy of the Tübingen School. Those modern researchers who stand in the tradition of Tübingen - Waitz and Strecker, and especially Schoeps and Lüdemann - have written much on the sources of the Clementines. Fourth, several opponents of the Tübingen School and those sceptical of source criticism of PsCl have agreed that the *AJ* may indeed be found in *R* 1. Support for an *AJ* source has, therefore, a broad base in the history of research.

Fifth, most of those who have held to an *AJ* source have usually given it slight treatment beyond identification. Some have noted distinct doctrines in the source, and others have studied it in the history of one tradition (Brown, Lüdemann). The chapter in Strecker's *Judenchristentum* is the fullest examination of *R* 1.33-71 that we possess. Finally, the treatment of *R* 1 has been primarily historical, dealing with such matters as the presence of a source, its scope, provenance, date, etc. The theology of *R* 1 has rarely been given treatment beyond a few passing comments on its christology, law observance, or other item.

Plan of the Present Work

Having reviewed and summarized past research into a proposed *AJ* source in *R* 1, we will offer a comprehensive and critical analysis of *R* 1.33-71. Chapter Two will assess the probability of an *AJ* source. In the course of this assessment, we will provide a full literary analysis of *R* 1 to make more precise and assured the limits of the hypothetical source offered by Strecker. We will also consider the question whether it is properly identified as the *AJ*. Chapter Three will provide fresh English translations of the *AJ* from the best Latin and Syriac texts. Chapter Four is an analytical commentary on the source, and will offer a precise understanding of its literary, historical and theological forms.

Chapter Five is a synthetic treatment of the *AJ* designed to examine its more important historical and theological issues as uncovered in the commentary. In this chapter we will also attempt to locate the *AJ* in the history of Christianity in the first and second centuries.

CHAPTER TWO

ISOLATION AND IDENTIFICATION
OF THE SOURCE

Introduction

In this chapter we will isolate and identify the proposed source behind *R* 1.33-71. The method to be employed analyzes *R* 1 to determine whether chapters 33-71 are of such a unique nature as to be based on a discrete source, one that stands apart from the rest of *R* 1 and PsCl as a whole.

A few cautions are in order here. First, we must emphasize that this source, even if isolated and identified with a convincing degree of probability, can only be hypothetical in nature. Second, we may not possess the source in its entirety, but only insofar as it has been preserved in *R* 1. Nor can we reconstruct the exact wording of our source. That is precluded by the successive redactions of the source by the authors of *G* and *R*, by the lack of the Greek original of *R* 1, and by the inexact nature of source criticism. Our aim is to recover the source with enough certainty to discern its basic literary form and the main lines of its material content.

As was indicated in Chapter One, some recent source criticism has cast doubt on the existence of the *KerygmataP*. It is beyond the scope of this study to defend or deny the existence of the *KerygmataP* or other sources in PsCl beyond the *AJ*. Our concern is the *AJ*, and here the work of Strecker still forms the consensus of research. A part of our task in this chapter is to refine and reinforce Strecker's source-critical labors into *R* 1.33-71.

Isolation of the Source

In this section, we will offer a source-critical analysis of *R* 1 in order to isolate the source that may lie behind 1.33-71. Our focus will be on the text, with occasional references as necessary to the source-critical labors of others. In most cases (exceptions are noted), the wording of the Latin and Syriac texts is substantially the same. In the argument over a source in *R* 1, the burden of proof is upon those who argue for a source. We intend to show that there is indeed sufficient evidence to demonstrate the probability of an *AJ* source in *R* 1.33-71.

Why would one suspect that there is a source behind *R* 1.33-71? Mainly because its material content is significantly different in ideology from other parts of *R* 1 and the rest of PsCl. This *ideological* criterion is, then, the first tool for source analysis. We cannot add to it the criterion of style, because we lack the Greek original, and stylistic peculiarities that may have existed in it are probably very inadequately reflected in the L and S versions. There is, however, a second tool for our source criticism: the *contextual* criterion. This is an analysis of the relationship of *R* 1 with other parts of PsCl, especially any extensive parallel passages, to determine if a source is present. Another part of contextual analysis is a careful study of the difficulties of the text. In source criticism, these difficulties have gone under the name "aporias" (from the Greek, "difficulty, perplexity"). R. Fortna has well described aporias as "the many inconsistencies, disjunctures and hard connections, even contradictions which the text shows . . . which cannot be accounted for by textual criticism."[1] The presence of one or more aporias in a passage may indicate a seam between literary strata, and the possible presence of a source. The reader will follow our source-critical analysis more easily by pausing here to read Book One of *Recognitions* in ANF, and by keeping it open for ready reference.

R 1 begins with the romance of Clement: his youth, schooling, and religious questionings (chaps. 1-3). He increasingly considered the question of immortality (chaps. 4-5). He first heard the Gospel

---

1 Fortna, *The Gospel of Signs* (SNTSMS 11; Cambridge: University Press, 1970) 2. Fortna's methodological approach to the Signs Source of the Fourth Gospel is, *mutatis mutandis*, applicable to the source criticism undertaken here, and our treatment in this paragraph owes much to his method (pp. 15-22).

secondhand (chap. 6), and then as preached by Barnabas (chap. 7). Clement was drawn to Barnabas' preaching, defended him before a hostile audience, and met him personally (chaps. 7-10). He then travelled to Caesarea and met Peter (chaps. 11-13). Clement explained his questionings, and Peter instructed him about the causes of his ignorance and its remedy in the True Prophet (chaps. 14-16). He became an attendant of Peter, who was pleased by his ability and progress (chaps. 17-19).[2] Peter and his associates then prepared for a debate with Simon the magician, their opponent, by rehearsing the main points of their belief "according to the tradition of the True Prophet" (1.21.7). This preparation continues from 1.22 through the end of *R* 1.

A major part of this preparation for the debate with Simon is a narration by Peter of events from the creation to the early church. This Petrine monologue begins at *R* 1.27.1 and ends at 1.74.5. Its first section runs from the creation to seven years after the death of Jesus (1.27.1 - 1.44.3); it is followed by a section of dialogue between Clement and Peter (1.44.4 - 1.53). The second section of Petrine monologue runs from 1.54 to 1.74.5. It covers the debate of the Twelve with the parties of the Jews in the temple, the speech of James and its aftermath, and Peter's final preparation to debate Simon.

An initial reading of *R* 1.27 - 1.44.4 might well suggest that it is a unified narrative. *R* 1 presents it as such, and several researchers from Hilgenfeld to Schoeps have argued for its integrity. Beside the formal unity of the Petrine monologue, there are two themes which would seem to bind this section into a unity: (1) an interest in the land of Judea (1.30.3; 1.31.2; 1.32.1,4; 1.34.4; 1.35.1,6; 1.37.3-4; 1.38.1,3); (2) polemics against idolatry (1.30.5; 1.35.2,5-6; 1.36.1), the temple (1.31.1; 1.37.2-3; 1.38.4; 1.39.3), and sacrifice (1.30.4; 1.36.1; 1.37; 1.39.1-2).[3]

But a close reading of the text has led Strecker to discern several aporias between 1.32 and 1.33 that indicate the beginning of a new source in 1.33.1. First, in 1.32 Abraham receives revelation from an angel, but in 1.33 from the True Prophet. Second, in 1.30 the Persians

---

2 Most of *R* 1.1-19 has close parallels in *H* 1.1-20, and has therefore been assigned by Strecker to *G* (*Judenchristentum*, 41).

3 Brown, "James," 198.

are said to exist at the time of Nimrod (cf. *H* 9.3 and *R* 4.29), but in 1.33 the Persians stem from Eliezer, one of the sons of Abraham. Third, the counting of the generations ends at 1.32, although the *Heilsgeschichte* continues.[4] Fourth, at 1.33 begins the parallel to the Stephen speech in Acts 7. Strecker also brings forward two important contextual evidences that a new source begins at 1.33.1: (1) Much of 1.27-32 is also presented in *R* 4.19-20, 27-30, chapters which are parallel to *H* 8.10-19, 9.3-7; (2) *R* 1.33-44 has no parallel in the rest of *R* or in *H*.[5]

Other factors suggest, however, that our source does not begin at 1.33.1, but rather at 1.33.3. 1.33.1-2 deals exclusively with the figure of the True Prophet. This True Prophet is prominent in what precedes 1.33 (1.16-18; 1.21.7; 1.25.5-7), but is largely absent from what follows, where the predominant figure is the Mosaic Prophet. Also, the content of the True Prophet's teaching in 1.33.1-2 has close parallels with the preceding material. "Knowledge of the Divinity" is echoed in "the knowledge of divine and eternal things" given by the True Prophet to those who seek it (1.16.2). All the other topics of the True Prophet's teaching - the beginning and end of the world, the immortality of the soul, the kind of life pleasing to God, and judgment - have close verbal parallels in the short span of 1.14.2-4. These topics are connected by Peter to the True Prophet, who alone can give certainty of these things (1.15-16) and a knowledge of the past, present, and future (1.21.7). Although he assigns 1.33.1-2 to our source, Strecker does admit, "Der gesamte Inhalt der Belehrung des wahren Propheten ist uberflüssig und wohl sekundär."[6] Thus, 1.33.1-2 is of a piece with what precedes it, from *G*, and is not the beginning of a new source.[7]

---

4 Not all the generations from Adam to Abraham are numbered in 1.29-32, but each time the text mentions some event the number of the generation in which it occurred is given. Generations twelve through twenty-one are all numbered in 1.30-32.

5 Strecker, *Judenchristentum*, 221. Strecker assigns 1.27-32 to *G*.

6 Ibid., 224. Strecker notes that "the kind of life pleasing to God" also has a close verbal parallel in *H* 8.10.3 (cf. *R* 4.9.2). We note that two other parts of 1.33.1-2 have verbal parallels with other parts of *R*: the True Prophet's knowledge of human thoughts (8.59.7); and the invisible celestial habitations (3.27.3). These verbal parallels show that these phrases may be a part of a literary stratum of PsCl other than our source.

7 All the aporias Strecker adduces to demarcate 1.33.1ff from 1.27-32 are fully applicable to a literary seam between 1.33.2 and 1.33.3. The only exception is a conflict between the revealer as an angel in 1.32 and as the True Prophet in 1.33; but the text, by mentioning "the things that had been told him" (1.33.1), connects these two revelations in a consistent fashion.

Two additional aporias also point to a seam between R 1.33.2 and 1.33.3. First, 1.33.3 is awkwardly connected with 1.33.1-2 in that it returns to a time before that spoken of in 1.33.1-2. Aside from this, the narrative in chaps. 33-34 moves in uniformly chronological order. Second, it is said in 1.33.3 and 1.34.1 that Abraham once lived in ignorance of God. But there is no previous mention of Abraham's ignorance in R 1. Rather, in 1.32.1 - 1.33.2 Abraham always has a knowledge of God, and progresses in further knowledge through revelations by an angel and the True Prophet. All these aporias and the demonstrable similarities between 1.33.1-2 and what precedes it in R 1 point to a literary seam between 1.33.2 and 1.33.3. At 1.33.3, therefore, our source begins.

R 1.34 continues the narration of the source. Abraham obtained Isaac through Sarah, Isaac begot Jacob, Jacob the Twelve Patriarchs, and the Twelve the Seventy-Two. Moses brought the people out of Egypt. At Sinai they worshipped an idol (chap. 35), and Moses then permitted them to sacrifice until the coming of the prophet like himself (chap. 36). The long history of Israel should have taught them that God does not desire sacrifice (chap. 37). Joshua led the people into Canaan, but they went from bad to worse in making kings for themselves and erecting a temple (chap. 38). When the Prophet like Moses came, he instituted baptism in place of sacrifice (chap. 39), but he was opposed by most of the people (chap. 40). The prophet was crucified and rose from the dead (chaps. 41-42). In seven years' time the church grew so numerous as to be a majority of the Jews, and was constantly asked by the priests to hold a public debate on the topic of whether Jesus is the Prophet like Moses, and thus the Messiah (chaps. 43-44.3). This entire passage of 1.33.3 to 1.44.3 has an integrity which is seen in its leading themes of the Mosaic Prophet and opposition to sacrifice.

The only recent researcher to take exception to the integrity of 1.33-43 has been S. Brown. He argued that 1.43.2, "For only about this does there seem to be a difference for us who believe in Jesus over against the Jews who do not believe," was added by the AJ author to his source. This statement is "an oversimplification which has been added under the influence of a tendency to diminish the differences between Jews and Christians."[8] This statement does indeed over-simplify the difference between Jews and "Christians" (note that this

---

8 Brown, "James," 198.

term does not occur in *R* 1). However, it is entirely consonant with the topic of the two debates of 1.55-65 and 66-71, which is if Jesus is the Messiah (1.55.1; 1.68.2). More importantly, as Epiphanius' account of the *AJ* is brief, with no direct quotation, it is difficult to see how Brown can accurately distinguish between tradition and redaction on such a precise point. More will be said in Chapters Four and Five about this sentence; for the present we may include it in our source.

At *R* 1.44.4 are indications of a literary seam that marks the end of the long monologue of 1.33.3 - 1.44.3. The form of the text abruptly shifts at 1.44.4 from monologue to dialogue as Clement reappears to question Peter. This dialogue form continues through 1.52. Strecker has enumerated several important evidences to show that 1.44.4 -1.53.3 is an interpolation by the *G* author.[9] To his evidence, we add the following aporias. First, from 1.44.6 to 1.45.5 the discussion seems to be oriented toward Gentile Christians, as the meaning of "the Christ" is given an explanation in terms of the name of the rulers of Gentile lands.[10] Second, "among the Jews a king is called Christ" (1.45.3) stands in contrast to the negative view of the Israelite kings in 1.38.4, as do the references to the kings in 1.46. Third, this explanation of "the Christ" also stands in contrast to 1.43.1 - 1.44.3, where both those Jews who believe in Jesus and those who do not believe share a common understanding of "the Christ" as the Prophet like Moses. Fourth, in 1.41.4 - 1.44 the Mosaic Prophet drops from view, and the True Prophet reappears (1.44.5-6). Fifth, in 1.44.4 - 1.53 "Christ" is most often used as a name ("Christ Jesus," 1.45.2; "the kingdom of Christ," 1.52.1,6; etc.), while in 1.33.3 - 1.44.3 it is a title ("Jesus is the eternal Christ," 1.43.1, 1.44.2). Sixth, a sharp aporia exists between 1.43.2, where the point of disagreement between believers and other Jews is whether Jesus is the Messiah, and 1.50.5, where the only point of disagreement is on the first and second coming of Jesus. Finally, 1.43.1 sees the *acceptance* of Jesus

---

9 The discussion of the title "Christ" and the emphasis on free will have no parallel in the source, but stem from *G*. The task of the angel to lead the people is suggested by *R* 1.45. *G* interpolated from the *KerygmataP*: (1) the changing form of the True Prophet; (2) the question of anointing; (3) the references to the false-pericope theory. *G* interpolated from the *AJ* the denial of sacrifice and the two-fold advent of Jesus (Strecker, *Judenchristentum*, 236).

10 Here we anticipate a position to be substantiated in Chapter Five, that our source is a Jewish-Christian document.

by most of the Jewish people as a divine confirmation of the church's confession of Jesus as Messiah, which 1.50.7 reverses by claiming that the *rejection* of Jesus by most of the Jews has been a confirmation of his coming. The cumulative weight of these aporias leads to the conclusion that 1.44.4 - 1.52 is an interpolation from a later hand into our source.[11]

If 1.44.4 - 1.52 is an interpolation, where does our source resume? At 1.53.3 a redactional device appears that may signal its resumption. This device, the "repetition," has been well summarized by Martyn as "a rule formulated by E. Hirsch, to the effect that authors who insert material into a literary piece which they are copying tend, before continuing, to repeat at the end of the insertion a key expression which occurred in that piece just prior to the insertion."[12] The repetition is most often used after longer interpolations, and is designed to help the reader resume the story. Such a repetition occurs at 1.53.4, and Strecker, Brown and Martyn see in 1.53.4 the resumption of our source.

But a closer reading of the text suggests that our source resumes, not at 1.53.4, but rather at 1.55.1. We note that 1.55.1 contains a repetition very similar to the one at 1.53.4, and 1.55.1 looks back to 1.44.2 in a more direct way than 1.53.4 does. This second repetition raises the possibility that 1.53.4-1.55 may be an interpolation from a later hand. Is there anything in the content of chap. 54 which would indicate its secondary nature?

A close reading of 1.54 reveals striking aporias in almost every sentence, indicating that it does not belong to our source. These aporias will be noted section by section in the following paragraphs.

Three items in the first section conflict with 1.33.3 - 1.43.3 and with the debate in 1.55-65 which chap. 54 introduces. (1) "Christ" is used more as a name than a title. (2) "The grace of baptism" is also present

---

11 Strecker, *Judenchristentum*, 41-2, traces the bulk of 1.44-53 to *G*, with some phrases from *R* and the *KerygmataP*.

12 Martyn, "Recognitions," 269. Martyn refers to Hirsch's *Das vierte Evangelium* (Tübingen: Mohr, 1936) on John 11:33-8. Compare also this description of the repetition: "die - auch sonst im hellenistischen Zeitalter nachweisbare - Technik des gleichendigen Einsatzes aufgezeigt: der Einschub endet, oft wörtlich, bei einer Aussage entsprechender der, bei der er den ursprünglichen Text unterbrach" (Hirsch, "Stilkritik und Literaranalyse im vierten Evangelium," *ZNW* 43 [1950] 133). See also B. O. Long, "Framing Repetitions in Biblical Historiography," *JBL* 106 (1987) 385-99.

in *R* 1.48.5 and 4.35.5 (cf. also 6.15.2-3, 7.35.2-3), but is not found in the source. (3) Each division among the people is called a "schism" (L: *schisma*; S: *plgwt'*).[13] This word is not used in 1.55-65, where the word "party" appears (L: *pars*; S uses neither word).

Beginning in 1.54.2 and lasting through 1.54.9, this chapter shows a strong interest in the origin of these sects. However, what follows in 1.55-65 does not take up the question of their *origin*, but only their *teachings*. Also, the wording of 1.54.2, "as more righteous than others, began to separate themselves from the assembly of the people," has a verbal parallel in *R* 6.11.2, where it is said of the Pharisees and scribes that they "seemed to be better than others, and separated from the people." This parallel shows that the wording of 1.54.2 may be drawn from a literary stratum of PsCl other than our source.

R 1.54.3 states that first Dositheus and then Simon were the authors of the sect of the Sadducees. This understanding is absent from 1.56, but is developed in detail in *R* 2.8-11 and *H* 2.24. In 1.54.4, the Samaritans are a religious party like the Sadducees and Pharisees, a misunderstanding which is avoided in the treatment of the Samaritans in 1.57.

Section five of 1.54 shows a mixing of the Prophet like Moses with the True Prophet: "They rightly expect from the predictions of Moses expect the one True Prophet." Such a mixing does not occur in the treatment of the Prophet like Moses in 1.33.3 - 1.43.3, nor will it occur in 1.55-65. Dositheus appears again as the one who foils the Samaritan's belief in Jesus. In 1.57.4, however, the refusal of the Samaritans to believe in Jesus as the Mosaic Prophet is traced rather to "the error of Mount Gerizim." In section six, the scribes and Pharisees are seen as one sect, but in the debate which follows they are two distinct groups (1.58-59).

1.54.7 traces baptism to John. In 1.33.3 - 1.43.3 and in the debate of 1.55-65, it is traced only to Jesus. John is never described by the source as "the Baptist," nor is his baptism mentioned (cf. 1.60). In section eight, "some" of the disciples of John proclaimed their own master as the Christ, while 1.60.1-4 presents the entire group of his disciples as doing so.

In conclusion, 1.54 is summarizing and superfluous. This chapter is not at all necessary for an understanding of 1.55-65. The order of the

---

13 The Syriac will be given in transliterated form, as it is thus somewhat intelligible to those who do not read Syriac, but are acquainted with other Semitic languages.

sects is drawn from 1.55-60, great emphasis is placed on their origins, and what is said about them is often contradictory with 1.55-65. The many aporias adduced above substantiate what is suggested by the repetition at 1.55.1: 1.54 does not belong to the source. Rather, it likely comes from the Recognitionist, to judge from his love of summaries and typically unskillful composition.

Chapter 55 resumes the narration of the source at the point at which 1.44.3 left off. In the debate in the temple, the disciples refuted the Sadducees (chap. 56), the Samaritans (chap. 57), the scribes (chap. 58), the Pharisees (chap. 59), the disciples of John (chap. 60),[14] and the high priest (chaps. 61-62). Chapter 63 is a summary of the debate, whose place in the source will be taken up shortly. Chapter 64 resumes the direct narrative of the debate as Peter predicted the destruction of the temple. This set off a near-riot, which was quelled by Gamaliel's promise to debate with the believers on the next day (chap. 65).

This entire section of R 1.55-65 has a literary integrity which is broken only by Chapter 63. Strecker enumerates good reasons for thinking this passage does not belong to the source. (1) It interrupts the speech of Peter.[15] (2) The summary of the theme of the debate in 1.63.1 is superfluous. (3) "Priests" are not mentioned in 1.55-62, but only the "high priest." (4) "The one only God" is suitable to Gentile Christian apologetics. (5) "The Son [of God]" and "grace" do not fit the source. (6) The "three-fold invocation" contradicts the source's uniform use of baptism in the name of Jesus. (7) "The Eucharist of Christ the Lord" is foreign to the source.[16]

To these aporias we add the following. (1) 1.63.1 implies that all the Twelve are fishermen (!). 1.62 calls only Peter a fisherman. (2) "The scribes and Pharisees, concerning the kingdom of heaven," is dependent upon 1.54.6-7, a passage which we have shown above to be secondary. (3) "All the people" conflicts with 1.55-65, for the debate is

---

14 Here only the disciples of John are refuted, not John himself. In PsCl, only R 1.60 has a positive view of John, calling him the "forerunner" of Jesus and a "prophet." 1.53.5 says that the time of John saw the division of the Jews into various sects. R 2.8 and its parallel in H 2.23-4 link John with Simon Magus and Dositheus, both arch-heretics.

15 Brown, "James," notes well that at the end of 1.62 and in 1.64 Peter's speech is in direct discourse, but 1.63 is in indirect discourse.

16 Strecker, *Judenchristentum*, 42-3.

not directed to the people as a whole, but only to the various groups addressed in the debate. (4) In 1.63, the Gentile mission is occasioned by the belief of the Jews; elsewhere, it is occasioned by their disbelief (1.42.1, 1.64.1-2). (5) Triadic language, absent from 1.22-44, 55-62, is found in 1.63.2-3. In view of these inconsistencies, 1.63 probably does not belong to our source.[17]

Resuming our tracing of the source, we note that 1.64, the conclusion of Peter's reply to Caiaphas, follows consecutively from 1.62. Chapter 65 presents the near-riot in the temple, which is arrested by Gamaliel. 1.66.1-3 is a transition between the end of the temple debate of the Twelve and the beginning of the disputation of James. Gamaliel set the terms of the debate (1.66.4 - 1.67). After the points of reference from Scripture were settled (1.68), James argued through seven successive days and convinced all the people that Jesus is the Christ, leading them to come for immediate baptism (1.69).

The reader may note in 1.69.5-7 the presence of language reminiscent of 1.63. Strecker has followed Rehm in seeing 1.69.5b-8a as secondary. In addition to the remarks of Rehm which argue for the Eunomian nature of 1.69.6-7,[18] we note several other aporias to show its secondary character. In 1.69.5 James is said to have taught "the people." However, James' teaching in 1.69 is, strictly speaking, not directed to the people, but to Caiaphas (note "to him," 1.69.1 [L]; S specifies no audience). "The name of the threefold blessedness" echoes the Trinitarian language of 1.63.3. Once again, "the True Prophet" appears. "Remission of sins" and "enter the kingdom of heaven" may be drawn from 1.55.3-4. Strecker, following Rehm and Waitz, holds that 1.69.5b-8a is an interpolation. The whole of sections 5-7 is rather an interpolation, since 1.69.8a, "But when he had spoken some things also about baptism" (so L; cf. S), contradicts 1.69.5b, which itself speaks about baptism. This aporia indicates that the source resumes here.

In Chapter 70 the source's narration of the debate continues. Just as James had convinced all his hearers and was about to present them

---

17 Strecker's sharp characterization of the content of this chapter as "clumsy patchwork" is entirely appropriate. He assigns it to the Recognitionist (Ibid., 42).

18 Rehm, "Entstehung," 96-7. Eunomius (d. 395) taught a form of extreme Arianism that stressed the complete unlikeness of the Father and the Son.

for baptism,[19] "an enemy" entered and upset the plan. He incited a riot, and then attacked James and threw him from the top of the steps. In 1.71, the whole church escaped from the temple. They returned to the house of James, and then went to Jericho. Meanwhile, "the enemy" received authority from the High Priest to go to Damascus to persecute the believers, but missed the church, which was still in Jericho.

We note disjunctures after 1.71 which indicate that our source has reached its end. Although the form of the Petrine monologue continues, the Clementine romance resumes. The cast of characters also shifts to that of *R* 1.11-26 and *R* 2: Zaccheus, Simon the Magician, Peter and Clement. On this evidence, we can conclude that our source, insofar as it is employed in *R* 1, concludes at the end of 1.71.

Our analysis of *R* 1 has shown several different evidences for a discrete source in chapters 33-71. These include the lack of parallels to our source in the rest of PsCl, the use of the redactional device of repetition, and many aporias that indicate the uniqueness of the content of our source, in its main lines of christology and in several smaller items. Because of the number of aporias we have adduced, it would be well to summarize them by gathering them into a table. (Unless noted, the references are to *R*.)

Table 2

Major Aporias between the Source
in *R* 1 and the Remainder of PsCl

The Source in *R* 1	Remainder of PsCl
1. Abraham knows God (1.33.3, 1.34.1)	Abraham in ignorance (1.32.3)
2. Persians from Abraham's son (1.33.3)	Persians antedate Abraham (1.30; 4:29)
3. Seventy-two enter Egypt (1.34.2)	Seventy enter Egypt (*H* 18.4.3)
4. Mosaic Prophet is main figure (1.36-37, 39-41, 56-59)	True Prophet is main figure (1.16-18, 21; 33.1)

---

19 This immediacy of baptism in 1.69.8 and 1.70.1 stands in marked contrast to the rest of PsCl, in which baptism is preceded by a time of fasting and other preparations; cf. *R* 2.72, 3.67; 6.15; 7.34; 10.71; *H* 3.73.1; 11.35.1.

The Source in *R* 1	Remainder of PsCl
5. Sacrifice comes from Moses, not the law (1.36.1)	Sacrifice comes from corruption of the law after Moses' death (*H* 3.46)
6. Kings viewed negatively (1.38.4)	Kings viewed positively (1.45.3-4; 1.46.2-4)
7. Sacrifice opposed by baptism (1.39.2)	Sacrifice opposed by false-pericope theory (*H* 3.45, 52, 56)
8. Moses has seventy-two disciples (1.40.3)	Moses has seventy disciples (*EpPt* 2.1)
9. Gentile mission result of unbelief of Jews (1.42.1, 1.64.2)	Gentile mission fol lows belief of Jews (1.63)
10. Jesus is magician (1.42.4, 1.58.1, 1.70.2)	Simon is magician (1.21; *R* 2-10 *passim*)
11. Point of disagreement is on Jesus' messiahship (1.43.2)	Point of disagreement is on Jesus' two comings (1.50.5)
12. Twelve report orally to James (1.44.1, 1.66.1)	Twelve report in writing to James (1.72.7)
13. "Christ" is predominately a title (1.43.1, 1.44.2, 1.59.3-5, 1.60.1-4, 1.68.2, 1.69.3)	"Christ" predominately a name (1.50.l, 6; 1.53.1; 1.54.1; 1.63.3)
14. Samaritans are not Jews (1.57)	Samaritans are a party like Sadducees and Pharisees (1.54.4)
15. Jesus established baptism (1.55)	John established baptism (1.53.5)
16. Mt. Gerizim causes unbelief of Samaritans (1.57.4)	Dositheus causes unbelief of Samaritans (1.54.5)
17. John and prophets viewed positively (1.59)	John and prophets viewed negatively (1.53; 2:8; cf. 1.46.4)
18. Baptism immediate upon belief (1.68.8; 1.70.1)	After belief, baptism preceded by fasting and other preparations (2.72, 3.67, 6.15, 7.34)

We have argued that the following sections of R 1 be assigned to our source: 33.3-44.3; 55-62; 64.1- 69.4; 69.8-71. Chapter Four, a commentary on the source, will confirm the source-critical analysis offered here.

The Unity of the Source

We now evaluate the unity of our source in the light of the arguments of those who have disputed its unity. Schoeps and Lüdemann have argued that only R 1.66-71 can rightly be called the *AJ*. For Schoeps, 1.66-71 stands as the *AJ* within the whole body of an "Ebionite Acts" in 1.27-71; for Lüdemann, 1.33-45 and 55-65 are later "doublets" of 1.66-71, authored by G with additions by R.[20] Does the content of 1.66-71 suggest a unity with or a disparity from the rest of the source in 1.33-65, and is 1.33-65 in fact a "doublet" of 1.66-71?

The material content of 1.66-71, while not sharing some of the leading elements of 1.55-65 such as opposition to sacrifice and Jesus as the Mosaic Prophet, does in other important respects show itself a piece with 1.33-65. Chapter 66 forms a smooth transition from 1.65 to 1.67. No discernible aporias appear at this juncture, as we might expect if chaps. 65 and 66 are from different literary strata. The same portrait of Gamaliel, both his status as a secret believer and his mission to protect his fellow-believers, is presented in 1.65.2-5 and in 1.66.4-7. The topic of the debates in 1.55-65 and 1.66-71 is the same: Is Jesus the Messiah? (1.59.3-6a; 1.60.1-4; 1.62.3-4; 1.68.2; 1.69.3). Both sections see baptism as the only entrance into the church (1.55.4; 1.69.8; 1.70.1). In both sections, the opposition charges that Jesus was a magician (1.42.4; 1.58.1; 1.70.2). Finally, both sections have a positive view of the prophets of the OT (1.59.4-6; 1.61.3; 1.68.3; 1.69.1). Judging from these shared elements of 1.66-71 and 1.33-65, most of which are distinct from the rest of PsCl,[21] chaps. 66-71 belong to the same literary piece as chaps. 33-65.

To view 1.33-65 as a doublet of 1.66-71 raises some difficulties which Lüdemann does not consider. First, if 1.33-65 is a part of G, why is

---

20 On Schoeps, see above, 19-20; on Lüdemann, 22-23.

21 Jesus as the Messiah and Mosaic Prophet, Jesus (not Simon) as a magician, the figure of Gamaliel, and a positive view of the OT prophets are all peculiar to 1.33-71. Jesus as Messiah and Mosaic Prophet is the main theme of this section.

there no parallel to it in the sections of *H* that derive from *G*? All of our source in *R* 1.33-71 is peculiar to *R* 1, having no significant parallels elsewhere in PsCl. This fact remains a strong contextual evidence for its unity. Second, if 1.33-65 was written by the author of *G* or *R* as a doublet of 1.66-71, why are several key themes not present in 1.66-71 introduced in 1.33-65 which cannot be found elsewhere in *G* or *R*? Jesus as the Prophet like Moses and explicit polemic against the temple and sacrifice are not found in 1.66-71, as one would expect if 1.55-65 were a doublet of 1.66-71. Third, several key elements of 1.66-71 are not taken up in 1.33-65: the debate to be drawn from Scripture (1.68.2 - 1.69.4); the two advents of Jesus (1.69.3-4); and anti-Paulinism (1.70.1 - 1.71.4). This too would be hard to explain if 1.33-65 were in fact a doublet of 1.66-71. While 1.66-71 and 1.33-65 share enough common elements to be seen as a part of the same source, as argued above, they also contain some differences which argue against viewing 1.33-65 as *literarily dependent* upon 1.66-71. In conclusion, we may say that Lüdemann's suggestion, which he holds as "plausible" but does not develop, raises more problems than it solves. The evidence indicates that 1.33-65 and 1.66-71 belong to the same source.

General Opposition to Source Criticism

We now turn to the matter of general opposition to source criticism of PsCl. What, if any, are the implications of opposition to source criticism for the isolation of an *AJ* source in *R* 1? We will consider the work of five scholars: Chapman, Schwartz, Rehm, Irmscher, and Wehnert. Because we have treated their work in Chapter One, our treatment here will be brief.

Chapman attacked the source-critical labors of Waitz, arguing that *KerygmataP* and *PP* are fictitious, but he did accept the presence of *G*. When he had to his own satisfaction disposed of the work of Waitz, he concluded that "The Clementines have no 'sources'." Chapman did not carry forth the debate over source criticism in a constructive manner, and he did not touch upon the question of an *AJ* source.[22]

Schwartz paid a good deal of attention to the *KerygmataP*, which he held a fiction, but the closest he came to a consideration of an *AJ* source is to deny that the report of Epiphanius in *Pan.* 30 can be related to *R*

---

22 Chapman, "Date," 26.

1.69. He traced the origin of *R* 1.55-71 to the Recognitionist, written on the basis of Acts 5 and 9. Schwartz's treatment of our source is limited to a few isolated and undeveloped comments.[23]

Like Chapman, Rehm held that source criticism beyond *G* is fruitless. He argued that *R* 1 was written by the Recognitionist from different sources. He did not enter explicitly into the question of the *AJ*. His treatment of *R* 1 is brief - less than one page - and the argument about its sources is not developed.[24]

Irmscher likewise held that source criticism beyond *G* is pointless. He did not offer or develop his reasons for opposition to source criticism beyond *G*. Although he knew of the work of Strecker, Irmscher did not enter into the question of the isolation of an *AJ* source.[25]

As a part of his literary study of PsCl, J. Wehnert surveyed the relationship of the material in *EpPt* and *Cont* with *H* by an exacting comparison of Greek vocabulary and style. From this analysis, he concluded that the *KerygmataP* source does not exist. Wehnert did not deal with the question of an *AJ* source.[26] But because *EpPt*, *Cont*, and most of *H* are only in Greek, and *R* 1 only in Latin and Syriac versions, it is difficult to see how the kind of linguistic analysis done by Wehnert could be applied to the question of an *AJ* source in *R* 1.

In summary, the general opposition to source criticism has only occasionally treated the question of an *AJ* source in *R* 1. This treatment has been cursory and not very well developed. Moreover, the opposition to *AJ* is not nearly as detailed, systematic and persuasive as the work of those who have argued for an *AJ* source. No compelling argument has been presented by opponents of source criticism of PsCl against the presence of an *AJ* source. Therefore, a consensus has existed since about 1945 among PsCl researchers that there is in fact an *AJ* source in *R* 1.

Identification of the Source

Our next task is to identify positively this source we have isolated. Unlike the *KerygmataP* referred to in *EpPet*, there is no indication in

---

23 Schwartz, "Beobachtungen," 184, 189.
24 Rehm, "Entstehung," 154-5.
25 Irmscher, "Pseudo-Clementines," 532-3.
26 Wehnert, "Literarkritik," 292-301.

R 1.33-71 or elsewhere in PsCl of any name for this source. Therefore, the search for its identity has focused on other early Christian literature.

The report of Epiphanius on the Ebionites and their literature furnishes us with enough evidence to relate our source to the *Ascents of James* he describes. In his *Panarion*, the last (ca. 377) and most comprehensive of all early Christian heresiologies, Epiphanius devoted a long chapter to the Ebionites.[27] As the text of *Pan.* 30.16.6-9 is important for comparison to *R* 1.33-71, it would be well to reproduce it here. Speaking of the Ebionites, Epiphanius says,

"(16.6) They call other works 'Acts of the Apostles,' in which there are many things full of impiety, from which they arm themselves in no cursory fashion against the truth. (7) Indeed, they adopt certain ascents and interpretations in the Anabathmoi Iakobou [[Ascents of James]], as speaking out against both the temple and the sacrifices, and against the fire which is on the altar, and many other things full of foolish talk; (8) and also in that work they are not ashamed with trumped up charges of evil-doing and deceit made by their false apostles accusing Paul of being a Tarsian, as he himself confesses and does not deny; but they said that they assumed that he was from the Greeks, basing their argument on the place where through regard for the truth he said, 'I am a Tarsian, a citizen of no insignificant city' [[Acts 21:39]]. (9) Then they say that he was a Greek, the son of a Greek mother and a Greek father, that he went up to Jerusalem and remained there a time, and that he desired to marry the daughter of the priest, and that on account of this he became a proselyte and was circumcised, and that he was angry when he could not marry such a maiden and that he wrote against circumcision, and against the sabbath and the Mosaic law."[28]

---

27 K. Holl, *Epiphanius (Anacoratus und Panarion)* (GCS 25; Leipzig: Hinrichs, 1915). Four English translations of *Pan.* 30.16.6-9, which deals with the *AJ*, have been offered. The first is by Klijn and Reinink, *Evidence*, 183-5; here Holl's text is also given. The second is by Brown, "James," 201. The third, and most careful, is by G. A. Koch, "A Critical Investigation of Epiphanius' Knowledge of the Ebionites: A Translation and Critical Discussion of Panarion 30" (Ph.D. dissertation, University of Pennsylvania; Ann Arbor: University Microfilms, 1976) 144-5. The most recent translation is by F. Williams, *The Panarion of Epiphanius of Salamis, Book One* (NHS 35; Leiden: Brill, 1987) 132-3. Williams uses Koch's translation as a base for his own translation of this section. A German translation is given in Strecker, *Judenchristentum*, 251.

28 Koch, "Investigation," 144-5. © 1976 by G. A. Koch. Reproduced by the permission of the author. The double brackets and their contents are from Koch.

Careful comparison of the content of this *AJ* as reported by Epiphanius with our source in *R* 1.33-71 yields the following similarities. (1) Both documents express an anti-sacrificial animus. (2) Both documents are anti-Pauline. In *R* 1.70-71, Saul/Paul is "the enemy," who attacks the church during the temple debate and later tries to persecute it. In *Pan.* 30.16.8-9, Paul is portrayed as opposed to the Mosaic law, and as a Gentile by birth. (3) In both documents, the order in treating these two features seems to be the same - first is the anti-sacrificial polemic, and second is anti-Paulinism. (4) Both documents speak of James' "ascents." *R* 1 says that James "went up . . . to the temple" (1.66.2) and stood on the steps (1.70.8; cf. 1.66.3; 1.55.2). *Pan.* 30.16.7 begins, Αναβαθμους δε τινας και 'υφηγησεις δηθεν εν τας Αναβαθμους Ιακωβου 'υποτιθενται, "They adopt certain ascents and interpretations in the *Ascents of James*."

But there are also dissimilarities between *Pan.* 30.16 and *R* 1.33-71. The *AJ* known to Epiphanius attacks Paul as a Gentile, and claims that his opposition to the law was a result of a frustrated attempt to marry the daughter of a priest. *R* 1.33-71 does not know this story, or describe Saul/Paul's background, but rather has him thwarting the conversion of the Jewish nation by James and following this up by continued persecution. Also, while the *AJ* known to Epiphanius seems to have only two main components of anti-sacrificial polemic and anti-Paulinism, and may deal primarily with early Christian times, the *AJ* in *R* 1 has a full treatment of sacred history, and (as we will show below) is a thoroughly christological document. But as the similarities outweigh the dissimilarities, it is most likely that these two documents are closely related to each other. Therefore, we can conclude with Strecker and a line of researchers back to Köstlin that it is probable that the source of *R* 1.33-71 can be identified as the Αναβαθμοι Ιακωβου.

What precisely does αναβαθμοι mean? Epiphanius, by pairing αναβαθμοι with 'υφηγησεις ("directions, teachings"), understands it to mean "steps in an argument." *Pan.* 30.16.6-9 does not say that James "ascended" to the temple, or spoke his anti-temple views from within the temple. Strecker, following T. Zahn, explains the αναβαθμοι of *Pan.* 30.16.7 by αναβασεις ("Aufsteige, ascents") and relates it to the "ascent" of James to the temple (*R* 1.66.2).[29]

---

29 Strecker, *Judenchristentum*, 251.

But αναβαθμος is not to be explained on the basis of αναβασις, as it is fully intelligible in itself. Its primary meaning refers to a step or stair, and in the plural to a flight of stairs. By extension, it can also mean "going up, ascents," or, as Epiphanius understands it, successive elements of teaching. The L and S versions of R 1 do not allow us to know with certainty if this word occurs in the source. Since there is only one "ascent" of James to the temple explicitly mentioned in R 1, the plural becomes problematic if αναβαθμοι is equivalent to αναβασεις. But it does make good sense if it is understood as "steps, stairs." Such stairs are referred to in R 1.66.3, where "the place which we were before" (so L; S: "the places of the preceding day") refers to the steps from which the Twelve spoke on the previous day (R 1.55-65). These stairs are also mentioned in the plural in R 1.70.8, where "the enemy" attacks James. The stairs thus are the place from which most of the action of 1.55-71 takes place. Therefore, we may conclude that the evidence favors interpreting αναβαθμοι of Αναβαθμοι Ιακωβου as ascents up the temple stairs, and by extension what transpired upon them. Αναβαθμοι Ιακωβου can thus be translated "Ascents of James," as recent researchers have done, if this meaning of αναβαθμοι is kept in mind.

Conclusion

The task of this chapter was to isolate and identify the proposed source behind R 1.33-71. Using the tools of source criticism, we have established the probability that such a source is contained in R 1.33-71, and that it can be identified as *The Ascents of James*. We have also shown that those who have doubted an *AJ* source in R 1 do not present compelling arguments against its presence. We now turn our attention in the subsequent chapters to the content of the *AJ*, beginning in Chapter Three with translations of its Latin and Syriac versions.

CHAPTER THREE

TRANSLATIONS OF *THE ASCENTS OF JAMES*

Introduction

In this chapter we will present translations of the *AJ* from the best critical editions of the Latin and Syriac versions of *R* 1. The only English translation of *R* in its entirety was done by T. Smith in 1868, and was based on the Latin editions of J. B. Cotelier and E. G. Gersdorf.[1] Our translation of L is from the critical edition of B. Rehm.[2] The translation of S is based on the critical edition of W. Frankenberg, which superseded that of P. de Lagarde.[3] The task of constructing a reliable edition of the S text is greatly simplified in that only two manuscripts are extant, in contrast to the more than one hundred surviving copies of L. The translations offered here are the first translations of the *AJ* from reliable texts of *R* into a modern language.

Another feature of Frankenberg's work, as its title implies, is a retroversion of *R* into Greek based on the S text. Frankenberg was criticized for this retroversion.[4] Although it conveys rather well the

---

1 Smith, *The Writings of Tatian and Theophilus; and the Clementine Recognitions* (ANF 3; ed. A. Roberts and J. Donaldson; Edinburgh: Clark, 1868; often reprinted, most recently by Eerdmans (Grand Rapids, 1986), in which the entire PsCl corpus is conveniently collected in vol. 8 of ANF; Cotelier (Cotelerius), *Ss. Patrum qui Temporibus Apostolicis Floruerunt* (Paris: Petri le petit, 1672); Gersdorf, *S. Clementis Romani Recognitiones* (Leipzig: Tauchnitz, 1838); reprinted in J.-P. Migne, *PG* 1 (Paris: Migne, 1857).

2 Rehm, *Die Pseudoklementinen II: Rekognitionen in Rufins Übersetzung* (GCS 51,2; Berlin: Akadamie, 1965).

3 Frankenberg, *Die syrischen Clementinen mit griechischem Paralleltext* (TU 48,3; Leipzig: Hinrichs, 1937); Lagarde, *Clementis Romani Recognitiones Syriace* (Leipzig: Brockhaus, 1861). I have followed Frankenberg's text even though at a few points the text of Lagarde may be superior; see Jones, "History," p. 5 n. 16.

4 The most notable criticism was by H. Lietzmann, the editor of TU, in the Preface of Frankenberg's edition.

---

general sense of the S, it cannot be relied upon as a guide to a careful English translation from S. The criticism of this retroversion has not impeached the value of Frankenberg's S text.

The aim of these translations is to render the L and S as literally as possible into idiomatic English. Textual variants and substantial differences in wording between the texts will be examined as necessary in the next chapter. Chapter and intra-chapter numbers have been preserved in each translation from the respective critical editions. Omission of those sections of *R* 1.33-71 that do not belong to the *AJ* is indicated by a line of dots. The translations have been put in parallel columns to facilitate comparison.

Translations of The Ascents of James

1.33.3 - 1.34.1 (L)

1.33.3 But when Abraham was still in ignorance, as we told you before, two sons were born to him. The one was named Ishmael, the other Heliesdros. From the one are descended the heathen nations, from the other the people of the Persians, (4) some of whom have adopted the life and manners of their neighbors, the Brahmins. Others settled in Arabia, some of whose descendants have also spread to Egypt. (5) From them some Indians and some Egyptians have learned to circumcise, and to be of a purer observance than the others, although in the passing of time most of them turned the proof and sign of purity into impiety.

1.34.1 He had received these two sons in the time in which he

1.33.3 - 1.34.1 (S)

1.33.3 But Abraham, when he was not in the knowledge of the Great One (as was related by the account which does not lie, and that True Prophet witnessed, as I have shown you again), had two sons. One was later called Ishmael; the other was Eliezer, of whom the nations of the Arabs and Persians are multiplied. (4) Some of them were joined with their neighbors, the Brahmins; and some from him who lived in Arabia were scattered to Egypt, because they were near it. (5) Hence some Indians and Egyptians have observed circumcision and were greatly purified with other purifications. But in the long span of time some of them turned the goodness of their purity into evil.

1.34.1 However, while he himself did not have knowledge,

1.34.1-6 (L)

still lived in ignorance of things. Nevertheless, when he obtained the knowledge of God he asked of Him, because he was just, that he might merit to have progeny by Sarah. She was his legal wife, although she was barren. (2) And he received a son, whom he named Isaac. From him Jacob was born, from Jacob in turn the twelve patriarchs, and from these twelve the seventy-two. (3) When famine fell, these came to Egypt with all their house. After being multiplied by the blessing and promise of God for four hundred years, they were persecuted by the Egyptians. (4) When they were persecuted, the True Prophet appeared to Moses. When the Egyptians did indeed resist the people of the Hebrews by not allowing them to leave and return to their native land, he worked ten plagues from heaven, and led the people of the true God out of Egypt. (5) Those of the Egyptians who survived, conspiring with the hatred of their king, pursued the Hebrews. (6) When they had overtaken them at the shore of the sea and intended to annihilate and destroy them all, Moses, having poured out a prayer to God, divided the sea into two parts. The water on the right and on the left was held as if frozen solid, and the people of God passed

1.34.1-6 (S)

he obtained two sons. When he was in the knowledge of the truth from God he prayed that, because he was just, Sarah would have a son. She was his lawful wife from his youth, although she was barren. (2) It was granted to her [to have] him whom he called Isaac. And Isaac begot Jacob, and Jacob the twelve, and the twelve the seventy-two. (3) But when, however, there was a famine, all their family went into Egypt. Within four hundred years they multiplied by the blessing and promise of God, and they were afflicted in wickedness by the Egyptians. (4) But when they were afflicted, the True Prophet, Moses, came to them. When the oppressing Egyptians did not allow the people of the Hebrews to depart and journey to the land of their fathers, he punished and scourged them with ten plagues from heaven; and thus he led them, the people who were loved by God, from Egypt. (5) Because of this, the Egyptian people who were left conspired in wickedness with their king. They followed and overtook the Hebrews. (6) They besieged them at once at the shore of the sea, and they desired together to destroy them by the sword. But when they were about to come near them, that prophet in his prayer to God divided the sea,

1.34.6 - 1.35.3 (L)

through as if the road were dry. But the Egyptians following them were killed after heedlessly entering. (7) For when the last of the people of the Hebrews came up, the last of the Egyptians also went down into the sea; and immediately the sea waters which had been held bound as if frozen were loosed by the command of him who had bound them. When they received their natural freedom, they exacted punishment upon the wicked people.

1.35.1 After this Moses, by the command of God, whose providence is over all things, led the people of the Hebrews out into the wilderness. Leaving the shortest road which runs from Egypt to Judea, he led the people in long wanderings in the wilderness, so that by the newness of changed habit he might abolish by the discipline of forty years the evils which had grown on them through long use of the customs of the Egyptians. (2) Meanwhile, they came to Mount Sinai, and from there the law was given to them with heavenly sounds and sights in ten written commandments. The first and greatest was that they worship only God Himself, and not set up for themselves another image or likeness to worship. (3) But when Moses went up to the mountain and

1.34.6 - 1.35.3 (S)

parting it in two, and so in this manner the people went over. And the multitudes of the Egyptians in their presumption all followed after them and died. (7) When the last of the Hebrews had gone up, the last of the Egyptians went down; then the sea, which had been made firm by the command of him who divided it, rushed back to its former nature. And the Egyptians who pursued received punishment in it.

1.35.1 Then Moses, by the command of God, who knows everything, led the great multitude of the Hebrews into the wilderness. He left the short way which leads from Egypt to Judea and led them by the long way of the wilderness, so that by forty years of wanderings he might purge the evil manner of life which grew on them through a long duration of time in Egypt, and at another time might be able to temper and change [them] by the giving of the law. (2) At last they came to Mount Sinai, and they heard with heavenly sounds the law of God, all ten commandments. The first of them is this, that while keeping the law they should keep only to Him, and not make for themselves the image of another [god] to worship. (3) But when Moses had been gone for forty

1.35.3-6 (L)

remained there forty days, the people who saw Egypt struck with ten plagues and the sea parted, and who went through on foot, and also were given manna from heaven for bread and were provided drink from the rock which followed them (which type of food was turned by the power of God into whatever taste anyone desired), (4) and although under the blows of a hot sky they were shaded by a cloud during the day so that they would not be burned, and by night were illumined by a column of fire so that the horror of darkness might not be added to the desolation of the wilderness - (5) when, I say, Moses delayed, these very ones, after making a golden calf's head after the type of Apis, whom they had seen worshipped in Egypt, worshipped it. Even after so many and so great miracles which they had seen, they were unable to scrape off and remove from themselves the evils of the old custom. (6) For this reason, Moses left the short road which leads from Egypt to Judea. He then led them on a great detour in the wilderness, to be able, if possible, as we mentioned before, to shatter the evils of the old custom by the change of a new arrangement.

1.35.3-6 (S)

days, those assembled, who saw Egypt punished with ten plagues, and who passed over through a divided sea on their feet, and who received heavenly manna for food, and who drank water from the rock which was following them (the taste of which were changed by divine power according to their desires), (4) and were travelling under the hot zone, a pillar of cloud shading them in the day because of the sun, and a pillar of fire giving them light in the night because of the darkness - (5) when Moses delayed, these made an idol in the image of Apis which they had seen in Egypt, an image of gold. They bowed down to it, those who after all sorts of demonstrations were not able to put away the evil customs from their hearts. (6) Because of this, Moses then came down from the mountain by the command of God, and left, and I said before, the shortest road which goes from Egypt to Judea. He led them in that vast wilderness, so that in the time of forty years he might by another time, in the giving of the law, be able to change those evils which clung to them from an extended time with the many customs of the Egyptians.

1.36.1 - 1.37.2 (L)

1.36.1 In the meantime, Moses, a faithful and wise steward, seeing how the evil of sacrificing to idols had grown so deeply on the people from their association with the Egyptians that it was not possible to cut from them the root of this evil, did indeed permit them to sacrifice. But he permitted this to be done only to God, in order to cut back, in a certain way, a part of the old ingrown evil. He left the other part to be corrected by another and at another time, by that one, namely, of whom he himself said, (2) "A prophet shall the Lord your God raise up for you like me; you shall hear him according to everything that he says to you. For whoever shall not hear that prophet, his soul shall be destroyed from his people."

1.37.1 To this purpose, moreover, he also established a place in which alone it would be permitted them to sacrifice to God. (2) All this he carried out with such a view that, when the right time should come and they should learn from the prophet that God desires mercy and not

1.36.1 - 1.37.2 (S)

1.36.1 Therefore, when Moses came down from Mount Sinai and saw that vice, as he was a good and faithful steward he discerned that it was not possible to take from the people all the sickness of the love of idol-worship which was in them from the long stay, and that they could not easily be ridded of it and bring it to an end because of their evil upbringing with the Egyptians. Because of this he did permit them to sacrifice; but he told them that they could do this only in the name of God, so that he could cut off and bring to an end one half of this sickness. But as for the correction of the other half, it was [reserved] for another time in the hand of someone else, as was right, in whose care it would be, in the one of whom he said, (2) "A prophet shall the Lord your God raise up for you like me; hear him in everything. Anyone who does not obey him shall surely die. It shall be known that this one has given up his soul to destruction."

1.37.1 And with these things he also set apart a place for them in which alone it was permitted to offer sacrifices. (2) All of this was promulgated to them until a more convenient time should come, when they would be able to understand that God desires mercy and not sacrifices. Then

1.37.2-5 (L)

sacrifices, they should see him who teaches them that the place divinely chosen as fitting to offer sacrifices to God is His wisdom. As for this other place which seemed for a time to be chosen and was often shaken by invasions and destructions by enemies, they should hear that it would finally be destroyed completely. (3) As a pledge of these things, even before the coming of the True Prophet who was to repudiate the sacrifices equally with the place, it was often devastated by enemies and burned with fire. (4) The people were carried into captivity in foreign nations and then brought back again when the took refuge in the mercy of God, in order that by this they might be taught that the one who offers sacrifice is thrust out and handed over into the hand of enemies, but those who do mercy and righteousness are without sacrifices freed from captivity and returned to their native land. (5) But it happened that only a few understood this. For although most were able to think of and perceive this, nevertheless they were held by the irrational common opinion. For correct understanding in the context of liberty belongs to the few.

1.37.2-5 (S)

that prophet who declares these things will be sent to them, and those who believe in him will be led by the wisdom of God to the strong place of the land, which is for the living. There they will be preserved from the war which will shortly come to their own destruction upon those who because of their division do not obey. (3) But this war did not come hastily or suddenly, as even before the arrival of the coming prophet they had been prepared for the abolition of sacrifices. For many times in the providence of God that war came upon them, (4) and they would be in captivity, and be carried away to another nation. Since they then did not have that place which the lawgiver permitted them for sacrifice, but were keeping his law without sacrifices, they were restored and redeemed. This [happened] many times to them, so that they might understand that when they keep the law without sacrifices, they were redeemed. But when coming to their place they offered sacrifices, they went out and were exiled from it, so that they would cease and offer sacrifices no more. (5) But they were slow to learn this, and it was good to only a few. Even the knowledge of those few was darkened by those multitudes who thought otherwise, who

1.38.1-5 (L)   1.37.5 - 1.38.5 (S)

were not able to perceive all this.
For to distinguish and understand the cause of this is not
given to the multitudes, but only
the few can understand it.

1.38.1 Therefore Moses,
having arranged these things,
put a certain one by the name of
Auses over the people, who was
to bring them back to their
homeland. He [Moses] himself
went up to a certain mountain by
the command of the living God,
and died there. (2) But his death
was such that to this day no one
has found the place of his burial.
(3) When, therefore, the people
reached the land of their fathers,
by the providence of God the
wicked nations who dwelt there
were put to flight at their first
incursion. They themselves took
up the inheritance of their fathers, as decided by lot. (4) Then
they were for some time
governed by judges, not by kings,
and remained in a rather peace-
able state. (5) But when they
made for themselves those who
were really more tyrants than
kings, then with royal ambition
they also built a temple in the
place which had been appointed
beforehand for them for the purpose of prayer. Thus through a
series of wicked kings succeeding one another in turn, the

1.38.1 Thus Moses, when he
had ordered and arranged these
things, appointed for them a
general of the army of the people
who was named Joshua, who
would lead them by the
strengthening word of God into the land of their fathers.
(2) When he went up before all
of them, he died, and no one to
this day has been able to find his
grave. (3) Then those multitudes
entered the land of their fathers,
and by the providence of God
they put to flight those evil
peoples as soon as they appeared. Then they entered into
the land of their fathers according to their tribes, taking possession of it in alloted portions.
(4) During the time of the judges
they did not have kings, and they
remained firmly in their places.
(5) But when they made for
themselves tyrants who really
were not kings, then they abolished for a temple that place
which had at first been appointed for them as a house of
prayer. They were taken captive
by force through the kingship, an
institution of their will and
making. Thus through time they

1.38.5 - 1.39.3 (L)	1.38.5 - 1.39.3 (S)

1.38.5 - 1.39.3 (L)

people fell way into ever-greater wickedness.

1.39.1 But the time began to approach for fulfilling what we have reported to have been lacking in those things instituted by Moses, and for the prophet whom he predicted to appear. From the first he warned them by the mercy of God to put an end to the sacrifices. (2) Lest perhaps they think that at the cessation of sacrifices there would be no forgiveness of sins for them, he established baptism by water for them. In it they would be freed from all sins by the invocation of his name, and for the future after a perfect life might continue in immortality because they had been cleansed not by the blood of animals, but by the purification of the wisdom of God. (3) Finally, this is given as a proof of this great mystery, that everyone who upon believing in this prophet predicted by Moses was baptized in his name, shall be kept uninjured in the destruction of war which hangs over the unbelieving nation and the place itself. But those who do not believe will become exiles from the place and kingdom, so that even against their will they may know and obey God's will.

1.38.5 - 1.39.3 (S)

were led away into increasing evil by those evil kings who were over them.

1.39.1 Thus when the time came near for the needed correction of what was lacking, the fitting time arrived in which that prophet who had been proclaimed beforehand by Moses was revealed. At his coming, because of the mercy of God he first warned them to cease and desist from sacrificing. (2) But lest they suppose within themselves that they were being deprived of the forgiveness of their sins through sacrifices, and this be troublesome for them, he appointed baptism by water for the forgiveness of sins. It was shown to them that it truly gives the forgiveness of sins and is able to preserve those who are perfect unto eternal life. (3) Then those who please God will in His inexpressible wisdom be preserved from the war which is coming to destroy those who do not believe. Just as they cannot do what they desire to do, so also when they are expelled from their place they will understand and be instructed against their will to do what pleases God.

1.40.1- 1.41.2 (L)

1.40.1 And so, with these things thus pre-arranged, he who was expected has come, bringing signs and miracles, the marks by which he should become known. (2) But even so the people did not believe, who had been taught for so many generations to believe such things. Not only did they not believe, but they added blasphemy to unbelief by saying that he was a glutton, a slave to the stomach, and led by a demon, even he who had come for their salvation. (3) Perversity so greatly prevails though the services of evil people, that without the wisdom of God aiding those who prize the truth, this impious error would have entrapped almost everyone. (4) Thus he first chose us twelve who believed in him, whom he named apostles, and then seventy-two other highly approved disciples, so that, by recognizing the similarity with Moses, the multitude might believe that this is the one Moses predicted, the prophet who was to come.

1.41.1 But lest someone claim that it is possible for anyone at all to imitate a number, what is to be said about the signs and wonders which he used to do? For Moses indeed worked wonders and healings in Egypt. (2) This prophet like

1.40.1 - 1.41.2 (S)

1.40.1 When, therefore, these things were thus appointed, he who is the good prophet appeared and worked signs. (2) Nevertheless the ancient people still did not believe, even though they had been prepared beforehand to believe. For those persons are most miserable of all, who desire to believe neither good nor evil about virtue; but this is how they do not believe, by despising them through accusations, and calling them gluttons and demons. (3) Thus does evil find victory through evil persons, that unless the wisdom of God had helped those who love the truth, these also would perhaps fall into error. (4) It was revealed to us that he who came first chose twelve apostles, and then seventy-two disciples, that through this the multitudes might understand that this is the coming prophet, whom Moses had already proclaimed.

1.41.1 But perhaps it is easy for anyone to make a number; but no one is able to make those signs and wonders which he did in his coming. For Moses did signs in Egypt. (2) And that prophet who arose even as he arose did signs among the

1.41.2 - 1.42.2 (L)

Moses, whose rise he himself predicted, although he healed every weakness and every infirmity in the common people, worked innumerable wonders and preached the good news of eternal life, was driven to the cross by wicked men. This deed, however, was turned into good by his power. (3) Finally, when he suffered the whole world suffered with him. The sun was darkened and the stars were disturbed; the sea was shaken and the mountains moved, and the graves opened. The veil of the temple was split, as if lamenting the destruction hanging over the place. (4) Nevertheless, although the whole world was moved, they themselves are still not yet moved to the consideration of such great things.

1.42.1 It was necessary, then, that the Gentiles be called in place of those who remained unbelievers, so that the number which was shown to Abraham would be satisfied; thus the preaching of the kingdom of God has been sent into all the world. (2) Thus, there is disturbance among worldly spirits, who always resist those who seek liberty, seeking the machinations of errors to destroy the building of God. But those who strive for the glory of salvation and liberty are made stronger by

1.41.2 - 1.42.2 (S)

people, drove out every sickness, and proclaimed eternal life. But by the folly of the evil stupidity of evil persons they brought crucifixion upon him, which very thing was changed by his power into grace and goodness. (3) For when he suffered, this whole world suffered with him. Even the sun grew dark and the stars were moved, the sea was troubled, and the mountains loosened and the tombs were opened. The veil of the temple was torn as if in mourning for the coming desolation of the place. (4) Because of these things, all the people were afraid and were constrained to question them. But some, although all the people were moved in their minds, did not move themselves to this matter.

1.42.1 It was right, on account of those who were not persuaded, that the Gentiles be called to be fullness of the number that was shown to Abraham; therefore this disorder came to be. (2) And the hostile power which frequently darkens and opposes those sons of freedom troubled all the people. He prepared a great testing of their goodness, so that those who wish to draw near to the word of salvation will be stronger than the strength which troubles them, and with their wills they will easi-

1.42.2 - 1.43.2 (L)

resisting and struggling against them with no small exertion, and they shall come to the crown of salvation not without the palm of victory. (3) In the meantime, after he had suffered, and darkness had overcome the world from the sixth hour to the ninth, when the sun returned things came back to normal. Wicked people once more went back to themselves and to their old customs, because their fear had ended. (4) For some of them, after guarding the place with all diligence, called him a magician, whom they could not prevent from rising; others pretended that he was stolen.

1.43.1 Nevertheless, the truth was victorious everywhere. For as a sign that these things were accomplished by divine power, as the days passed we who had been very few became many more than they by the help of God. At last the priests became very much afraid that, to their own embarrassment, the whole people would perhaps, by the providence of God, come into our faith. Sending to us frequently, they used to ask us to discuss with them about Jesus, whether he were the prophet whom Moses predicted, who is the eternal Christ. (2) For only about this does there seem to be a difference for us who believe in

1.42.2 - 1.43.2 (S)

ly receive victory in salvation. (3) While he suffered, there was darkness from the sixth hour to the ninth. But when the sun appeared, and matters returned firmly as they were before, evil ones of the people returned to their ways. (4) For some of them said about him who had suffered, and who was not found although they had guarded him, that he was a magician; thus they were not afraid to dare to lie.

1.43.1 But the uprightness of the truth was victorious; for because they lied that we were fewer than they, they were not upright. For by the zeal of God we more and more were steadily increasing more than they. Then even their priests were afraid, lest perhaps by the providence of God the whole people might come over to our faith, to their own confusion. Sending to us frequently, they asked us to speak to them about Jesus, if he were that prophet who was prophesied by Moses, who is the eternal Messiah. (2) For only on this is there a difference between us, we who believe in Jesus, and those sons of our faith who do

1.43.2 - 1.44.3; 1.55.1 (L)

Jesus over against the Jews who do not believe. (3) But while they frequently asked about this, and we were looking for an opportune time, one seven-year period was completed since the passion of the Lord. The church of God founded in Jerusalem was abundantly multiplied and grew through James, who was ordained bishop in it by the Lord and governed it with most righteous administrations.

1.44.1 But when we twelve apostles had assembled with a vast multitude on the day of the Passover, after each one of us had entered the church of the brothers and James had asked about the things that had been accomplished by us in every place, we reported briefly as the people listened. (2) During this time Caiaphas the high priest was sending priests to us, asking us to come to him, so that we might either teach him a reason that Jesus himself is the eternal Christ, or he himself would teach us that he is not, that the whole people might agree upon one faith or another. He frequently appealed to us to do this. (3) But we often delayed, always seeking a more opportune time.

. . . .

1.55.1 Nevertheless, as we were beginning to say, since the

1.43.2 - 1.44.3; 1.55.1 (S)

not believe. (3) But while they asked us many times, and we were looking for a fitting time, one week of years was completed from the passion of Jesus. The church in Jerusalem which was established by our Lord was increased, being governed uprightly and steadily by James, who was made bishop in it by our Lord.

1.44.1 When we twelve apostles had gathered on the days of the Passover with the great assembly in Jerusalem, that we might gather with our brothers in the festival, each one of us was asked by James to tell us about the most important of those things which we had done among the people. Each one briefly reported to us. (2) Caiaphas the high priest sent priests to us apostles and asked us to come to him, that either we should persuade him that Jesus is the eternal Messiah, or he should convince us that he is not, and thus all the people should come to one and the same faith. (3) Many times he sought for us to do this, but we not a few times declined, as we were seeking a more suitable time.

. . . .

1.55.1 Since, therefore, the high priest with the rest of the

1.55.1 - 1.56.1 (L)

high priest frequently asked us through the priests that we might have a discussion about Jesus, when an opportune time came and it pleased the whole church, we went up to the temple. (2) When we were standing on the steps together with our faithful brothers, the people were completely silent. First the high priest began to exhort the people to listen patiently and quietly, and at the same time be witnesses and judges of those things which were to be said. (3) Next, extolling with many praises the rite of sacrifice which had been given by God to the human race for the forgiveness of sins, he contested the baptism of our Jesus as recently introduced contrary to this. (4) But Matthew, opposing his arguments, clearly showed that whoever does not obtain the baptism of Jesus shall not only be deprived of the kingdom of heaven, but also will not be free of danger at the resurrection of the dead, even if he is defended by the advantage of a good life and a right mind. After having continued with these and similar things, Matthew was silent.

1.56.1 But the party of the Sadducees, which denies that there is a resurrection of the dead, was indignant. One of

1.55.1 - 1.56.1 (S)

priests had asked us often about these things which concern Jesus, either to teach or learn in the counsel of all, when all the church was assembled we went up to the temple. (2) We were standing upon the steps with all our believing multitude, in the silence of every man and in great quietness. First the high priest began to appease the people, [that] as those who are in the love of the truth they humbly be willing to seek it, because they had been chosen witnesses and judges of the debate which was to come. (3) But as he was greatly desirous to find those who desired the sacrifices, supposing that they give the forgiveness of sins, he accused the baptism which was given by Jesus to us. (4) But Matthew refuted this one who spoke thus, [saying] that not only will he who is not baptized be rejected from the kingdom of heaven, but also will be in danger in the resurrection of the dead; even if he is good in manner of life and upright in mind, he will not have eternal life. As they were in quietness, when he had said those things and witnessed others like them, he then was silent.

1.56.1 Then the Sadducees, who do not believe in the resurrection of the dead, were enraged when they heard [this].

1.56.1 - 1.57.3 (L)

them cried out from the middle of the people, saying that those who suppose that the dead ever arise are greatly mistaken. (2) Andrew my brother taught in response to him that it is not an error, but a most certain matter of faith, that the dead arise, according to the teaching of him whom Moses predicted as the prophet who was to come. (3) In case they did not see that he indeed was the one whom Moses foretold, "About him," he said, "let it first be inquired, so that when it will be clearly demonstrated that it is he, there will be no further doubt about these things which he taught." When he proclaimed to them these and other similar things, Andrew was silent.

1.57.1 But a certain Samaritan, speaking against the people and God, asserted that neither are the dead raised nor is that worship of God in Jerusalem to be maintained, but rather Mount Gerizim is to be venerated. He added this also against us, that our Jesus is not he whom Moses predicted, the prophet who was to come. (2) James and John, the sons of Zebedee, vehemently opposed him and another who followed him in these same ideas. (3) Although they had a command not to enter their cities nor bring the word of

1.56.1 - 1.57.3 (S)

One of them shouted from the middle of the multitude and said, "This is an error, to think that the dead ever arise." (2) Against him Andrew my brother spoke, and showed that it is not an error for us to believe that the dead are raised, because he who was foretold by Moses as the prophet who was to come, who is Jesus, showed before in this matter that the dead are raised. (3) But if one does not believe that he is the prophet foretold by Moses, who was to come, it first ought to be inquired into, if this one is he. And when we know that it is he, it ought to be easy to learn everything in his teaching. When he had said these things and witnessed others like them, he then was silent.

1.57.1 But one Samaritan, who thought and considered against the people and God, said that the dead are not raised, and Mount Gerizim instead of the holy place of Jerusalem is the house of worship. As an enemy he said against Jesus that he is not the one foretold by Moses, the prophet who was to come. (2) Against this one and another who helped him, James and John, the sons of Zebedee, spoke wisely. (3) For even though they had a command not to enter their city nor speak with them, they continued even preaching to them, yet so that the speech of these people, if not refuted, would not harm the faith of others, they responded so wisely and strongly that they put them to permanent silence. (4) For James made a speech on the resurrection of the dead, with the favor of the whole people; while John showed that if they should cease from the error of Mount Gerizim, they would then know that Jesus is the one expected to come according to the prophecy of Moses. (5) For just as Moses did signs and wonders, Jesus certainly did also; and there is no doubt that the likeness of the signs witnesses that he is the one to come, as he himself said. After they had proclaimed these and many other similar things, they were silent.

though they were not to speak with them, and were silent no more, lest they think they attained victory and revile the true faith of many. Wisely, therefore, as though from silence, they spoke with them. (4) Because of this love of believing in the resurrection of the dead and of honoring the holy place of Jerusalem, James blamed them for thinking wickedly in not believing that the dead arise. His brother showed that they act foolishly in that which is difficult for them. Then he argued these things, that by praising Mount Gerizim they dishonor the holy place of Jerusalem. After these things he immediately argued that if they knew the teaching of Jesus, they would then believe in the resurrection of the dead and honor the place of Jerusalem. (5) "Because of this," he said, "it is necessary first to know if this one who did signs and wonders like Moses is the one whom Moses announced beforehand, the prophet who was to come." When he had said those things and witnessed others like them, he then was silent.

1.58.1 And behold, a certain one of the scribes, shouting from the middle of the people, said, "The signs and wonders which your Jesus worked, he worked as a magician, not as a prophet."

1.58.1 And one of the scribes shouted from the middle of the people and said, "Your Jesus did signs and wonders as a magician and not as a prophet." (2) Against this one Philip

1.58.2 - 1.59.5 (L)

(2) Philip vehemently opposed him, showing that by this reasoning he accused Moses also. (3) Since Moses worked signs and wonders in Egypt similar to those of Jesus in Judea, it cannot be doubted that whatever was said about Jesus may also be said about Moses. When Philip had proclaimed these and many other similar things, he was silent.

1.59.1 Then a certain Pharisee, when he heard this, accused Philip, because he said that Jesus was equal to Moses. (2) In responding to him, Bartholomew firmly taught that we do not say that Jesus is equal to Moses, but greater. (3) For Moses was indeed a prophet, as was Jesus; but Jesus was the Christ, as Moses was not. Thus without a doubt he who is both a prophet and the Christ is greater than he who is only a prophet. And when he had continued with these and many other similar things, he was silent. (4) After him James the son of Alphaeus made a speech to the people in which he showed that one should not believe in Jesus because the prophets predicted him. Rather, one should believe the prophets, that they truly were prophets, because the Christ bears witness to them. (5) For the presence and

1.58.2 - 1.59.6 (S)

spoke, and said, "By this saying you accuse Moses also, (3) because he did signs and wonders in Egypt in the way that Jesus did here." He said these things so that he might understand that what he said about Jesus could also be said about Moses. When he had said these things and witnessed others like them, he then was silent.

1.59.1 But one of the Pharisees, when he heard these things, condemned Philip, because he said that Jesus is equal to Moses. (2) Bartholomew spoke against him, and showed that we do not say that he is an equal to Moses, but that he is greater than Moses. (3) For Moses was a prophet, which Jesus is also; but that which Jesus is, the Messiah, Moses was not. Therefore, that which Moses is, Jesus is also; but that which Jesus is, Moses is not. When he had said those things and witnessed others like them, he then was silent. (4) After him James the son of Alphaeus spoke and taught, "One ought not to believe in Jesus because the prophets who proceeded him foretold him, but in the prophets, that they were prophets, because the Messiah witnesses to them. (6) For it is not right that faith receive witness from the lessers about the great and vir-

1.59.5 - 1.60.3 (L)

coming of the Christ show them truly to have been prophets. (6) For the testimony of faith ought to be given, not by the inferiors to the superior, but by the superior to the inferiors. After continuing with these and many other similar things, James also was silent. (7) After him Lebbaeus began to accuse the people vehemently. Why did they not believe in Jesus, who had done so much good to them by teaching the things of God, by comforting the afflicted, by healing the sick, [and] by relieving the poor? But for all these good things, they returned hatred and death. When he had proclaimed these and many other similar things to the people, he was silent.

1.60.1 And behold, one of the disciples of John ["the Baptist"] asserted that John was the Christ, and not Jesus: "Inasmuch," he said, "as Jesus himself declared that John was greater than all men and prophets. (2) If therefore," he said, "he is greater than all men, he must without doubt be held to be greater than both Moses and Jesus himself. (3) But if he is greater than all, he himself is the Christ." In answering him, Simon the Cananaean declared that John was certainly greater than all prophets and all who are the

1.59.6 - 1.60.3 (S)

tuous one, but by the witness of the great and virtuous one the lessers are made known." But when he had said these things and witnessed others like them, he then was silent. (7) After him Lebbaeus condemned the people in many things, that they did not believe in Jesus, who had helped them by exhortation and his healing and his consolatory discourses. In spite of these things they killed him and hated him, he who helped them in everything and did good things for them. When he had said those things and witnessed others like them, he then was silent.

1.60.1 And one of the disciples of John ["the Baptist"] came near, saying that he was the Messiah, and Jesus was not. "For Jesus himself said about him that he was greater than the prophets who were beforetime. (2) If then he is greater than Moses, it is evident that he is also [greater] than Jesus, because Jesus arose as Moses did. Thus John, who is fittingly greater than these, is the Messiah." (3) Against him Simon the Canaanite argued that John was greater than those prophets who are among those born of women, but he was not

1.60.3 - 1.61.2 (L)

sons of women, but he is not greater than the Son of Man. (4) Therefore Jesus is certainly also the Christ, but John is only a prophet. There is as much difference between him and Jesus as between a forerunner and him whose forerunner he is, even as there is a difference between him who gives the law and him who observes the law. After continuing with this and other similar things, the Cananaean also was silent. (5) After him Barnabas, who is also [called] Mathias, who was substituted as an apostle in place of Judas, began to admonish the people not to have hatred toward Jesus nor blaspheme him. (6) For it is much more proper, even for one who does not know or is doubtful about Jesus, to love him rather than hate him. For God has put a reward on love, a punishment on hatred. (7) "Even this," he said, "that he assumed a Jewish body and was born among the Jews, how has this not been an incentive for all of us to love him?" When he had explained completely these and other similar things, he ceased speaking.

1.61.1 Then Caiaphas attempted to find fault with the teaching of Jesus, claiming that he said vain things. (2) "For he said that the poor are blessed, and promised earthly rewards,

1.60.3 - 1.61.2 (S)

[greater] than he who is the Son of Man. (4) Therefore Jesus is also the Messiah, but that one was only a prophet. But all these things about Jesus are as distant from comparison with these things about John, as he who is sent as a forerunner is distant from him whose forerunner he is, and he who does the work of the law from him who lays down the law. When he had said those things and witnessed others like them, he then was silent. (5) And after this Barabbas, who became an apostle in place of Judas the betrayer, advised the people that they neither hate Jesus nor reproach him. (6) For it is more virtuous, since they do not know that Jesus is the Messiah, that they not hate him, since God has appointed a reward for love and not for hatred. (7) For since he has taken a body from the people of the Jews and became a Jew, God brings not a little loss of death upon him who hates him. When he had said those things and witnessed others like them, he then was silent.

1.61.1 Then after the counsel of Barabbas, Caiaphas condemned the teaching of Jesus, (2) "Because he said many vain things in his coming, that he gives blessing to the poor and

1.61.2 - 1.62.3 (L)

and placed the highest gift in an earthly inheritance, and promised that those who observe righteousness will be satisfied with food and drink; and many things similar to these he is charged with teaching." (3) In responding to him, Thomas argued that his charge is mistaken. He showed that the prophets, in whom he too believes, taught more things, but did not show how these things would be or how they were to be understood; but Jesus showed how these things ought to be taken. And when he had said these things and other similar things, Thomas also was silent.

1.62.1 After this Caiaphas again looked at me, at one time as if warning, but at another time as if accusing. He said that I ought in the future to cease from the preaching of Christ Jesus, lest this lead me into destruction, and lest being deceived by error myself, I should also deceive others by my error. (2) Then he further charged me with arrogance, because although I myself was ignorant, a fisherman and a rustic, I dared to assume the office of teacher. (3) When he had said these things and other similar things, I responded in these words, that there was certainly less danger to me if, as he himself claimed, this one

1.61.2 - 1.62.3 (S)

promised earthly rewards, that those of virtue will inherit the earth and that they will be satisfied by eating and drinking, and things similar to these." (3) Against him Thomas spoke, and showed that he is wickedly angry at Jesus. He showed that the prophets, those who believed beforehand, also spoke things similar to these, but they did not show how the people are able to receive them; but he [Jesus] also showed and made known how they are to receive them. And after saying those things, and witnessing others like them, he then was silent.

1.62.1 After this Caiaphas looked at me, in part as if counseling me, in part as if condemning me. He said, "Be silent, and do not proclaim Jesus as the Messiah, because you are bringing destruction upon your soul, as you yourself are going astray after him, and you are leading others astray." (2) He condemned me again as arrogant, "Because although you are ignorant and are a fisher by trade, you are teaching." (3) When he said these things and things similar to them, I also said words such as these to him: "My danger is less if, as you say, this one is not the Messiah, for I accept him as a teacher of the law. But there is were not the Christ, because I accepted [him as] a teacher of the law. But he was in great danger if this one is indeed the Christ, as he certainly is. (4) For I believe in him who has appeared; but for whom else does he reserve his faith - for one who has never appeared? (5) "But that even I, as you say, an uneducated and ignorant man, a fisherman and a rustic, have more understanding than the wise elders, this," I said, "ought even more to strike terror in you. (6) For if in disputing I overcame you wise and erudite men by some kind of erudition, it would be seen that this knowledge came to me over a long time, and was not granted by the grace of divine power. (7) But now when, as I have said, we ignorant men convince and overcome you wise men, is it not apparent to anyone who has sense that this is not the work of human cleverness, but of divine will and gift?"

. . . .

1.64.1 "For we," I said, "know for a certainty that God is very much angered by the sacrifices which you offer, all the more since the time of sacrifices has at last been completed. (2) Because you do not wish to acknowledge that the time for offering victims is now past, therefore the temple will be destroyed, and the abomination

not a little danger, but great danger for you, if he is the Messiah, which he in truth is. (4) For I believe in him who has appeared and been revealed, but you are keeping your faith for someone else whom you do not know. (5) But if, as you have said, I am an ignorant and uneducated man and a fisherman, and I confess I know more than the wise sages," I said to him, "this ought rather to alarm you greatly. (6) For if we had gone out for instruction, and then refuted you wise men, this would be a work of time and diligence which is of natural disposition and not of the power of God. (7) But because we who are unlearned overcome by our refutation you who are wise, in whose judgment would this not be apparent that this thing about us is not of the sons of men, but is of the will of God, to whom everything is possible?" But I said these things to him, and things similar to them.

. . . .

1.64.1 "For we know that He is very angry because of your sacrificing, because the time of sacrifices is now complete. (2) Therefore the temple will be destroyed, and they will set up the abomination of desolation in the holy place. Then the Gospel will be made known to the Gentiles as a witness, for the healing of the divisions which exist, and

1.64.2-4; 1.65.1-3 (L)

of desolation will be set up in the holy place. Then the Gospel will be preached to the Gentiles as a witness against you, so that by their faith your unfaithfulness may be judged. (3) For all the world at various times suffers from various diseases, either generally through all, or through an individual one especially. Therefore it needs a physician to visit it for its health. (4) We therefore witness to you and we announce that which has been hidden from every one of you. Yours is to consider what is advantageous for you."

1.65.1 When I had said these things, the whole multitude of the priests was in an uproar, bcause I had foretold to them the destruction of the temple. (2) When Gamaliel, a leader of the people (who was secretly our brother in the faith, but by our plan was among them) saw this, because they were greatly angered and were moved with monstrous fury against us, he arose and said, (3) "Be quiet for a little while, O men of Israel; for you do not perceive the trial which is hanging over us. Therefore leave these men alone. If what they are doing is of a human plan it will quickly end; but if it is of God, why do you sin without a cause and not gain anything? For who is able

1.64.2-4; 1.65.1-3 (S)

your divisions as well. (3) For because the whole world in each generation is sick with evil desire either secretly or openly, that physician who was sought visited for its health. (4) Behold, we thus witness to each one of you about all that you lack. Yours is now to decide what is helpful for you to do."

1.65.1 When I had said these things, the whole multitude of the priests shouted about this, that I had openly spoken about the destruction of the temple. (2) But then Gamaliel, a leader of the people who for our advantage was secretly our brother in the word of faith, noticed that many were gnashing their teeth in the great rage with which they were filled against us. He said to them, (3) "Be quiet and keep silence, O men, sons of Israel, for we do not know what sort of trial this is that stands over us. Therefore leave these men alone. If this thing is of the sons of men, it will fail; but if it is of God, why would you sin uselessly when you are not able to accomplish it? For the will of God always fit-

1.65.3 - 1.66.4 (L)

to overcome the will of God? (4) Now therefore, as the day is already turning toward evening, I myself will dispute with these men tomorrow in this same place as you listen, so that I may openly oppose and clearly refute every error." (5) By these words their furor was somewhat held back, particularly in the hope of their expectation that on the next day we would be publicly convicted of error. And so he dismissed the people in peace.

1.66.1 But we, when we had come to our James, explained everything that was said and done. When we had eaten, we stayed with him, making supplication to Almighty God through the whole night, that the discourse of the coming disputation may show the undoubtable truth of our faith. (2) Therefore, on the next day James the bishop went up together with us and with the whole church to the temple, where we found a large multitude that had been waiting for us since the middle of the night. (3) Therefore we stood in the place where we were before, so that by standing in a prominent [place] we might be seen by the whole people. (4) Then, when there was perfect silence, Gamaliel, who as we said above was of our faith, but by permission remained among them, so

1.65.3 - 1.66.4 (S)

tingly conquers in everything. (4) Now because this day is passing away, I desire to speak with them tomorrow here in your presence in order to refute their word of error." (5) While these were gnashing their teeth and were filled with rage and anger, they became silent in the supposition that on the next day we would be convicted of error in the presence of them all. When he had promised this to them, he dismissed the people in peace.

1.66.1 When we had come, we related these things that were said to James. When we had told him, we took food, and all of us spent the night with him. During the whole night we prayed that on the next day our word of truth would prevail and conquer in the coming debate. (2) On the next day, James the bishop went up to the temple with all our multitude, and we found there a great multitude which had been waiting for us. (3) Then we all were standing in the places of the preceding day, as thus in the high places we were visible to all the people. (4) When there was a great quiet, Gamaliel, who, as I said before, was secretly among them for our assistance although he was our brother, so that when they in one mind were plotting against us, he would be able to know it and keep it from us, or

1.66.4 - 1.67.4 (L)

that if they should ever attempt anything wicked or impious against us, either would restrain them by a wisely adopted plan, or would warn us so that we would be able either to take care or deflect it; (5) - he therefore, as if he were acting against us, first while looking at James the bishop addressed him in this way:

1.67.1 "If I, Gamaliel, consider it a disgrace to neither my learning nor advanced age to learn something from children and the unlearned, if perhaps there may be something of usefulness or salvation to acquire (for he who lives according to reason knows that there is nothing of more value than the soul), should this not be prized and desired by all, to learn what one does not know, and teach what one has learned? (2) For it is very certain that neither friendship nor kindred relationship nor lofty royal power ought to be of more value to one than truth. (3) And so, brothers, if you know anything further, do not hesitate to bring it before all the people of God, that is, to your brothers, as the whole people is listening willingly and in complete silence to what you say. (4) For why should the people not do this, when they see even me as an equal with them

1.66.4 - 1.67.6 (S)

in fitting counsel would change it by his intercession against those who opposed us, (5) nevertheless first wisely spoke as our enemy, and he proclaimed in such a way that he might persuade the people, and that they would hear in love the true words which were spoken. Looking at James the bishop, he began his discourse thus:

1.67.1 "I Gamaliel, who am old, and who have honor among teachers of the truth, am not ashamed to learn from children and unlearned ones something about salvation and helpful for my life, for to those who have a discerning mind there is nothing more excellent than their soul." (2) And he declared that neither kings nor friends nor kindred nor fathers nor anything else is more excellent than the truth. (3) As if enticing and coaxing us, he said, "If you know anything, do not be reluctant to give it to your people, because you are brothers in the matter of the worship of God. (4/5) Let us commit our soul, brothers, in faith to the love of the true narration, as God desires to fill up through these things what is lacking in us or in you. (6) But if perhaps you fear the deceit of those prejudiced men among us who indiscriminately stir up division, and you do not wish to

1.67.4 - 1.68.2 (L)

willing to learn from you, if perhaps God has revealed something further to you? (5) But if
you lack in anything, likewise do
not hesitate to be taught by us, so
that for both sides God may
complete anything that may be
lacking. (6) But if any fear may
perhaps disquiet you because of
some of us whose minds are
prejudiced against you, and because fearing their treacheries
you do not dare to speak openly
what you think, I will free you
from the cause of such fear: I
swear to you by Almighty God
who lives forever that I will
allow no one to lay hands on you.
(7) Since, therefore, you have all
these people as a witness of this
my oath, and hold our sealed
covenant as an appropriate
pledge, let each one of you without any delay declare what he
has learned; and let us, brothers,
listen earnestly and in silence."

1.68.1 In saying these things,
Gamaliel did not greatly please
Caiaphas. Seemingly holding
him suspect, he began to insert
himself subtly into the disputations. (2) For smiling at what
Gamaliel had said, the chief of
the priests asked James, the
chief of the bishops, that the con-
versation about the Christ be
drawn from no other place but
the Scriptures, "That we may
know," he said, "whether Jesus

1.67.6 - 1.68.2 (S)

speak openly what is lacking in
us, I also take away this cause,
and I swear to you by the living
God that I will not allow anyone
to lay hands upon you. (7) Since
you have these multitudes who
have come near and are standing
[here] as witnesses and medi-
ators, and the oath has been
given to you as a pledge, let there
by no delay in each one of you
saying what you have learned,
and we will listen as lovers of the
truth."

1.68.1 When Gamaliel said
these things, Caiaphas was not
much pleased. I thought he supposed something in his mind
against him, and took it upon
himself to probe and question.
(2) As if quietly mocking
Gamaliel and James the head
bishop, the chief of the priests
asked that the debate and disputation about the Messiah be
drawn only from Scripture, "So
that," he said, "we may know if

72THE ASCENTS OF JAMES

1.68.2 - 1.69.4 (L)

is himself the Christ or not." (3) Then James said, "First we must inquire from what Scriptures we are principally to have the disputation." (4) Then, after he was with difficulty finally overcome by reason, he answered that it must be had from the law; and after this he also made mention of the prophets.

1.69.1 Our James began to show him that whatever things the prophets say were taken from the law and were spoken in accordance with the law. (2) He also made some comments about the Books of Kingdoms, how and when and by whom they were written, and how they ought to be used. (3) And when he had discoursed fully about the law, and brought to light in a very clear exposition everything which concerns the Christ, he showed by most abundant arguments that Jesus is the Christ, and in him are fulfilled all the predictions which concern his humble coming. (4) For he taught that two comings of him are foretold: one in humility, which he has fulfilled; the other in glory, the fulfillment of which is hoped for, when he will come to give the kingdom to those who believe in him and who observe everything that he commanded.

. . . .

1.68.2 - 1.69.4 (S)

Jesus is certainly he who is anointed, or not." (3) And James said, "First we must seek from where the debate ought rightly to be made." (4) But after great coercion he was rightly compelled to agree to this, that the debate be made from the law.

1.69.1 James likewise spoke in his speech about the prophets, and showed that everything they said was taken from the law, and is truly in agreement with the law. (2) Then he also spoke about the Books of Kingdoms, how and when and by whom they were written, and how one ought to use them. (3) Then he again spoke in his speech about the law and showed how those things are in them. At the end of his speech he spoke about the Messiah, and completed great arguments without measure from every place that Jesus is the Messiah, in whom everything about his humble coming is fulfilled. (4) For there are two comings of him: one in humbleness, in which he has come; but the second in glory, in which he will come and rule over those who believe in him, who do all those things that he commanded.

. . . .

1.69.8 - 1.70.5 (L)

(8) But when he had said some things about baptism also, through seven continuous days he persuaded all the people and the high priest that they should hasten immediately to receive baptism.

1.70.1 When the matter was at the point that they would come and be baptized, a certain hostile man, entering the temple at that time with a few men, began to shout and say, (2) "What are you doing, O men of Israel? Why are you so easily led away? Why are you led headlong by men who are most miserable and deceived by a magician?" (3) While he was saying these things and adding more to them, and as he was overcome by James the bishop, he began to incite the people and raise dissensions, so that the people could not hear those things which were being said. (4) Therefore he began to disturb everything by shouts, and to undo those things which had been arranged with much labor. At the same time he accused the priests, and inflamed them by revilings and reproaches, and like a madman incited everyone to murder, saying, (5) "What are you doing? Why are you stopping? O sluggish and idle ones, why do we not lay our hands on

1.69.8 - 1.70.8 (S)

(8) He also said many things about the Paraclete and baptism, and persuaded all the people with the chief priest through seven complete days that they should immediately hasten and come now for baptism.

1.70.1 Then a certain man who was an enemy came into the temple and toward the altar, while shouting and saying, (2) "What are you doing, O men of Israel, that you are so quickly carried off by miserable men who go astray after a magician?" (3) But while he was saying other things like these, he heard James speaking other things against them and overcoming them. He began to make a great tumult, so that the good things that were being said properly could be neither examined in quietness nor understood, and so be believed. (4) Then he shouted even more about the foolishness and feebleness of the priests, and reviled them, (5) saying, "Why do you delay? Why do you not immediately seize all of them who are with him?" (6) When he had said these things, he first jumped up and seized a brand from the altar, and began to strike with it. (7) When the rest of the priests saw him they did likewise. (8) Many were in flight, and some were falling by the

1.70.5 - 1.71.4 (L)

them and dismember them all?"
(6) And when he had said these
things, seizing a brand from the
altar he began to murder. (7)
Others also, when the saw him,
were carried away by a similar
madness. (8) There was loud
shouting by all, the murderers
and the murdered alike. Much
blood flowed. There was a confused flight, during which that
hostile man attacked James, and
threw him down headlong from
the top of the steps. As he
believed him to be dead, he was
not concerned to beat him further.

1.71.1 But our colleagues
lifted him up, for they were both
more in number and greater in
strength than the others. But because of their fear of God, they
allowed themselves to be slain by
the few rather than slay others.
(2) But when evening came the
priests closed the temple. We
returned to the house of James,
and after passing the night there
in prayer, we went down before
the light to Jericho, about five
thousand persons. (3) Then after
about three days one of the
brothers came to us from
Gamaliel, of whom we spoke
before. He brought secret news
to us, that the hostile man had
received authority from
Caiaphas the high priest (4) to
pursue all who believe in Jesus

1.70.8 - 1.71.3 (S)

sword. Some of them were consumed, and many died. Much
blood of those killed was shed.
That enemy threw James from
the top of the stairs, and when he
fell he was as dead, so he did not
strike him a second time.

1.71.1 When they saw what
had happened to James, they
came up and rescued him. For
although they were more
numerous than them, because of
their fear of God they would
rather endure killing than kill
[others]. Although they were
greater and stronger than them,
because of their fear of God they
were seen as fewer. (2) When
evening came, the priests closed
the temple. We came to the
house of James and prayed
there. Before dawn we went
down to Jericho, about five
thousand persons. (3) After
three days, one of the brothers
came and related to us what had
happened after we were in the
temple. Those priests who were
with him were convinced that he

1.71.4-6 (L)

and travel to Damascus with his letters, so that there also by using the help of unbelievers he might bring ruin to the faithful. Another reason why he was especially hastening to Damascus was that he believed Peter had fled there. (5) About thirty days later he stopped while passing through Jericho to Damascus, when at that time we had gone out to the tombs of two of our brothers. (6) Each year these were whitewashed by themselves, a miracle by which the fury of many against us was held back, as they saw that we were held in memory by God.

1.71.3-6 (S)

should be as a priest in all their plans, because they did not know that he was a fellow-believer with us. He told us, therefore, that the hostile man had gone before the priests and asked Caiaphas the high priest to destroy all those who believe in Jesus. (4) He had gone to Damascus taking letters from them, so that there the unbelievers would help him destroy those who believe. Now he wanted to go there first because he thought that Peter had gone there. (5) But after thirty days he passed by us there in Jericho < ... > to two of our brothers in the night in the place we had buried them, whose tombs were every year suddenly whitened. (6) And the anger of many was suppressed, as they knew that the sons of our faith were worthy of divine remembrance.

CHAPTER FOUR

A COMMENTARY ON *THE ASCENTS OF JAMES*

Introduction

In this chapter we will offer a commentary on *The Ascents of James*, considering both its Latin and Syriac versions. This commentary will be in two parts, Notes and Comment. The Notes will offer discussion of several technical matters: textual problems; grammar and translation; differences between L and S; literary forms; relationships with other literary strata of PsCl, with the biblical tradition, and with early Judaism; and the interpretive comments on the *AJ* by other researchers. The Comment will offer an interpretation of the main lines of meaning of the three large sections of the *AJ*, and will consider how each section fits into the whole. These sections of the *AJ* are the *Heilsgeschichte* from Abraham to the early church (1.33-44), the debate of the Twelve with the Jewish parties in the temple (1.55-65), and the speech of James and its aftermath (1.66-71).

As indicated in Chapter One, most treatment of *R* 1 has been carried out with a source-critical or tradition-critical aim. The only researchers to deal exegetically with an extended portion of *R* 1 have been H.-J. Schoeps, in his *Theologie*,[1] and G. Strecker, in a chapter of his *Judenchristentum*. These two works, especially that of Strecker, offer valuable exegetical comments on the text. However, neither can be characterized as a commentary on *R* 1 or the *AJ*, offering a sustained and systematic treatment of the text.

---

1 Pp. 384-417 give a treatment of 1.54-71. See also Schoeps's *Aus früchristlichen Zeit* (Tübingen: Mohr, 1950) 1-37, a treatment of 1.27-34.

Before we begin the commentary, we will consider the provenance, authorship, date and occasion of the source.

Provenance

Several pieces of evidence suggest that the *AJ* was written in the region of Pella in Transjordan. First, the witness of the *AJ* to the Pella tradition (1.37[S], 39) has rightly led several researchers to point to this area.[2] While Pella is not mentioned by name in the *AJ*, other key elements of the Pella tradition are present, leading us to infer that Pella may be meant. Perhaps the name of Pella is not mentioned because the community of the *AJ* would not need to be reminded of its location.

Second, the affinity of the *AJ* to what is known of Aristo of Pella (fl. ca. 150) may suggest that the two were geographically proximate. Aristo was a Jewish Christian who taught a pre-existence christology, knew of the decree of Hadrian expelling all Jews from Jerusalem and environs, and argued with a Jew about whether Jesus is the Messiah.[3] All these are also found in the *AJ*.

Third, the *AJ* was used as a source by the author of *G*. Since *G* is usually given a provenance in lower Syria, this may be an indication that the *AJ* originated in this area or near it. A Pellan provenance of the *AJ* would be consistent with the provenance of *G*. This is not by itself a weighty piece of evidence, as *G* could have picked up and used a document that originated in almost any area. When added to the two arguments above, however, this third argument has a certain corroborative value in establishing Pella as the most likely provenance of the *AJ*.

Authorship

In its present setting in *R* the *AJ* is pseudonymous. As noted in Chapter One, it has been recognized since the eighteenth century that Clement of Rome, the purported author, had no part in the authorship of *R*. No one seeking to recover the sources of *R* 1 has argued that Clement had a role in writing these sources.

---

2 Strecker, *Judenchristentum*, 253-4; Martyn, "Recognitions," 270-2; Lüdemann, "Successors," 168, 173.

3 The literary remains of Aristo can be found in ANF 8, 749-50.

The question of the *AJ*'s authorship is complicated by our not knowing if the *AJ* was written in the first or third person. Peter is not presented by the *AJ* as its author, because his name stands in 1.71.4 unaltered by later redactors. If the *AJ* were written in the first person, it is possible that it was written under the name of James, as his name is in the title. But it seems more likely that the *AJ* was originally in the third person, because the *heilsgeschichtlich* form found in 1.33-44 is almost invariably in the third person, as are narratives such as 1.55-71.

Therefore, we cannot with any certainty identify the author of the *AJ*. No clues are left in the present form of *R* 1, and the report of Epiphanius on the *AJ* does not mention any author. Despite this uncertainty, the commentary will show that the *AJ* does reflect, if not the mind of one identifiable author, the history and theology of a community.

Date

The *terminus a quo* of the *AJ* can be established by two pieces of evidence. First is the *AJ*'s use of the NT. It has many borrowings from Matthew, Luke and Acts.[4] Moreover, Martyn has argued strongly that the *AJ* uses a tradition of expulsion of Jewish Christians from the synagogue that is traceable to the Fourth Gospel.[5] Because the *AJ* employs the text and tradition of the canonical Gospels and Acts, it must be dated from at least the end of the first century. Second, as Strecker argues, the *AJ* probably refers in *R* 1.39 to the Hadrianic decree of ca. 135, by which all Jews were expelled from Jerusalem and environs.[6] Thus the earliest possible date of the *AJ* is 135.

---

4 Martyn, "Recognitions," 266, reports that Rehm has twenty-six references to Matthew, ten to Luke and five to Mark. Almost all of these are within the bounds of the *AJ*. Lüdemann, *Paulus,* 2.242, lists five references to Matthew, one to Luke, and refers to Strecker for references to Acts. The commentary in this chapter will uncover eleven references to Matthew, five to Luke, and sixteen to Acts.

5 Martyn, "Recognitions," 281-91.

6 Strecker, *Judenchristentum*, 253.

The *terminus ad quem* cannot be as precisely fixed. Since the *AJ* was interpolated by the author of *G*, it must have been written before *G*, which is usually dated ca. 260.[7] Another source of PsCl, the *KerygmataP*, is also older than *G*; it is usually dated ca. 200.[8] Because both the *AJ* and *KerygmataP* were used independently by *G*, we have no redactional evidence that one is older than the other. While any time between 135 and 260 is therefore possible as the date of the *AJ*, its similarities with the thought of Aristo indicate that the *AJ* could fit very well into the middle of the second century. Thus, we may conclude with most researchers that a date somewhere in the second half of the second century is most likely.

Occasion

Why was the *AJ* written? No explicit reason is given in the text, and we are left to read clues it may contain. As we will see in the Commentary below, it certainly was not written as a missionary tract to Jews, as that mission had been destroyed by Paul. Nor does the *AJ* seem to be directed to Gentiles, even though it knows a law-observant mission to them. Rather, it is more likely that the *AJ* was written for its own church. The *AJ* reminds its community that the true line of faith goes from Abraham to Moses to Jesus. This line extends through Jesus to James and the Jerusalem church he leads, and then to those communities that are the true descendants of James' church, like that of the *AJ*. The *AJ* is also concerned to distinguish this true line from two false lines: Judaism, now consigned to permanent unbelief in Jesus; and the law-free Great Church, as symbolized by Paul.

---

7 Ibid., 254.

8 It is not possible to say with Strecker, *Judenchristentum*, 254 n. 1, that because the *AJ* knows no Gnostic elements it therefore "repräsentiert sich sachlich ein ursprünglicheres Judenchristentum" than the *KerygmataP*. This lack of Gnostic elements may also be due to a lack of contact or conflict with Gnosticism, and a lack of Gnostic elements does not necessarily show one source of PsCl to be earlier or more original than the other.

Notes to R 1.33.3 - 1.44.3 [9]

1.33.3 *But when Abraham was still in ignorance* (L) / *But Abraham, when he was not in the knowledge of the Great One* (S). The beginning of the *AJ* as we have it in *R* 1.33 speaks of Abraham's time of "ignorance." The L of 1.33.3 does not specify what Abraham was ignorant of. However, the L of 1.34.1 states that he was "in ignorance of things," and contrasts this with his obtaining "the knowledge of God." S says that Abraham did not have "the knowledge of the Great One." We have read the S *rbwt'*, "greatness, size, majesty," as a reference to God. Since in 1.34.1 both L and S will explain this ignorance of Abraham as ignorance of the knowledge of God, this is evidently the meaning in 1.33.3 also.

(as was related by the account which does not lie, and that True Prophet witnessed, as I have shown you again) (S). Here the role of the True Prophet is to bring a true account of Israel's past. This is consistent with the role of the True Prophet elsewhere in PsCl as a revealer of divine truth (cf. *R* 1.16.2, 1.21.7). The mention of the True Prophet and his absence from L argue that this passage was added by S. While the punctuation of S gives no pertinent indication, the content of this passage clearly indicates that it is parenthetical.

Abraham [had] two sons. Ishmael is known from OT tradition as the son of Abraham by Hagar. But why is Eliezer, Abraham's servant, also called Abraham's son by birth? Schoeps, *Zeit*, 26, is probably correct in attributing Eliezer's sonship to a misunderstanding of Gen 15:2-3, where Abraham calls Eliezer "a slave born in my house" and his heir. However, Gen 15:4 makes it clear that Eliezer is not Abraham's

---

9 The format of the Notes is as follows. The text to be treated is given first, in italics. Where it is short, or L and S are similar, the text is given on (a) full line(s). Where the text is longer and L and S differ, necessitating treatment of both in the Notes, the translations are put in parallel columns. A full reference number is given for the first text on each page. Footnotes are provided for works not yet fully cited; for works cited, a short form of citation is given in the text.

son. Other midrashic treatments of Abraham's offspring more clearly preserve the distinction between Ishmael and Eliezer.[10]

The two forms of the name "Eliezer" call for comment. "Heliesdros" is the Latinized form of the Greek Ελιεζερ. For the different forms of this name in PsCl, cf. *R* 2.1.2, 3.68.1; *H* 2.1.2 and 2.16.5, noting the variant readings in the MSS. The S form of Eliezer is spelled exactly as in Gen 15, *'ly'zr*.

<table>
<tr>
<td>

1.33.3 (L) *From the one [Ishmael] are descended the heathen nations, from the other [Heliesdros] the people of the Persians,* (4) *some of whom have adopted the life and manners of their neighbors, the Brahmins.*

</td>
<td>

(S) *One was ... Ishmael; the other was Eliezer, of whom the nations of the Arabs and the Persians are multiplied.* (4) *Some of them were joined with their neighbors, the Brahmins.*

</td>
</tr>
</table>

In L, the descendants of Ishmael are *barbarae*, "heathen, foreign, strange." Interpreted against the *AJ*'s Jewish background, "heathen" is to be understood as "gentile." From the Jewish perspective, of course, not only are the descendants of Ishmael *barbarae*, but all non-Jews, including the descendants of Eliezer. Drawing on OT tradition (cf. Gen 16:11-15), S identifies the descendants of Ishmael as the Arabs. Despite some variations between L and S on the descendants of these two sons of Abraham, the main lines are the same. From Ishmael come the Arabs, some of whom migrate to Egypt; from Eliezer come the Persians, who associate with the Brahmins.

Unique to the *AJ* is the notion that the Persians are descended from Eliezer. In *R* 4.27.2 and 9.3.2, they are descended from Ham, the son of Noah, and thus would antedate Eliezer. By "Brahmins," the text seems to mean the people of India as a whole, not just the ruling caste: (1) "Brahmins" is associated with "Persians," here a nation; (2) The language soon shifts to "some Indians."

---

10 One exception is Philo's *Who is the Heir?* 39-40, as Strecker, *Judenchristentum*, 224, points out; but see also sections 1-2 and 61-2 of Philo. Cf. also the passages given in the article "Eliezer" in *EncJud* 6.618-9, and in L. Ginzberg, *Legends of the Jews* (7 vols.; Philadelphia: Jewish Publication Society, 1925) 1.293; 5.260 n. 282. According to the Hurrian law reflected in the Nuzi tablets, which is often cited as a parallel to Gen 15:2-3, a childless man could adopt a grown man to be his heir. This heir was considered his son by law. In *R* 1.33.3 Eliezer is not adopted, but is a son by birth.

1.33.5 *From them some Indians and some Egyptians have learned to circumcise, and to be of a purer observance than the others, although in the passing of time most of them turned the proof and sign of purity into impiety* (L). Here the *AJ* explains the origin of circumcision among these two gentile nations. This practice stems ultimately from the two sons of Abraham, Ishmael and Eliezer. It has done some limited good, resulting in these nations being purer than those who are not circumcised, but through time this purity has been lost. While L states that "most" (*quam plurimi*, "most, as many as possible") turned circumcision to impurity, S states that "some" did this. But both agree in implying that this circumcision did no lasting good, because it came from the sons born to Abraham in his time of ignorance. For the OT account of the circumcision of Ishmael and (by implication) Eliezer, see Gen 17:23-27.

Circumcision is mentioned only here in the *AJ*, but in a very positive manner. Even though the Gentile nations have abused it, circumcision is still the "proof and sign of purity" (L) and leads to "goodness" (S). This view of circumcision can be contrasted with the attitude of some Fathers of the Great Church, who used the practice of circumcision among the Gentiles as an argument against its continuing validity for the church.[11] Also, this passage shows no sign of the bitter struggle over circumcision that marks several writings of the NT. While not enough evidence exists in 1.33.5 to conclude that the community of the *AJ* practiced circumcision, the positive view of circumcision makes it possible.

1.34.1 *When he obtained the knowledge of God he asked of Him, because he was just, that he might merit to have progeny by Sarah* (L). Does the "he" in "because he was just" refer to God or Abraham? The two readings of L give quite different answers. The first, *quia erat iustus*, "because he was just," is a clear reference to Abraham's state. It implies that Abraham's righteousness was the basis of his request for a son. This view is substantiated by the mention in the next clause of Abraham's "merit." The other reading, *qui erat iustus*, "who was just," is an equally clear reference to God: Abraham, knowing God to be just, made his request for a son by Sarah. [*Q*]*uia* is the better reading because it is the more difficult and better-attested in the MS tradition; it is rightly preferred by Rehm. S clearly refers to Abraham as just.

---

11 See the references in Strecker, *Judenchristentum*, 224.

Our translation follows its word order exactly: ". . . he [Abraham] prayed that, because he was just . . ." On the basis of the MS evidence of L and the reading of S, we may conclude that "he" refers to Abraham. When Abraham knows God, he becomes just, and this is the basis of his successful prayer for a son by Sarah.

Genesis and early Jewish midrash upon it have no reference to a prayer of Abraham for a son by Sarah.[12] Instead of Abraham's prayer, Genesis records disbelief at God's unexpected promise of a son (Gen 17:15-21; 18:1-15).

1.34.1 *Sarah would have a son* (S). Both MSS of S literally read in 1.34:1-2, "he prayed that, because he was just, from Sarah who was his lawful wife from his youth although she was barren, a son would be to her. And it was granted her to have . . . Isaac." Frankenberg emends the two occurrences of "her" to read "him" by removing the diacritical dot over the second letter in the word *lh* ("to her"). This conjectural emendation removes the awkwardness of "from Sarah . . . a son would be to her." It also brings the first sentence of 1.34.2 into agreement with 1.34.1 by granting the answer of the prayer to Abraham, who made it. Against Frankenberg, "her" is to be preferred as the more difficult and well-attested reading. Whatever reading is adopted, the sense of the passage is the same: God grants Abraham's prayer to have a son by Sarah.

the twelve . . . the seventy-two. "The twelve" refers to the twelve sons of Jacob, the patriarchs of the tribes. "The seventy-two" is the number of the Hebrews who entered Egypt (cf. Gen 46:26-7; Exod 1:5). This second number is peculiar in Jewish and Christian tradition to the *AJ*. As Strecker, *Judenchristentum*, 224-5, points out, the MT has this number as seventy, and the LXX as seventy-five. Philo also has seventy-five (*Migration of Abraham* 36), as does Acts 7:14. In the only other reference in PsCl to this number, *H* 18.4.3 has it as seventy.

"Twelve" and "seventy-two" become more important later in the *AJ*, where a parallel is drawn between the two groups chosen by Moses to assist him and the two groups of Jesus' disciples (1.40.4). The *AJ* has

---

12 The medieval Jewish exegete Rashi (1040 - 1105) approximates this prayer in his *Commentary on Genesis* as he comments on Gen 21.1, "The Lord visited Sarah": "This scripture adjoins the preceding one to teach you that anyone who seeks blessing for his fellow man, when he himself is in need of that very thing, is answered first. As it is said, 'Abraham prayed,' and then 'and the Lord remembered Sarah.' God remembered Abraham before he heard Abimelech." I owe this reference to David Marcus.

altered the number of the Hebrews who entered Egypt to seventy-two to make it match the seventy-two sent out by Jesus. See the second Note on 1.40.4 for further comment on these numbers. All of 1.34.2, with the exception of "seventy-two," is drawn from Acts 7:8, where Abraham, Isaac, Jacob and "the twelve patriarchs" are also given in short order.

1.34.3 *promise of God.* "The blessing and promise of God" cause the people to multiply in Egypt. The meaning of "the promise of God" is uncertain, as no promise has yet been mentioned. Acts 7:17 also links the promise of God with the growth of the people in Egypt. In Acts, however, "promise" refers to possession of the Promised Land.

four hundred years. This number of the years the Hebrews spent in Egypt is from Gen 15:13 via Acts 7:6. Gen 15:13-16 is quoted and this number is given in *H* 3.34.4.

.4 *The True Prophet.* L reads "the True Prophet appeared to Moses," and S reads "the true prophet, Moses, came to them." Because "the True Prophet" appears in both L and S, it probably was in the Greek MSS used in translating *R* into these versions. As we saw in Chapter Two, the True Prophet belongs to other strata of PsCl. He is not mentioned elsewhere in the *AJ*, where the dominant figure is the Prophet like Moses.

he punished . . . them (S). Literally, "he put upon their heads." The S idiom "to put upon the head" has the implication of killing a person. Thus in 1.34.5 only some of "the Egyptian[s] . . . were left" after the plagues.

.5 *their king.* The use of "king" to describe the Pharaoh hints of the anti-royal sentiment to come in 1.38.4. Exod 14:1-29, on which 1.34.5-7 is based, refers in both the MT and the LXX in all but one verse (8) to "Pharaoh." The *AJ* avoids this name, and by using "king" links the evil king of the Egyptians with the later kings of the Israelites.

.7 *received punishment* (S). The same idiom is used as in 1.34.4, with death explicit here as the punishment the Egyptians suffered. In S, "the Egyptians who pursued received punishment in it" (1.34.7) is a restatement of ". . . the Egyptians . . . all followed after them and died" (1.34.6).

1.35.1 *Then Moses, by the command of God, who knows everything, led the great multitude of the Hebrews into the wilderness* (S). God planned the wilderness wanderings to rid the Hebrews of the evil they learned in Egypt. In Exodus, the wanderings come after the idolatry at Sinai, with the aim that all the members of that idolatrous generation should die before the entry into the Promised Land. In the *AJ*, the wanderings begin immediately after the exit from Egypt, because the people's idolatry was learned in Egypt. Philo, *Life of Moses* 1.29, also speaks of Moses' immediately taking the "long road" to Canaan, and gives two reasons: to prevent an easy return to Egypt; and to test the loyalty of the people in the desert when supplies were low.

1.35.2 *The law was given to them with heavenly sounds and sights in ten written commandments* (L) / *They heard with heavenly sounds the law of God, all ten commandments* (S). The "heavenly sounds"[13] and "sights" which accompany the Decalogue are probably the thunder, lightning, fire and earthquake (Exod 19:16-19; Deut 4:11, 5:22). S implies that the whole Decalogue was spoken to the people. In L, the law was given "in ten written commandments." This variation between L and S is probably an unintended reflection of the difficulties in the narratives of the giving of the Law in Exodus 19-20 and Deuteronomy 5. M. Greenberg sums up exegetical opinion on these passages: "The accounts apparently combine different versions of the event: (a) God spoke with Moses and the people overheard; (b) He spoke with Moses and then Moses transmitted his words to the people; (c) God spoke to the people directly."[14] Greenberg's version (b) is suggested by L, while version (c) is explicit in S. In both Exodus and Deuteronomy, we should add, the Decalogue is also written down.

Jewish tradition also varies on whether God spoke some or all the Decalogue to the people of Israel. Ginzberg, *Legends*, 6.45 n. 243, cites many aggadic works to show a general agreement in early Judaism that God spoke the first two commandments (i.e., Exod 20:1-6) directly to the people, but disagreement over whether he spoke the rest. Josephus says the entire Decalogue was spoken by God (*Ant.* 3.5.5 §91). Philo states that all the commands were spoken by the "voice of God" (*Life of Moses* 2.6). He calls the Decalogue "those he gave in his own person and by his own mouth alone" (*On the Decalogue* 5).[15] Compare also Acts 7:38, "the angel who spoke to him [Moses] at Mount Sinai, and with our fathers," and Acts 7:53, "you who received the law as delivered by angels."

---

13 We have translated S's *bnt ql'* (literally, "daughters of the voice") as "sounds," but it could also mean "voices."

14 "Decalogue," *EncJud* 5.1436.

15 More in accord with his own aversion to anthropomorphism, Philo also says that God did not speak, but willed into being an incorporeal voice to pronounce the Decalogue (*On the Decalogue* 9).

1.35.2 *the first* [commandment]. The division of the Decalogue into ten commandments was also a problem in early Judaism. The *AJ* here gives as the first commandment the twin injunctions of Exod 20:3-6 not to worship another god or make an image to worship. In retelling the Jewish legends surrounding the Decalogue, Ginzberg gives as the first commandment Exod 20:2, "I am the Lord your God . . . ," and as the second Exod 20:3-6, the injunctions against worshipping other gods and idolatry (*Legends*, 3.94-109). This division "is the only one known in rabbinic sources" (*Legends*, 6.43, n. 234). Modern Jewish worship still uses this division.[16] On the other hand, Philo (*On the Decalogue* 12) and Josephus (*Ant.* 3.5.5 §91) give vv 2-3 as the first commandment, and vv 4-6 as the second. The *AJ* has a third enumeration, one that like rabbinic tradition combines into one commandment the injunctions against worshipping another god and idolatry, but unlike rabbinic tradition calls this the first commandment.[17]

.3 *the people . . . were given manna from heaven for bread and were provided drink from the rock which followed them (which type of food was turned by the power of God into whatever taste anyone desired)*(L). Two originally distinct Jewish legends are combined by the *AJ*: the miraculous taste of the manna, and water from the following rock.

The legend of the miraculous taste of the manna first appears in the first century BC at Wis 16:20-21. Well attested in rabbinical literature, it is not found in either the Hebrew Scriptures or the NT. According to the legend, one only had to think of a certain food before eating the manna, and it tasted like that food. As Maiberger, *Manna*, 1.239, notes, this legend developed despite Numbers 11, which states that the Hebrews grew tired of the taste of the manna, "like the taste of cakes baked in oil" (v 8). This strongly implies that its taste did not change.

The *AJ* develops the legend of miraculous taste a step further by extending it to the waters of the rock. The taste of both manna and water were changed by divine power according to the desires of the people. This development is unique in Jewish and Christian literature. Strecker, *Judenchristentum*, 225, seems to limit the miracle of taste to

---

16 See, e.g., *Gates of Prayer: The New Union Prayerbook* (New York: Central Conference of American Rabbis, 1975).

17 This problem has a parallel in later Christian tradition, as the Roman Catholic and Lutheran churches view Exod 20:3-6 as the first commandment, but the Orthodox and Reformed churches give Exod 20:3 as the first and vv 4-6 as the second.

the manna when he states that *quae species cibi . . . saporem* refers to the manna. But *cibus*, as an inclusive term for food, refers here to both bread (*panis*) and drink (*poculum*).[18] If the *AJ* had wanted to restrict the miracle to the manna, it could have said *quae species panis*. The mention of the taste-miracle after the mention of both bread and water also indicates that the author sees both as miraculous. S states unambiguously that the taste of both manna and water "were changed" (note the plural).

The legend of the following rock is probably a midrashic expansion of Num 21:17. It is well-attested in Jewish literature, most notably at *t. Sukkah* 3:11 and in Pseudo-Philo's *Bib. Ant.* 10:7. The basic form of the legend tells of a well or a rock which accompanied the Hebrews during the wilderness wanderings, providing them water.[19] In line with the legend, the *AJ* implies that the rock followed them continually. This is supported by the continual aspect of the compound S verb *nqyp' hwt*, "was following."

Is there a relationship between the *AJ*'s use of these legends of the manna and water and the Apostle Paul's in I Cor 10:4? In contrast to other sources which sometimes cite a well, both have in common the mention of a rock, and both say this rock followed the people and gave them drink. Moreover, Paul, like the *AJ*, ties the manna and water together: both are "spiritual." But three differences between Paul and the *AJ* can be discerned. First, Paul does not mention the taste-miracle, which is most important for the *AJ*. Second, Paul calls the rock πνευματικη, "spiritual," which the *AJ* does not. Most importantly, Paul interprets the rock christologically: "and the rock was Christ." The *AJ* does not make such an interpretation. Therefore, the *AJ* is probably not literarily dependent upon I Cor 10:4; rather, both draw independently from the legend.

1.35.4 *cloud . . . fire.* In the OT, the purpose of the pillar of fire and the (pillar of) cloud is to lead the people night and day on their way through the wilderness. Once it is said that the pillar of fire gives light

---

18 The variant reading for *cibi, sibi* ("to them") is probably caused by the similar sound and by interference with the *sibi* found thirteen words before *cibi* in 1.34.1.

19 E. E. Ellis (*Paul's Use of the Old Testament* [Edinburgh: Oliver & Boyd, 1957] 66-70) gives a hypothetical reconstruction of this legend, and full references to its use in the OT and Jewish literature; see also Str-B 3.406-8. For the most recent treatment of Moses and the giving of water in the Targums and Midrash, see G. Bienaimé, *Moïse et le don l'eau dans la tradition juive ancienne* (AnBib 98; Rome: Biblical Institute, 1984).

to illumine the people (Exod 13:21). The point of 1.35.3-4 is that God took complete care of the people, so they did not need to turn to another god.

1.35.5 *Apis.* The golden calf is associated by the *AJ* with the Egyptian fertility god Apis, who was represented as a sacred bull. In the Greco-Roman era, Apis was connected to the story of the dying and rising of Osiris, and thus was called Osiris-Apis or Serapis. Here the older name is kept. The cult of Apis is also mentioned at *R* 5.20.2-3 and its parallel in *H* 10.16.2, but is not connected with the Hebrews' idolatry. The *AJ*'s linking of their idolatry with a specific Egyptian deity reinforces its point about the old evil customs of the Egyptians clinging to Israel. J. Hahn reports that some "speculations" in the modern history of exegesis have sought to relate the calf to Apis, but rejects this as untenable.[20] Speaking of Jewish exegesis, Ginzberg, *Legends,* 6.53, n. 271, remarks, "The identification of the golden calf with the Apis of the Egyptians frequently mentioned by early Christian authors (comp., e.g.,*Apostolic Constitutions* 6.20; Lactantius,*Divinae Institutiones* 4.10) is unknown in the old rabbinic sources."

.6 *For this reason* (L) / *Because of this* (S). Section six offers a closure to this chapter by repeating much of section one and tying the wilderness wanderings to the result of idolatry.

1.36.1 *faithful steward.* Moses is called "a faithful and wise steward" (L) / "a good and faithful steward" (S) because he knows that he cannot end all the evil customs obtained by the people in Egypt. Therefore he ends only one half of the evil, the worship of other gods. He leaves the other half, sacrifice, to a future prophet like himself (1.36.2). "Faithful steward" probably stems from Num 12:7 (L), where God calls Moses "faithful in my whole house." The L phrase *fidelis et prudens dispensator* stems from Luke 12:42, πιστος οικονομος 'ο φρονιμος, which the Vg renders *fidelis dispensator et prudens*. (In Luke, though, there is no reference to Moses.) Compare also Heb 3:3,5, where the faithfulness of Moses is emphasized, and *R* 2.52.3, where Moses is the πιστος οικονομος. Strecker, *Judenchristentum,* 226, gives other references to this expression in other early Christian literature.

permit them to sacrifice. Moses permits sacrifice to God as a concession to the weakness of the people. Sacrifice is temporary, to be done away with at the coming of the Prophet like Moses. In his essay,

---

20 *Das "Goldene Kalb"* (Frankfort: Lang, 1981) 318-9.

"Concessions to Sinfulness in Jewish Law,"[21] D. Daube examines several institutions which, although having legal status in the Mosaic code, are nonetheless seen in early Judaism as morally wrong, and given only because of the wickedness or weakness of the people. Among these are the slavery of Hebrews, polygamy and divorce. Daube also examines other concessions not given Mosaic status, such as the establishment of the monarchy. Jewish tradition did not view sacrifice as a concession to sin, but the *AJ* draws on this legal category to argue against sacrifice. Once again, the *AJ* is on common ground with second-century Great Church theology. As Strecker, *Judenchristentum*, 226, notes, this view of sacrifice as a concession to Israel's sinfulness is shared by some Fathers of the Great Church (Justin, *Dial.* 19.6; 22.1,11; Irenaeus, *Adv. Haer.* 4.26.1; *Didascalia* 1.6.8).

Strecker also draws attention to the telling difference between the *AJ*'s view of sacrifice and the law and the view of PsCl passages which he includes in the *KerygmataP*. These passages explain the presence of sacrifice and temple in the law by the theory of false pericopes (see, e.g., *H* 3.45-56, especially chaps. 45, 52, and 56). They trace sacrifice to the falsified law, but not to Moses; the *AJ* traces it to Moses' concession, but not to the law. Thus both the *AJ* and these passages share an anti-sacrificial animus, and they agree that sacrifice is not rightly a part of the law.

1.36.1 *a part . . . the other part* (L) / *one half . . . the other half* (S). The first item in these pairs is idolatry, which Moses ended. The second is sacrifice itself, left by Moses for the coming Mosaic Prophet.

.2 *of whom he himself said* (L) / *the one of whom he said* (S). The speaker is Moses.

"*A prophet shall the Lord your God raise up for you like me; you shall hear him according to everything that he says to you. For whoever shall not hear that prophet, his soul shall be destroyed from his people*" (S). Here the *AJ* draws on Acts 3:22 in describing the Mosaic Prophet. Acts 3:22 is itself drawn from the words of Moses in Deut 18:15,19 and Lev 23:29. It is also cited in *H* 3.53.3; but as Strecker, *Judenchristentum*, 226, remarks, *R* draws more strongly than *H* on Acts 3:22. The *AJ* alters Acts 3:22 by replacing its "from your brethren as he raised me up" with "like me," which is the reading of Deuteronomy 18. This alteration serves to emphasize the identity of the Prophet as "like Moses."

---

21 JJS *10* (1959) 1-13.

1.36.2 *shall surely die* (S). Literally, "shall die in death."

A prophet... like me. The Prophet like Moses is an eschatological figure in early Judaism, the NT, and other early Christian literature. It has been well-researched, chiefly by O. Cullmann, H. Teeple, J. Jeremias, and F. Hahn.[22] Since it is beyond the bounds of this work to treat all the evidence for the Prophet like Moses, we may summarize the consensus of this research as a background for our commentary.

Slim but suggestive evidence in post-biblical Judaism indicates that among its many different eschatological figures was a Prophet like Moses. This Prophet like Moses is sometimes distinguished (e.g., by Jeremias) from the expectation of a return of Moses (*Moses redivivus*) or a "New Moses," but such a fine distinction may not have been made in ancient times. Teeple, *Prophet*, 43-5, points to the NT, especially Mark 9 and Rev 11:3-13, as evidence that the Prophet-like-Moses expectation has Jewish origins.[23] After reviewing the NT, Jewish and Samaritan sources, Hahn concludes that two features mark this figure: certification by miracle, and an emphasis on a teaching role, especially teaching on the law. The *AJ* prominently features both.

Researchers into the Mosaic Prophet in early Christianity have focused on Acts 3:22 and 7:37, in which "the primitive community found affinities between the story of Moses and that of Jesus" (Jeremias, "Moyses," 868). Many other NT writings, especially Matthew, John and Hebrews, develop their distinctive christologies with traditions about Moses. These writings may contain allusions to Deut 18:15, but this text is cited explicitly only in Acts. The *AJ*'s explicit use of this text shows that it draws and develops the Prophet-like-Moses category from Acts.

---

22 Cullmann, *Christology*, 13-50; Teeple, *The Mosaic Eschatological Prophet* (SBLMS 10; Philadelphia: Society of Biblical Literature, 1957; the University of Chicago dissertation on which this book is based contains an appendix on "The Prophet in the Clementines" which is unfortunately omitted from the book); Jeremias, "Moyses," *TDNT* 4 (1967) 848-73; Hahn, *The Titles of Jesus in Christology* (Philadelphia: Westminster, 1965) 352-406.

23 Teeple also points to *Mid. Deut. Rab.* 3 and the Jerusalem Targum on Exod 12:42 (fifth century). Schoeps, *Theologie*, 96, places *Mid. Deut. Rab.* in the late first century; but it is probably much later, as Teeple argues.

While the story of Moses is used in extra-NT Christian literature
mainly in moral exhortation (e.g., in *I Clement* and *Barnabas*), the
Mosaic Prophet is found in only a few writers, and plays a minor role
in them. Teeple can cite only Clement of Alexandria (*The Pedagogue*
1.7) as a second-century witness to the Prophet like Moses christology.
Clement applies Deut 18:15 to Joshua and through him to Jesus, noting
the similarity of their names in Greek.[24] The Logos christology is
everywhere the leading christology in Clement's writings. Other christological categories, including the Mosaic Prophet, play only a small
role. In contrast to this spare usage of the Mosaic Prophet in the NT
and in other early Christian literature, the *AJ* has the most highly-
developed use of the Mosaic Prophet christology in early Christianity.

1.36.2 *It shall be known that this one has given up his soul to
destruction* (S). S adds this sentence to the end of the quotation,
building it from the words "soul" and "destruction" which it omitted
from the first sentence of 1.36.2. This second sentence serves to
reinforce the penalty of death for not heeding the Prophet like Moses.
"His soul" (*npšh*) can also be translated "his life."

1.37.1 *a place.* Moses establishes a place to which sacrifice is
restricted, thus limiting its evil. The tabernacle, though not named, is
probably in view here.[25] Since the words used here for "place" (*locus,
dwkt'*) are used later in the *AJ* for the temple, the temple is also by
extension in view. This passage alludes to Deut 12:5-14, in which
Moses is said to restrict sacrifice in the Promised Land to one place.
See the Note on 1.38.5 for more on the relationship of the tabernacle
and temple in the *AJ*.

.2 *the right time* (L) / *a more convenient time* (S). Moses is said to
permit sacrifice to God until a fitting time should come. This is the time
of the Mosaic Prophet, in which the ministry of Moses will be completed by the abolition of sacrifice.

---

24 Teeple, *Prophet*, 90-2. References he cites from Great Church writers of the third
   and fourth centuries include Terullian's *Against Marcion* 4.22; Novatian's *On the
   Trinity* 9; Cyprian's *Treatise* 12; Lactantius' *Divine Institutions* 4.17; the *Acts of
   Archelaus* 41; and the *Apostolic Constitutions* 5.20.
25 For a full treatment of the antecedents of the tabernacle in the *AJ*, see C. R. Koester,
   "The Tabernacle in the New Testament and Intertestamental Jewish Literature"
   (Ph.D. dissertation, Union Theological Seminary [New York]; Ann Arbor:
   University Microfilms, 1987).

1.37.2 *God desires mercy and not sacrifices.* This quotation of Hos 6:6 (LXX) is found on the lips of Jesus in Matt 9:13 and 12:7. As the *AJ* identifies it as the words of the Prophet, the citation is from Matthew rather than directly from Hosea. This saying will play a large role through 1.39. Hos 6:6 is also quoted by Rabban Johanan ben Zakkai, the chief editor of the Mishna, to argue that "acts of lovingkindness" are "another atonement as effective" as sacrifice (*'Abot R. Nat.*, A 4).

(L) . . . *they should see him who teaches them that the place divinely chosen as fitting to offer sacrifices to God is His wisdom. As for this other place which seemed for a time to be chosen and was often shaken by invasions and destructions by enemies, they should hear that it would finally be destroyed completely.*

(S) *Then that prophet who declares these things will be sent to them, and those who believe in him will be led by the wisdom of God to the strong place of the land, which is for the living. There they will be preserved from the war which will shortly come to their own destruction upon those who because of their division do not obey.*

After the citation of Matthew, L and S diverge widely for the remainder of 1.37.2. L is comprised of two contrasting statements: (1) the place chosen by God for sacrifice is His wisdom; (2) the "other place," the temple, is not chosen, and will be destroyed. Since the second of these statements is less problematic, we will begin with it. The temple "seemed for a time to be chosen," because it was the place for sacrifice allowed by Moses. (Here the tabernacle drops from view, its place taken by the temple.) In reality, it was only a concession from Moses, being neither permanent nor divinely approved. The "invasions and destructions" visited by God upon it were a sign of its ultimate and complete destruction. "They should hear that it would finally be destroyed completely" is a reference to the words of the Mosaic Prophet, who prophesied the temple's total destruction. This anti-temple animus stands in sharp contrast to the many OT statements approving of the temple. Aside from numerous OT references to the temple as the "house of God" or the "temple of God," the story of the dedication of Solomon's temple in 2 Chronicles 7 states that God is said to "have chosen this place for myself as a house of sacrifice" (v 12).

L's statement in 1.37.2 that God's "wisdom" is the "place divinely chosen as fitting to offer sacrifices" has no parallel in the rest of the *AJ* or in PsCl. Given the *AJ*'s strong animus against sacrifice, it may be a reference to a non-literal, "spiritual" sacrifice. This could be a veiled allusion to baptism, considering those baptized as "sacrifices." Such a reading gains some support from 1.39.2 (L only), where baptism is called "the purification of the wisdom of God." But the *AJ* has no other positive reference to sacrifice, and no other hint that those baptized are considered sacrifices.

W. Harter, "Causes," 113-4, 127, gives the L of 1.37.2 as a witness to the Pella tradition. He does not explicate this passage in any detail, but seems to follow Lüdemann's analysis. But Lüdemann ("Successors," 161-73) correctly notes that only the S of 1.37.2 contains a witness to the Pella tradition. A careful reading of 1.37.2 (L) shows that the only similarity between this passage and the Pella tradition is a mention of the destruction of Jerusalem. It says nothing of a flight to safety, refuge in a safe locale, the preservation of believers and the destruction of unbelievers, etc.

The S of this passage is indeed a witness to the Pella tradition. Since a fuller treatment of the Pella tradition will be given at 1.39, where it occurs in both L and S, we will give only a brief treatment of it in here. The basic meaning of 1.37.2b is that those who believe in the Prophet like Moses will be preserved in a special place, given by "the wisdom of God" (perhaps divine revelation, in any case not connected to sacrifice), from the destruction soon to come upon the Jewish nation. This "strong place" is "of the land." While Pella was a part of the Decapolis in NT times, it was within the old tribal territory and in the Northern Kingdom, and so could be considered "of the land." This place is also "for the living," i.e., a place in which they will be kept alive. Here they will be "preserved from the war" which will destroy the temple. As the "destruction" (*'bdn'*) to come upon the nation looks back to the last word of chap. 36, it leads the reader to interpret the destruction of the war as the punishment promised earlier for those who do not obey the Mosaic Prophet. S points to "their division" as a special cause of this disobedience. This may be an allusion to the sectarian divisions within the Jewish nation, which the *AJ* will draw on in 1.55-65.

1.37.3 *the True Prophet* (L). As "true" is lacking in S, its presence in the original can be doubted. The reference is to the Mosaic Prophet, who in the *AJ* "was to repudiate the sacrifices" (L). Apart from this passage, the True Prophet does not have this role in PsCl.

often (L) / *many times* (S). The *AJ* here views war, the destruction of the temple, captivity and return as repeated several times before the coming of the Prophet. It may allude to Psalm 106:41-3: "He gave them into the hands of the nations ... many times he delivered them." In fact, the temple was destroyed and the people exiled and restored only once before Jesus' coming, in the sixth century BC. But from the longer perspective of the *AJ*, the temple was destroyed in AD 70, and an exile was imposed by Hadrian in 135. This longer perspective is anachronistic, of course, because the time of the *AJ* is ostensibly seven years after Jesus' death. It is used to establish the principle articulated in the last half of 1.37.4: Israel should have learned from these repeated events that God does not approve of sacrifices. God punishes those who offer them, but restores to their land those who "keep the law without sacrifices" (S) / "do mercy and righteousness ... without sacrifices" (L).[26] The L form is an allusion to Matt 9:13, 12:7.

.4 *the lawgiver* (S). This lawgiver who permitted sacrifice is Moses (cf. 1.37.1).

---

26 This notion that Israel was more faithful in exile and oppression by her enemies than when in possession of the land has been remarkably stated (though without the specific animus against sacrifice, of course) by P. Johnson (*A History of the Jews* [New York: Harper & Row, 1987] 840): "It is notable that when the Israelites, and later the Jews, achieved settled and prosperous self-government, they found it extraordinarily difficult to keep their religion pure and incorrupt ... Only in adversity did they cling resolutely to their principles and develop their extraordinary powers of religious imagination, their originality, their clarity and their zeal."

1.37.5 (L) *But it happened that only a few understood this. For although most were able to think of and perceive this, nevertheless they were held by the irrational common opinion. For correct understanding in the context of liberty belongs to the few.*

(S) *But they were slow to learn this, and it was good to only a few. Even the knowledge of those few was darkened by those multitudes who thought otherwise, who were not able to perceive all this. For to distinguish and understand the cause of this is not given to the multitudes, but only the few can understand it.*

While the wording of L and S diverges somewhat in 1.37.5, the meaning is plain. Only some understood the principle (stated in 1.37.4) that God punishes with exile those who offer sacrifices, and restores to their land those who obey without sacrifices. Even these few were held back by the multitude who did not understand this. Therefore, the nation did not turn from sacrifices after its exile. The smallness of those who perceive the truth may foreshadow the true number of those who believe in Jesus; see the fourth Note on 1.43.1.

1.38.1 *Moses.* After the digression in 1.37.2-5, the narrative resumes the story of Moses.

Auses (L) / *Joshua* (S). "Auses" is drawn from the LXX of Num 13:16 (Αυση). In S, the spelling of "Joshua" is the same as "Jesus" (*yšw'*), just as it identical in Greek (Ιησους). Strecker, *Judenchristentum*, 228, notes that in early Christian literature the name Joshua was often explained by the name Jesus (e.g., in Justin's *Dial.* 113.1). But we should add that the *AJ* has no such explanation, because it patterns Jesus not after Joshua, but after Moses.

1.38.1-2 deals with the events of the transition from Moses to Joshua. Moses first "arranged these things," i.e., the provision for sacrificing until the coming of the Prophet. Then he appointed Joshua "general of the army of the people" (S), or, as L puts it more simply, "over the people" (cf. Deut 31:7,23; Num 27:18ff.). L then contrasts "the living God" and the dying of Moses. The phrase "to this day" is drawn from Deut 34:6, and reapplied to the time of the *AJ*. The secret burial of Moses serves here, as in Jewish aggada in general, to emphasize the importance of the life of Moses in the history of Israel (Ginzberg, *Legends*, 330, 473). But the *AJ* has no hint of an unusual death or burial that would lead to hopes of a *Moses redivivus*.

1.38.3 *When, therefore, the people reached the land of their fathers,*
by the providence of God the wicked nations who lived there were put to
flight at their first incursion (L). *[P]atria terra,* "the land of their fathers,"
could also be translated "homeland." The *AJ* has a positive attitude to
the land of Israel (1.34.4; 1.35.1,6; 1.37.3-4; 1.38.1-3).

The grammar of L allows *per providentiam dei* to go with either what
precedes or follows it, but Rehm is probably correct in punctuating this
sentence to place it with what follows. S clearly places "the providence
of God" with what follows. See the references to the providence of God
in 1.35.1 (L) and 1.37.3 (S).

At their first incursion (L) / *immediately when they appeared* (S).
This draws upon the OT tradition of immediate and total conquest, as
presented in Joshua 1-12. The gradual settlement and conquest in-
timated in Judges 1 is not in view. In the *AJ*, the rapidity of the conquest
is a sign of divine providence and blessing on Israel, and a punishment
of the evil nations who lived there.

by lot (L) / *in alloted portions* (S). For the OT account of the
distribution of the land by lot, see Joshua 13-21, especially 13:1 and
14:1-2.

.4-.5 judges . . . kings. When the judges rule, the people inhabit their
land. With the kings, they build a temple for sacrifice, and they are
taken captive. This is a restatement of the *AJ*'s prominent theme of the
evil of sacrifice. The kingship is deprecated here because of its close
association with temple and sacrifice.

.5 But when they made for themselves those who were really more
tyrants than kings, then with royal ambition they also built a temple in the
place which had been appointed beforehand for them for the purpose of
prayer. Thus through a series of wicked kings succeeding one another in
turn, the people fell away into ever-greater wickedness (L). Here the
anti-kingship polemic of the *AJ* reaches its highest intensity. The kings
do not even deserve that name - rather, they were "tyrants." The evil of
the kingship is shown in the building of the temple to replace the place
which had been appointed for prayer. After its building, a "series of
wicked kings" led the Israelites into ever-increasing wickedness. This
reflects the reticence toward the kingship found in Samuel 8 and Deut
17:14-20, but the *AJ* connects it with the building of the temple, as these
OT passages do not do. Acts 7:45-47 also links the building of the
temple and the kingship in a negative way.

This section states that the "place / house of prayer," probably the
tabernacle although it is never named, was replaced by the temple.
"They" who abolished the "place / house of prayer" and built a temple

are those who established the kingship, the people of Israel. Thus it is not only the kings themselves, but the people of Israel as well, who turn away from God by building the temple. In the Bible, the term "house of prayer" always means the temple (Isa 56:7; Mark 11:17, par. Matt 21:13 and Luke 19:46). This passage strongly implies that the tabernacle had no sacrifices, while the evil of the temple consists in the onset of sacrificing. Such an implication is contradicted by 1.37.1, where the institution of sacrifice dates from the time of Moses, and the tabernacle is the one approved place for this sacrifice. See the Notes above on 1.37.1 and 1.37.1-2.

1.39.1. *Thus when the time came near for the needed correction of what was lacking, the fitting time arrived in which that prophet who had been proclaimed beforehand by Moses was revealed* (S). The time for the "fulfilling" (L) or "correction" (S) of what was lacking in the arrangement of Moses is the time of the Prophet like Moses, as in 1.36.1. Here he is called "the prophet predicted [S "proclaimed"] by Moses." This variation of the Mosaic Prophet title will reappear at 1.39.3 (L), 1.40.4, 1.41.2 (L), 1.43.1, 1.56.2-3, and 1.57.1,4 (S .5).

mercy... sacrifices. Another allusion to Hos 6:6 is present in "mercy" and "sacrifices." The Prophet shows God's mercy by warning the people to put an end to sacrifice, lest the punishment of destruction described in 1.37 come upon them. That he "first" warned them so indicates that this was the Prophet's primary and continual message.

.2 *baptism by water.* The prophet established baptism as the replacement of sacrifice. John the Baptist is not mentioned here, for baptism's origin is traced only to the Prophet. He is the one who, according to the plan of Moses, is to end sacrifice. Baptism brings the forgiveness of sins, as sacrifice did previously. Strecker, *Judenchristentum*, 229, notes well that the replacement of sacrifice by baptism is unique in the Clementines to the *AJ*. For that matter, it is unique in early Christianity to the *AJ*. However, Lüdemann, "Successors," 168, errs when he states that in the *AJ* "Jesus replaces circumcision by baptism." As we have seen in 1:33, circumcision is held in positive regard in the *AJ*; baptism does not replace *circumcision*, but *sacrifice*.

L has in "by the invocation of his [the prophet's] name" in the staement of forgiveness through baptism. Baptism "in the name of Jesus" is well-attested in the Acts (2:38; 8:16; 19:5), and is the rule elsewhere in the NT where a specific formula is given (Rom 6:3, I Cor 1:13-15; Gal 3:27). [27] Apart from the *AJ*, the PsCl knows only the triadic formula of baptism, which is found in the NT only in Matt 28:19. Two other second-century witnesses to baptism in the name of Jesus are *Did.* 7:1 and Justin's *Apol.* 1.61. For another reference in the *AJ* to baptism in the name of Jesus, see 1.39.3 (L). Although not a part of the *AJ*, 1.73.4 refers back to the *AJ* at 1.69.8 - 1.70.1, where baptism in the name of Jesus is implied.

How is the absence of "in the name of Jesus" from S's treatment of baptism to be explained? Although its absence from S casts some doubt on its genuineness, it is highly unlikely that *G* or *R* added it, as both hold firmly to the triadic formula. Nor is it likely that Rufinus added it in his translation of *R* into Latin, as the triadic (now fully Trinitarian) formula was well-established in the Great Church by the end of the fourth century. As baptism in Jesus' name is more likely omitted from 1.39.2 by S than added by L, we may conclude that it belongs to the *AJ*.

1.39.2 *because they had been cleansed not by the blood of animals, but by the purification of the wisdom of God* (L). This is not found in S, and is likely an explanatory addition by L. L develops the replacement of sacrifice by baptism by juxtaposing cleansing "by the blood of animals" with "the purification of the wisdom of God." As we saw in the third Note on 1.37.2, "the purification of the wisdom of God" is baptism. Given the exclusively christological connection of baptism in the *AJ*, "the wisdom of God" may have a hint of wisdom christology.

---

27 The conclusion of W. Heitmüller (*Im Namen Jesu* [FRLANT 2; Göttingen: Vandenhoeck & Ruprecht, 1903]) on the early Christian usage of baptism has been succinctly restated by P. Feine ("Baptism" *New Schaff-Herzog Encyclopedia*, ed. S. M. Jackson [12 vols.; Grand Rapids: Baker, 1951] 1.436): "The Greek phrase *baptizein en* or *epi toi onomati Iesou* means that the act of baptism takes place with the utterance of the name of Jesus; *baptizein eis to onoma Iesou* means that the person baptized enters into the relation of belonging to Christ" [with no implication of the use of Jesus' name at baptism]. Here in the *AJ*, to judge from L's "by the invocation of his name," the name of Jesus was formally used.

1.39.3 Finally, this is given as a proof of this great mystery, that everyone who upon believing in this prophet predicted by Moses was baptized in his name, shall be kept uninjured in the destruction of war which hangs over the unbelieving nation and the place itself. But those who do not believe will become exiles from the place and kingdom, so that even against their will they may understand and obey God's will (L).

R 1.39.3, together with 1.37.2 (S), has been seen by modern interpreters as a witness to the Pella tradition. The full form of this tradition is found in Eusebius (*Hist. eccl.* 3.53), and can be summarized as follows: The Jerusalem church was warned by an oracle at the beginning of the revolt of AD 66-70 to flee the city; they did so, traveling to Pella in Transjordan, while their Jewish compatriots were destroyed in the war. Since the publication in 1957 of S. G. F. Brandon's *The Fall of Jerusalem and the Christian Church,*[28] which was the first challenge to the generally-accepted historicity of the Pella tradition, a good deal of controversy has occurred over the historicity of the tradition and whether it is found in the NT. The state of the question, with full references to the secondary literature, is well presented by the recent contributions to the debate by Lüdemann and Harter.[29] To examine the entire history of the Pella tradition or the question of whether it is reflected in the NT is beyond the scope of this study. We here will examine *R* 1.39.3 in its context in the *AJ*, and relate this text to the wider Pella tradition.

1.39.3 develops 1.39.2 by pointing to a future demonstration of the divine replacement of sacrifice by baptism. All who believe in the Prophet and receive his baptism will be preserved from the coming war. Those who do not believe will be destroyed, along with their "nation and place itself" (L). Those unbelievers who do survive will be exiled from the "place," the temple. This exile refers to the decree of Hadrian made ca. 135, after the Bar Cochba revolt, as Eusebius (*Hist. eccl.* 4.6.3) relates: "From that time forward the whole nation was wholly prohibited from setting foot upon the country round about Jerusalem, by the decree and ordinances of a law of Hadrian, which forbade them even from afar to gaze upon the soil inherited from their fathers."

---

28 London: SPCK.

29 Lüdemann, "Successors," 161-73, disputed the interpretation of Mark 13:14-20, Luke 21:20-24, Matt 24:15-22 and Rev 12:3b-6, 13-16 to support the presence of the Pella tradition in the NT. Harter devoted a chapter of his "Causes" (pp. 109-65) to defending the historicity of the Pella tradition and finding it in these passages.

The *AJ* does not explain the destruction of Jerusalem as punishment for the death of Jesus, but rather as a punishment for the refusal to believe in him as Messiah and put an end to sacrifice. The last clause of 1.39.3 looks back to 1.37.3-4, where exile is also seen as a time for those who had trusted in sacrifices to follow "the will of God." The community of the *AJ* sees itself as that community preserved from war. It also sees the destruction of the temple and expulsion of the Jews as a divine sign of the correctness of the replacement of sacrifice by baptism, and (implicitly) of the status of Jesus as the Mosaic Prophet. The *AJ* evidently views both the destruction of AD 66-70 and the expulsion of 135 as two events in the same divine plan, and has telescoped them together.

When coupled with 1.37.2 (S), 1.39.3 offers a glimpse into the developing Pella tradition. Several key elements of its full, Eusebian form are present in the *AJ*: mention of divine guidance to flee the city (1.37.2); the coming of war; the destruction of the unbelievers and preservation of believers.[30] Already at the time of the *AJ*, therefore, most key elements of the Pella tradition have been assembled. The only major element that is lacking is the explicit attachment of the flight to Pella.[31]

1.40.1 *And so, with these things pre-arranged* (L) / *When, therefore, these things were thus appointed* (S). The expression "these things" refers back to 1.39, especially the establishment of baptism as the replacement of sacrifice. This is indicated in S by the use of the same verb "to appoint" (*hrq*, in Ethpe'el) in 1.40.1 as in 1.39.2 ("he appointed baptism").

he who was expected has come, bringing signs and miracles, the marks by which he should become known (L) / *he who is the good prophet appeared and worked signs* (S). In S "good" is to be contrasted with the evil manner in which evil people treated the prophet (1.40.2-3). L has the more conventional "he who was expected."

In L, "signs and miracles" (*signa et prodigia*) are "the marks by which he should become known," the proof of his status as the Mosaic Prophet. Although "the marks by which he should become known" is lacking in S, the first clause of section two in S implies that these signs should have led to belief in this prophet: "But nevertheless not thus did

---

30 For other later attestations of the Pella tradition, see Lüdemann, "Successors," 163-6.
31 See above, p. 78, for the implication of the lack of mention of Pella for the provenance of the *AJ*.

the ancient people believe . . ." (similarly L). These "signs" allude to the
accreditation of Moses to the people of Israel by signs and wonders
(Exod 4:1-9,17; Acts 7:36). The signs worked by the Prophet like Moses
should have reminded the people of the signs worked by Moses. This
parallel between the miracles of Jesus and Moses will be developed
more fully in 1.58.

1.40.2 *But even so the people did not believe, who had been taught
for so many generations to believe such things* (L). Since the time of
Moses, his prediction of the Prophet like himself (1.36) and the experience of Israel with captivity and return (1.37) have been known,
and should have led the Jews to believe in the Prophet when he came.
The unbelief that greets the Prophet is the culmination of the continued
disobedience and unbelief of Israel (1.37.5; 1.38.5).

*For those people are most miserable of all, who desire to believe
neither good nor evil about virtue* (S). This contradicts the rest of 1.40.2.
"The most miserable" of all people are here said to be those "who desire
to believe neither good nor evil about virtue," i.e., are indifferent to it.
But the rest of 1.40.2 (S) states that these same people call those who
are virtuous "gluttons and demons," thus believing evil about virtue.
Because this passage has no parallel in L and contradicts the rest of
1.40.2, it was probably not a part of the Greek text, but was likely added
by S.

(L) *Not only did they not
believe, but they added blasphemy to unbelief by saying that
he was a glutton, a slave to the
stomach, and led by a demon,
even he who had come for their
salvation.*

(S) *. . . but this is how they do not
believe, by despising them
through accusations, and calling
them gluttons and demons.*

L clearly represents these charges of gluttony and demon-posses-
sion as blasphemy against the Prophet alone. By its plurals, S includes
others, possibly the disciples, as the object of these calumnies.

These charges are drawn from the Gospel accounts of charges
against Jesus by his opponents. "Glutton" is from Matt 11:19; "led by a
demon" is from Matt 11:18, where it is spoken of John the Baptist.
Compare also John 7:20, 10:20, and Mark 3:30, where a similar charge
is laid against Jesus. Martyn, "Recognitions," 273-4, notes that "led by
a demon" could be drawn from John 7:20, but concludes that all these
charges against the Prophet are drawn from Matthew. In L, "a slave to

the stomach" (*ventri servientem*) is epexegetical on "a gluttonous man," and emphasizes it. It has a close parallel in Rom 16:18, "serve . . . their own belly," which in the Vg is *serviunt . . . ventri*. This is more likely a common expression than an allusion to Romans.

1.40.3 *the wisdom of God.* Here wisdom brings enlightenment to "those who prize [S: love] the truth." Like 1.37.2 and 1.39, wisdom is personified, but the *AJ* does not identify wisdom with the Prophet like Moses.

.4 *us.* The first person narration by Peter (cf. 1.26) surfaces here for the first time in the *AJ*. Strecker, *Judenchristentum*, 232, is probably correct in arguing that the first person was interpolated by *R* into 1.40.4 on the basis of the first-person narration of *G*.

It was revealed to us that he who came first chose twelve apostles, and then seventy-two disciples, that through this the multitudes might understand that this is the coming prophet, whom Moses had already proclaimed (S). The Twelve are called "apostles" in Mark 6:30, Matt 10:2, and Luke 6:13. But only in Luke 6:13 is it said, with 1.40.4 (L), that Jesus named them apostles. By choosing the twelve apostles, the Prophet imitates Moses' selection of twelve assistants (Num 1:1-17, 24-25).[32]

The Prophet also imitates Moses by selecting seventy-two disciples. This alludes to Luke 10:1, 17, where some MSS read "seventy," others "seventy-two." The *AJ* draws on the latter reading. The textual problems of Luke 10:1, 17 are examined carefully by B. M. Metzger in his essay, "Seventy or Seventy-Two Disciples?"[33] Metzger speaks of "the predominance in Syria of the tradition that there were seventy-two disciples" (p. 71), but "It appears that '72' is read by witnesses that are generally accounted to be primary witnesses of each of several text-types" (p. 74). He concludes that "Perhaps all that one can say with assurance is that both '70' and '72' were widespread in the early centuries" (p. 75). Thus the use of "seventy-two" cannot be reliably tied to any particular locale, giving us additional evidence of the provenance of the *AJ*. If our dating of the *AJ* is correct, it would push the

---

32 Rehm, *Pseudoklementinen*, 32, and Strecker, *Judenchristentum*, 231-2, refer only to Num 11:16, the choosing of the seventy-two. But it is clear that the *AJ* sees the parallel between Moses and Jesus in the choosing of both twelve and seventy-two. On the meaning of Moses' selection in its own time and its interpretation in Hellenistic times, see W. Horbury, "The Twelve and the Phylarchs," *NTS* 32 (1986) 503-27.

33 Metzger, *Historical and Literary Studies* (NTTS 8; Grand Rapids: Eerdmans, 1968) 67-76.

earliest citation of seventy-two disciples into the second century, earlier than Metzger seems to place its first citation in the MS tradition
(pp. 74-5).

The several uses of "seventy-two" in the *AJ* seem to have their start
at this point. On the basis of this number of Jesus' disciples, the *AJ*
frames a parallel to Moses by using "seventy-two" as the number of
"disciples" that Moses picked. This number is read even further back
into Israelite history at 1.34.2, where it is made the number of those
who went into Egypt. The similarity between Moses' and Jesus' seventy-two disciples should have led "the multitude," the Jewish people as
a whole, to acknowledge Jesus as the Prophet like Moses.

The *AJ*'s characteristic use of "seventy-two" contrasts sharply with
the use of "seventy" in *EpPt* 2.1, where the "seventy brothers" are
compared to the seventy (not seventy-two) appointed by Moses. This
comparison is not used by *EpPt*, as by the *AJ*, to promote a Prophet-
like-Moses christology. Rather, it is a technique to keep "the books of
my [Peter's] preaching pure." Compare a similar use in *H* 2.38.1 and
3.47.1.

1.41.1 *But lest someone claim that it is possible for anyone at all to
imitate a number, what is to be said about the signs and wonders which
he used to do? For Moses indeed worked wonders and healings in Egypt*
(L). The first clause may reflect an actual counter-argument heard by
the *AJ* community against the argument of 1.40.4: Jesus' choosing of
the same number of disciples as Moses is not persuasive, because a
number is easily imitated.

The author replies with a surer argument in the Prophet's signs and
wonders,[34] and links these with the miracles done by Moses in Egypt.
On the "signs and wonders" done by Moses, see Exod 4:8-30, 7:3; Deut
4:34, 6:22, 7:19, and especially 34:10-12, "signs and wonders . . . in the
land of Egypt." L's mention of Moses' "healings" (*sanitates*) in Egypt
is an effort to conform the signs and wonders of Moses to those of
Jesus, and thus make the similarity between them stronger. The OT has
no record of Moses working healings in Egypt, and Ginzberg's *Legends*
is also silent on it.

Although the Fourth Gospel characteristically calls Jesus' miracles
"signs," only once does "signs and wonders" occur (4:48). The combination of "signs and wonders" is common in Acts (2:19, 22, 43; 4:30; 5:12;

---

34 Justin Martyr also argues explicitly from Jesus' miracles to his messianic status in
Dial. 69.

6:8; 7:36; 14:3; 15:12). The *AJ*'s use of this phrase is probably drawn from Acts, especially Acts 7:36, which also has Moses doing signs and wonders in Egypt.

1.41.2 *This prophet like Moses, whose rise he himself predicted, although he healed every weakness and every infirmity in the common people, worked innumerable wonders and preached the good news of eternal life* (L). This passage alludes to Deut 18:15. "Rise" and "arose" are references to the coming and ministry of the Prophet, not to his resurrection.

Rehm, *Pseudoklementinen*, 32, does not note the scriptural allusion in "healed every weakness and every infirmity in the common people" (L). It is drawn from Matt 4:23, "healing every disease and every infirmity among the people." The *AJ* and the Vg share the wording *omnem languorem et omnem infirmitatem*. "Preached the good news of eternal life" (*vitam evangelizaret aeternam*) is reworked from Matt 4:23b, "preaching the good news of the kingdom."

the evil stupidity of evil persons (S). S expands the emphasis on evil in L's reference to the death of Jesus. Despite the healings worked by the Prophet, and his preaching of eternal life, he was crucified by evil persons, in whom the power of evil found its greatest victory (cf. 1.40.3).

which very thing was changed by his power into grace and goodness (S). What is the meaning of "by his power"? Three interpretive possibilities can be suggested. First, it could refer to a salvific meaning in the crucifixion, but this would contradict the *AJ*'s association of salvation only with baptism. No other passage in the AJ speaks of a salvific significance of the cross.

A second interpretive possibility is suggested by S at the beginning of 1.41.3. The wording "For when" suggests that the death of the Prophet "was changed by his power to grace and goodness" in that "when he suffered the whole world suffered with him." But this was only an incomplete effect. Some were never moved to question the meaning of the Prophet's death (1.41.4). Moreover, soon after his death no more effect was felt, as people went back to their wicked ways (1.42.3). The *AJ* is unlikely to call such an incomplete and temporary effect "grace and goodness."

A third possibility points to a reference to the resurrection of the Prophet, that he raised himself "by his power." This would follow consecutively from the Prophet's passion and death. The wording of 1.42.4 (L) corroborates this interpretation: "they could not prevent [him] from rising." Also, the charge in 1.42.4 that Jesus raised himself from the dead by the power of magic may reflect a claim by the *AJ* community that Jesus raised himself from death. While "by his power" remains rather ambiguous, it likely refers to Jesus' raising himself "by his power" from the dead.

1.41.3 *the whole world suffered with him.* The portents in nature are seen by the *AJ* as contemporaneous with the crucifixion. They end upon Jesus' death (1.42.3). "The sun was darkened" is drawn from Matt 27:45, Mark 15:38, and especially from Luke 23:44-45, which alone of these three accounts explicitly mentions "the sun." (The *AJ* seems to draw on the textual tradition that underlies the variant reading "darkened" in Luke, not "eclipsed.) "The stars were moved" (so S; L: "shaken") is an expansion on the portent of darkness. When the sun grew dark, the stars were now visible during the day, and were put off their courses. Thus the whole heavens "suffered with him." The portent of the shaking of the sea is an expansion of Matthew's account of the shaking of the earth, meant to bring "the whole world" into the effect of the crucifixion. The shaking of the mountains is linked as in Matt 27:51b-53 (where "the earth shook") to the opening of the tombs. As these last two portents are given only in Matthew, the *AJ* is dependent on the Matthean account, and is an expansion of it. There seems to be no literary relationship between the *AJ* at this point and the second-century *Gospel of Peter*, which makes the rending of the temple veil contemporaneous with Jesus' death (5.20) and places the earthquake after it (6.21).

The veil of the temple was torn as if in mourning for the coming desolation of the place (S). For the NT references to this event, see Mark 15:31, Matt 27:51, and Luke 23:45. According to D. Silva, three different meanings of the rending of the temple curtain in the Synoptics have been proposed in the history of research: (1) It was a sign of the destruction of the temple; (2) It was a sign of the abrogation of the temple and its sacrifices; (3) It was a sign that through Jesus' death the way to God was now open (as also in Heb 10:19, 20).[35] The first is explicit in the *AJ* at 1.41.3. "As if lamenting" (L) / "as if mourning" (S) refers to the Jewish custom of tearing clothing in mourning. Here the

---

35 "The Temple Curtain and Jesus' Death in the Gospel of Luke," *JBL* 105 (1986) 239-50. See also the articles by M. deJonge, "Het Motief van het gescheurde Voorhangsel van de Tempel in een aantal vroegchristelijke Geschriften," *NedTTS* 21 (1967) 257-76, and "Two Interesting Interpretations of the Rending of the Temple-Veil in The Testaments of the Twelve Patriarchs," *Bijdragen* 46 (1985) 350-62.

mourning is not for Jesus, even though it is associated with his death. Rather, it is for the temple and the terrible destruction of life that will accompany its end.

1.41.4 (L) *Nevertheless, although the whole world was moved, they themselves are still not yet moved to the consideration of such great things.*

(S) *Because of these things, all the people were afraid and were constrained to question them. But some, although all the people were moved in their minds, did not move themselves to this matter.*

While these portents were occurring, all who witnessed them were compelled to consider their meaning. L points out the irony in the disbelief that greeted the Prophet. Although "the whole world," understood as the physical universe, was moved, "they themselves are still not yet" (*etiam nunc*, "yet, still, until now") moved to consider such great portents. DeJonge, "Motief," 259, correctly understands "they themselves" to be the unbelieving Jews.

The S of 1.41.4 is somewhat awkward, but the meaning is plain. "These things," the portents, forced "all the people" to question their meaning. But despite this, "some . . . did not move themselves to this matter." "This matter" probably refers not to "these things," the portents, but to the last phrase of section three, the coming destruction of the temple. In other words, the questioning of the portents at Jesus' death did not move them to see the evil of the sacrifices and the temple.[36] This persistent unbelief stands in continuity with the dark history of Israel as portrayed in the *AJ*, and its restatement here sets the stage for the Gentile mission in the next chapter.

---

36 The *Gospel of Peter* 8.28-30 says that the effect of the portents on the common people continued after Jesus' death, and led them to conclude that he was righteous. This shared motif of the effect of the portents may indicate that the *AJ* is in touch at this point with the traditions behind the *Gospel of Peter*.

1.42.1 (L) *It was necessary, then, that the Gentiles be called in place of those who remained unbelievers, so that the number which had been shown to Abraham would be satisfied; thus the preaching of the kingdom of God has been sent into all the world. (2) Thus there is disturbance among worldly spirits, who always resist those who seek liberty, seeking the machinations of errors to destroy the building of God. But those who strive for the glory of salvation and liberty are made stronger by resisting and struggling against them with no small exertion, and they shall come to the crown of salvation not without the palm of victory.*

(S) *It was right, on account of those who were not persuaded, that the Genitles be called to the fullness of the number that was shown to Abraham; therefore this disorder came to be. (2) And the hostile power which frequently darkens and opposes those sons of freedom troubled all the people. He prepared a great testing of their goodness, so that those who wish to draw near to the word of salvation will be stronger that the strength which troubles them, and with their wills they will easily receive victory in salvation.*

1.42.1-2 digresses from the narration of the death of the prophet to make a statement on the Gentile mission and the opposition which it aroused. The beginning of 1.42.1 indicates that this mission is a result of the unbelief of the Jews. That there were Jews who did not believe in the prophet brought about a diminishment of "the number shown to Abraham." This reference to Gen 15:5 was not mentioned in the *AJ*'s treatment of Abraham in 1.33, but the clear implication here is that this was the number of the whole Jewish people. The unbelief of most Jews necessitated a Gentile mission to complete their number. In the *AJ*, "Believing Gentiles replace not the Jews as a nation, but the unbelieving Jews within the nation" (Skarsaune, *Proof*, 330). This section articulates the cause of the Gentile mission, but is not concerned with its nature, e.g., whether it is a law-observant or law-free mission.[37] See the second Note on 1.64.2 for more on the Gentile mission.

---

37 For more on the Gentile mission in the *AJ*, see J. L. Martyn, "A Law-Observant Mission to Gentiles: The Background of Galatians," *SJT* 38 (1986) 307-24, especially 310-11.

The wording of section two varies between L and S, but the same idea is present. Those who wish to attain salvation will achieve it, and be victorious over the powers which oppose them. In L, these powers are called "worldly spirits" (*mundani spiritus*), which could mean either supernatural or human opposition. Strecker, *Judenchristentum*, 223, seems to interpret it in the latter sense when he labels this an "Anspielung auf die (durch Juden veranlassten?) Christenverfolgerung." S's "the hostile power" may imply a supernatural opposition, as *mstyn'* ("hostile, opposing, adversarial") is related to the *stn'* ("Satan"). The hostile power acts in his role as adversary by preparing "a great test of their goodness." Of course, the human and supernatural side of opposition are not mutually exclusive.

1.42.3 *darkness.* The narrative of the passion resumes from 1.41. The mention of darkness in 1.41.3 is elaborated here with "from the sixth to the ninth" hour. Darkness is contemporaneous with the crucifixion (Matt 27:45; Mark 15:33; Luke 23:44-45). When the Prophet died, the darkness and other portents ceased, and "evil ones among the people" (S), unbelievers among the Jews, went back to their previous manner of life. Fear of the portents had held their evil in check; when the portents ended, so did this restraint.

.4 (L) *For some of them, after guarding the place with all diligence, called him a magician, whom they could not prevent from rising; other pretended that he was stolen.*

(S) *For some of them said about him who had suffered, and who was not found although they had guarded him, that he was a magician; thus they were not afraid to dare to lie.*

Here is the most important example of what happened when evil people returned to their ways. "Some of them" were guarding Jesus' tomb, but they could not find him (so S) or prevent him from rising from the dead (so L). The *AJ* sees this guarding of the tomb as done by Jews. Matt 27:62-66 and 28:11-15, on which the *AJ* draws, are ambiguous on whether the guard is Roman or Jewish, but most commentators seem to prefer the former.

Jesus' resurrection led to the charge that it was accomplished by the power of magic. S labels this a daring lie. L identifies as a lie the charge, drawn from Matt 28:13, that Jesus' body was stolen from the tomb. The NT does not contain any explicit statement that Jesus was called a magician by his opponents. M. Smith has argued that Jesus was indeed seen by many of his contemporaries as a magician, but that

for apologetic reasons this was omitted from the Gospel tradition.[38]
While we cannot enter into this question here,[39] it is enough for our
purpose to note that Jewish opponents of the church did label Jesus a
magician. The tractate *Sanhedrin* of the Babylonian Talmud says in a
famous passage, "On the eve of the Passover Yeshu was hanged. For
forty days before the execution took place, a herald went forth and
cried, 'He is going forth to be stoned because he has practiced sorcery
and enticed Israel to apostasy. Anyone who can say anything in his
favor, let him come forward and plead on his behalf.' But since nothing
was brought forward in his favor, he was hanged on the eve of the
Passover."[40] The key word in this passage for our study is "practiced
sorcery" (*ksp*), which can also be translated "practiced magic." [41] This
passage links Jesus' "magic" to the charge of apostasy. The charge
against Jesus of magic is also found in *b. Sanh.* 107b and *b. Sota* 47a.[42]

Although these passages from the Babylonian Talmud cannot be
dated to the second century, the charge that Jesus worked miracles by
magic can. Justin is an important witness to the charge that Jesus was
a magician. His *Dial.* 69 reports that Jews "in every part of the empire"
call Jesus "a Galilean magician." Another witness from the time of the
AJ is Celsus, who wrote ca. 180 an anti-Christian work which has not
survived, but which is known from Origen's reply to it in his *Against
Celsus*. Celsus had charged that Jesus was a magician (*Against Celsus*
1.28, 32, 69). He probably drew on Jewish tradition for his story of
Jesus, in which he said that Jesus learned magical powers in Egypt.

---

38 *Jesus the Magician* (San Francisco: Harper & Row, 1978).

39 For a different approach to the problem of the relation of magic and the traditions
about Jesus, see J. M. Hull, *Hellenistic Magic and the Synoptic Tradition* (SBT 28;
London: SCM, 1974).

40 *b. Sanh.* 43a, from *The Babylonian Talmud* ed. I. Epstein (London: Soncino, 1969),
vol 21.

41 J. Levy, "Zaubern, zauberei treiben," *Wörterbuch über die Talmudim und Midraschim*
(4 vols.; Berlin: Hart, 1924) 2.423. Levy gives *b. Sanh.* 43a as an illustration,

42 References from Str-B 1.1023. While these passages refer to Jesus as being a
magician during his life, some have argued that a passage in *b. Sanh.* 106a may be a
reference to Jesus' raising himself from death by magic. This would correspond to
the charge laid against Jesus in the *AJ*. The passage reads, "R. Simeon b. Lakisch
[third century] said: 'Woe to him who makes himself alive by the name of God'."
R. T. Hereford (*Christianity in Talmud and Midrash* [London: Williams & Norgate,
1903] 74-5) sees this as a covert allusion to Jesus, as also does Smith, *Jesus*, 120. But
this saying is tantalizingly vague, and nothing in its context points to Jesus. That it
does refer to Jesus can only be a possibility. Jewish legends of a later age, particularly
the *Toledoth Yeshu*, do indeed contain this charge.

From this evidence we may conclude that the Jewish tradition charging Jesus as a magician is traceable at least to the second half of the second century. The *AJ* is in contact with these Jewish traditions that label Jesus a magician, and may preserve an early witness to the charge that Jesus raised himself from the dead by magical powers.

1.43.1 *the truth was victorious.* This is the truth of Jesus' messianic status, especially of his resurrection. The truth was victorious over the lie of 1.42.4, that Jesus raised himself by magic. S also relates "the truth" to the lie "that we were fewer than they," a topic that both L and S will pick up later in 1.43.1.

they were not upright (S). Literally, "its uprightness was not to them" (*l' npqt lhwh*). The lie against the church indicates that its opponents were not in the right. Events soon publicly showed them to be wrong - the growth of the church contrasts with the relatively diminishing number of those Jews who did not believe in Jesus.

we ... they. Here begins a "we / they" contrast that will last through the *AJ*. "We" are those Jews "who believe in Jesus" (1.43.2), the "church in Jerusalem" (1.43.3). "They" are "the Jews / sons of our people who do not believe" in Jesus (1.43.3). In the *AJ*, "we who believe in Jesus" is the most common description of the church. Absent from the *AJ* and the rest of the PsCl is the name "Christian." This is scarcely unexpected, as (according to Acts 11:26) the name "Christian" probably was of Gentile origin. Its usage was not shared by most Jewish Christians in at least the first two centuries.

For by the zeal of God we more and more were steadily increasing more than they. Then even their priests were afraid, lest perhaps by the providence of God the whole people might come over to our faith, to their own confusion (S). The growth of believers to the point that they outnumbered the rest of the Jews is seen as a sign of divine approval. Indeed, in time "the whole people" would have come to believe in Jesus as Messiah, had not something happened to prevent it. In the first chapters of Acts, the believers are also said to increase rapidly, but with no suggestion that they became a majority of the Jews.

The priests of the temple try to prevent this total conversion by arranging a public debate at which they expect to defeat the church and thwart its growth. The priesthood directly represents the cult of sacrifice which the church seeks to end. Thus the complete conversion of the Jewish people would lead to the priests' "embarrassment" (L) or "confusion" (S), i.e., to their downfall. This is the very thing that almost happens late in the *AJ* at 1.70.

1.43.1 *sending to us frequently.* In 1.43.3 it said that the requests from the priests for a discussion about Jesus continued over a seven-year period. The discussion requested is to be "with them," with the priests (1.43.1, 1.44.1). But the debate that finally results is not only with the priests, but with all the parties of the Jews (1.55-65). The NT and other early Christian literature preserve no such request or discussion.

whether he [Jesus] were the prophet whom Moses predicted, who is the eternal Christ (L). Here the Prophet like Moses is explicitly identified for the first time as the Messiah. From this point on, this will be the *AJ*'s chief christological category. *Christus aeternus* (L) / *mšyh' dmn 'lm* (S) may be drawn from John 12:34, as Rehm, *Pseudoklementinen*, 33, notes. But as Martyn, "Recognitions," 274, remarks, "The thought of the Messiah's eternity is . . . much too widespread to allow us to move beyond the mere possibility" of dependence on John 12:34. "The eternal Messiah" will reappear in 1.44.2.

The precise meaning of "Jesus the eternal Messiah" is difficult to discern. Does it mean "from eternity past," "from Jesus' birth and forevermore," or both? L's *Christus aeternus* contains no clue. S has interpreted the original to mean "from eternity past," as it uses an idiom, *dmn 'lm,* that means "of yore, from forever." While it is not possible to decide certainly on "eternal Messiah," the reading of S has more affinity with another passage in the *AJ* which explicitly posits pre-existence of the Messiah (1.60.7).[43] Thus "from eternity past" is the likely meaning.

.2 *a difference.* Here and throughout the *AJ* the only difference between "we who believe in Jesus" and those who do not believe in him is said to be belief in Jesus as Messiah.[44] This is the main point of the

---

43 Pre-existence language is found in *G* at 1.45.4, *homo factus est* (also the wording of the Nicene Creed!). This passage also calls the True Prophet "the Son of God, the beginning of all things," which implies creation through him. As Strecker, *Judenchristentum*, 234, remarks, the idea of the pre-existence of Jesus is not found in the *KerygmataP*.

44 Epiphanius also says of the Jewish-Christian sect of the Nazoreans, "They have no different ideas [from the Jews] , but confess everything as the Law proclaims it and in Jewish fashion, except for their belief in Christ" (*Pan.* 29.7.2). The Nazoreans did not reject sacrifice or temple; hence the statement that the only difference between some Jewish Christians and the other Jews is belief in Jesus as Messiah is even truer for the Nazoreans than for the community of the *AJ*. Epiphanius in this passage also points out the predicament, from the Great Church perspective, of Jewish Christianity as a whole: "They disagree with the Jews because they have come to faith in Christ; but since they are still fettered by the Law . . . they are not in accord with the [Great Church] Christians" (*Pan.* 29.7.5, 8-9).

debate in 1.55-65 and the speech of James in 1.66-70. The reader of the *AJ* has already learned that there are other differences as well: sacrifice, the temple, and baptism the most important. The statement here that the only difference is over the messianic status of Jesus is not an attempt to gloss over these differences. The meaning of 1.43.2 seems to be that the messianic status of Jesus is the major difference between "us" and "them," and the others flow from it. This characterization of the difference between two faiths is, of course, from the perspective of the community of the *AJ*. It may not be shared by "those . . . who do not believe in Jesus."

1.43.3 *one seven-year period* (L) / *one week of years* (S). As noted above on 1.43.1, these requests were made repeatedly over seven years. They were continually refused by the church until the proper time should come. The frequency of requests by the priests for a meeting is emphasized by the recurring mention of them in 1.42-44 and 1.55.1.

Lord. "Lord" (*dominus, mr'*) occurs only in this chapter in the *AJ*. That it refers to Jesus is shown by "the passion of the Lord" (L).

the church. Here for the first time the company of believers is called "the church." This church is "in Jerusalem" (so S; L: "founded in Jerusalem"). It is based in and centered on Jerusalem, even though the *AJ* knows also that a Gentile mission has gone "into all the world" (1.42.1-2).

James. James is the relative of Jesus, although this relationship is never stated in the *AJ*. James appears here and will be prominent in the remainder of the *AJ*. He has been "ordained bishop" of the church by "the Lord," the Lord Jesus. The time of this ordination is not specified, but the *AJ* implies that James has always been bishop of the church. The growth of the church mentioned in 1.43 is due to his government, done "uprightly and steadily" (S) and "with most righteous administrations" (L). The pre-eminence of James will be taken up again in Chapter Five.

1.44.1 *we twelve apostles.* Here the first-person narration is applied to the Twelve, as in 1.40.4.

Passover. This passover is probably in the *AJ*'s reckoning the seventh anniversary of "the passion of the Lord" (1.43.3). The church is not only gathered in Jerusalem at the time of the Passover, but is "gathered in the festival" (S). It celebrates the Passover feast with the rest of the Jewish nation.

1.44.1 (L) . . . *James had asked us about the things that had been accomplished in every place, we reported briefly as the people listened.*

(S) *. . . each one of us was asked by James to tell us about the most important of those things which we had done among the people. Each one briefly reported to us.*

James has the Twelve report to him in the presence of the whole church about their activities "among the people" (S). This expression implies that their activity was among the Jews, as "the people" signifies the Jews. L's "in every place" should probably be read in the light of S's "among the people." James' able governance of the church is illustrated by this request for reports from the Twelve. In the *AJ* these reports are oral and in the hearing of all. Elsewhere in the PsCl, James requires a written report every year (*R* 1.17.3, 1.72.7; *H* 20.2-3; *EpCl* 19).

.2 *Caiaphas . . . was sending priests* (L) / *Caiaphas . . . sent priests* (S). On the occasion of the gathering of the church, there is a renewed request for a meeting with those Jews who do not believe in Jesus. Earlier "the priests" made this request (1.43.1). Now Caiaphas the high priest makes it, asking "us to come to him." This proposed meeting takes on the format of a debate between the church and Caiaphas on the question, "Is Jesus the Messiah?"

While the NT has not a hint about his request for a debate, several passages speak of "the high priest" (Matt 26:3, 57; Mark 14:53; Luke 3:2; John 11:49, 18:13-4, 24; Acts 4:6). The *AJ*'s knowledge of Caiaphas as the high priest some seven years after Jesus' death could be drawn from either Matthew or John, as both say explicitly that Caiaphas is the high priest at the time of Jesus' death. Caiaphas is also mentioned as high priest in Josephus (*Ant.* 18.4.3 §95).

faith. "Faith" is appropriate as a description of both Jewish Christians and Jews, as what separates them (in the *AJ*'s view) is faith or the lack of it in Jesus as Messiah. Here this word is used almost in the sense of "religion." This affords the reader a glimpse of the wide gulf that by the time of the writing of the *AJ* separates its community from Judaism.

.2 *frequently* (L) / .3 *many times* (S) Note that the section divisions vary between S and L, but the wording is the same. This passage restates 1.43.3, applying it now to Caiaphas and the response of the Twelve to him.

Comment on R *1.33.3 - 1.44.3*

Having discussed technical matters in the Notes, we now comment on the main lines of the meaning of *R* 1.33.3 - 1.44.3, and on its relation to the *AJ* as a whole. Particular attention will be given to the literary form of 1.33-43, the Prophet like Moses, and the replacement of sacrifice by baptism.

The literary form of *R* 1.33-43 is that of the *Heilsgeschichte*, a narrative sketch of redemptive history. Such sketches are found in the OT (e.g., Psalms 105 and 106) and in the NT (e.g., Acts 7; 13:17-31; and Hebrews 11).[45] At first glance, this *Heilsgeschichte* in *R* 1.33-44 seems to be a straightforward and routine recitation of redemptive history from Abraham through the early church. It begins with Abraham and his offspring and proceeds through Isaac, Jacob and the seventy-two members of Jacob's family who went down to Egypt and multiplied there. Moses led the people in the Exodus and wilderness wanderings. He predicted a prophet like himself. Joshua led the people into their land, where they were governed first by judges and then by kings. When the Prophet like Moses came, he urged the people to end sacrifice and instead receive baptism. He met unbelief, opposition and finally crucifixion, but was raised from death. The church founded by Jesus grew rapidly over a seven-year period until it outnumbered those Jews who did not believe in Jesus as Messiah. At this point the *Heilsgeschichte* ends. 1.44.1-3 is a transition from 1.33-44 to the temple debate of 1.55-65.

A closer examination of 1.33-44, however, shows that this sketch of salvation history from Abraham to the early church is really a *heilsgeschichtlich* treatise on Moses and the Mosaic Prophet. The treatment of Moses extends from 1.34.4 to 1.38.2, and the treatment of the Mosaic Prophet from 1.39.1 to 1.42.4. Thus, more than three-quarters of this section of the *AJ* is devoted to these two figures. The emphasis on Moses serves to exalt his role as giver of the law. The law is seen as instrumental in changing the "old habits" of the Israelites learned in Egypt. More importantly, this emphasis on Moses is used to support the anti-sacrificial polemic of the *AJ* - Moses granted sacrifice only as a concession to Israel's weakness, when he saw that even the law could not cure the sickness of sacrifice.

---

45 The *AJ*, like Psalm 106 and Acts 7, has a *Heilsgeschichte* which is predominantly negative in tone.

This section of the *AJ* also emphasizes Jesus' status as the Prophet like Moses. This stress is accomplished in several ways. First, the *AJ* refers continually to the "Prophet like Moses," and explicitly identifies this Prophet as Jesus only at the end (1.43.1). The title "Prophet like Moses" is even used in the part of this *Heilsgeschichte* that deals with the story of Jesus (1.39-42), where we might expect "Jesus" to be used. Second, the *AJ* refers to the parallels between Jesus' and Moses' prophetic careers (1.40.1, 4; 1.41.1-2). Third, the *AJ* explicitly asserts that Jesus is the Prophet like Moses (1.39.3; 1.43.1). He should be believed in by all Jews because of the two proofs of divine approval offered in the life of the early church, its preservation during the war (1.39.3) and the remarkable numerical growth of the first believers (1.43.1).

In the Notes to 1.33-43, many allusions to the Stephen speech in Acts 7 were discerned. It would be well to review these allusions here in a more systematic fashion, and to draw whatever conclusions can be drawn from them.

Like the Stephen speech, the *AJ* starts its *Heilsgeschichte* with Abraham (1.33.3-1.34.1). In 1.34.2, Abraham, Isaac, Jacob and the Twelve are all listed in short order, as in Acts 7:8. In 1.34.3, the people of Israel sojourn for four hundred years in Egypt, as Acts 7:6. Also in 1.34.3, as in Acts 7:17, the promise of God to multiply the seed of Abraham is linked to the growth of the Israelites in Egypt. In 1.34.4-7, Moses is said to do wonders and signs in Egypt, at the Red Sea and in the wilderness for forty years, as in Acts 7:36. 1.35.2, like Acts 7:38, speaks of the giving of the law at Sinai; there may be a further connection in Stephen's "angel speaking to Moses and our fathers" to the *AJ*'s reference to all the people hearing the law (1.35.2, especially in S). In 1.35.5, the people make an idol and worship it, as in Acts 7:41. In 1.36.1-2 and in Acts 7:37 there is a reference to the Prophet like Moses. As we have seen, this is the leading christological category in the *AJ*, and (aside from "the righteous one" of Acts 7:52) it is the only christological title in the Stephen speech. In 1.37.1, the Tabernacle is built according to the direction of Moses, as in Acts 7:44. In 1.38.3, Joshua and the conquest of the land are mentioned, as in Acts 7:45. In 1.38.4, the temple is built contrary to the will of God (Acts 7:47). In both the *AJ* and Acts, the narrative jumps directly from the kings of Israel and their building of the temple to Jesus.

In addition to these eleven detailed allusions, the *AJ* shares the most striking theme of the Stephen speech - opposition to the temple. Both claim that it is not God's house, and was built and continued by the sin of Israel. Moreover, both hold that the cult of sacrifice is an error (Acts 7:41-42; *R* 1.36-39). Both have a strong emphasis on Moses (Acts 7:20-44; *R* 1.34.4-38.2). Some differences appear between Acts 7 and *R* 1.33-43, chief of which is the lack of christological emphasis in Acts 7 compared with the first section of the *AJ*. But the numerous similarities are sufficient to suggest a marked literary relationship between this section of the *AJ* and the structure, content and theology of the Stephen speech.

We turn now to the christology of *R* 1.33-44. We have argued above that the Mosaic Prophet is the leading christological figure in this section of the *AJ*. The Prophet-like-Moses figure is used in this section of the *AJ*, as it will be in the section to follow (1.55-65), to argue that Jesus is the Messiah. Other christological titles occur as well. Next to the Prophet like Moses in importance in this section is "Messiah." This term appears in 1.43.1 and 1.44.2, where it is used by the emissaries of the priests, who ask the Twelve to debate with them about whether Jesus is "the Christ" (L) / "the Messiah" (S). Also, the term "Lord" appears at the end of this section, where it applies to Jesus. It has a special connection with his governance of the church ("the church of the Lord," "ordained bishop in it by the Lord," both in 1.43.3). "Lord" occurs only here in the *AJ*, and is always used absolutely, never in a compound name (e.g., "the Lord Jesus").

The question of the relationship of Jesus and the Law of Moses is raised in the course of these christological affirmations. According to the *AJ*, Jesus came to do away with sacrifice and thus to rid Israel of the last "old evil" which had clung to them since the Exodus. The *AJ* says nothing about Jesus coming to "perfect" or "fulfill" the law. Jesus does not give a "new law," nor is he portrayed as a "New Moses." He is simply the Prophet like Moses, the one whom Moses foretold. He comes to end the sacrifices, which Moses himself knew to be wrong.

The final topic to be considered in the Commentary on 1.33-44 is the anti-sacrificial animus of this section, and its promotion of baptism as the replacement of sacrifice. This is a major theme of 1.33-44, second only to the status of Jesus as Prophet like Moses.

The practice of sacrifice is implied in chap. 35 to be an evil before it is explicitly labelled so in chap. 36. At 1.35.1 there is mention of the "evils" that clung to the Israelites because of their long stay in Egypt, and in 1.35.5 the people make and worship an idol in the form of the Egyptian god Apis. The chief evil learned in Egypt is sacrificing to idols. While Moses is able to eradicate idolatry, he could not root out sacrifice, but left this to the Prophet like himself (1.36.1). Moses does manage to curb the pervasiveness of the evil of sacrifice by limiting it to one place (1.37.1). Then, over the long period of Israelite history between Moses and the Prophet, God showed them in exile and restoration that sacrifice had no divine sanction (1.37.3-5). When the Prophet came, he rejected both the sacrifices and the temple (1.37.3).

The *AJ*'s strong rejection of sacrifice is followed by an endorsement of baptism to take its place in assuring the forgiveness of sins. In the third Note on 1.37.2 (L), we saw that baptism may be referred to as a form of "spiritual sacrifice," one to replace animal sacrifice. At 1.39 the real argument for baptism begins. Baptism was instituted by the Mosaic Prophet to replace sacrifice, and the proof of its divine approval is that those who are baptized are kept safe during the war that comes upon those who sacrifice. That 1.39 interrupts the flow of the *heilsgeschichtlich* narrative, describing the Prophet's provision of baptism before he actually comes (1.40), is an indication of the importance of baptism in the *AJ*.

These two themes will continue to be prominent in the remainder of the *AJ*. The anti-sacrificial animus will continue through the debate of the Twelve with the sects of the Jews in 1.55-65, as will the emphasis on baptism as its replacement. The speech of James in the temple (1.66-71) has no animus against sacrifice, but a summons to baptism is the culmination of his appeal to the Jews.

What is the relationship between the opposition to sacrifice and the argument for baptism in the *AJ*? A clue may be found in the way that sacrifice is viewed solely as a way to forgive sins. The Jewish sacrificial system was of course much wider than that. Sacrifices were also offered for other purposes, such as in thanksgiving, upon taking solemn vows, etc. As baptism in the NT and in other early Christian literature is closely associated with forgiveness, the community of the *AJ* probably looks upon sacrifice from the viewpoint of its practice of baptism.

Notes to R 1.55 - 65

1.55.1 *Nevertheless, as we were beginning to say, since the high priest frequently asked us through the priests that we might have a discussion about Jesus, when an opportune time came and it pleased the whole church, we went up to the temple* (L). The mention of the high priest's request for debate looks back to 1.44.2-3, and indicates that the *AJ* resumes at 1.55.1. (See above, pp. 35 - 37.) L's "As we were beginning to say" refers to 1.53.4, which is not part of the *AJ*. This phrase was likely added by Rufinus, the L translator, who sensed the redundancy of this redactional device in 1.55.1.

Why is the time for debate now "opportune"? The reason cannot be that seven years have now passed, or that the high priest himself requests the debate, as these are mentioned in 1.43.3 - 1.44.2, where "a more opportune time" was not present (1.44.3). L associates the coming of the "opportune time" only with "it pleased the whole church" to debate. S states that the church went up to the temple for debate "since . . . the high priest . . . had asked us often." But this can hardly be the reason, for 1.43.1-3 and 1.44.2-3 also state that such a request had "often" been made and refused, as an opportune time was not yet present. Thus, the frequency of the request to debate does not of itself indicate an opportune time for such a debate.

1.55.1-2 *we . . . our.* These pronouns refer to the Twelve, not the whole church. This becomes clear in 1.55.2, where "we" is distinguished from "our faithful brothers."

.2 *We were standing on the steps together with our faithful brothers* (S). Earlier the believers in Jesus are said to outnumber those Jews who do not believe (1.43.1). Thus, it is physically impossible that they all could be accommodated in the temple at once, let alone all stand on the steps with the Twelve. "Multitude" (S: *knš'*) is used of the Jerusalem church in Acts 4:32, 5:14, 6:2, 5, where the Greek word is $\pi\lambda\eta\theta\sigma\varsigma$; the Peshitta uses *knš'* in all but 6:5. The use of "multitude" reinforces the *AJ*'s claim of the size of the church.

Where in the temple were these steps? Although it is difficult to know precisely the plan of the temple, in which there were several flights of stairs,[46] or if the *AJ* author knew an accurate plan, it is probable that these steps were in the sanctuary. They led from the Court of Israel (for Jewish men) to the Court of the Priests. The Mishnah also refers to steps and a platform in this area (*m. Mid.* 3:6). To judge from 1.70, the *AJ* sees these steps as near the altar of burnt offering, indicating a location within the inner courts of the temple.

in the silence of every man and in great quietness (S). This hendiadys emphasizes the completeness of the silence of the people as the debate begins. L's "completely silent" is equivalent in meaning, though without the emphasis of S.

---

46 See the comprehensive article by W. F. Stinespring, "Temple, Jerusalem," *IDB* 4.534-60, especially 557.

1.55.2 *the people.* While 1.55 gives no description of the people present in the temple for the debate, it becomes evident as the debate proceeds that "the people" are representative of the whole Jewish nation and its different religious groups. The people are "witnesses" because they hear the debate, and "judges" because according to 1.44.2 they are to decide which faith will be followed.

.3 *Next, extolling with many praises the rite of sacrifice which had been given by God to the human race for the forgiveness of sins ...*	(S) *But as he was greatly desirous to find those who desired the sacrifices, supposing that they give the forgiveness of sins ...*

The wording of the first half of 1.55.3 differs in L and S. L has the high priest (here unnamed, but earlier in 1.44.2 and in 1.68.1-2 said to be Caiaphas) "extolling with many praises the rite of sacrifice." He claims that it had been "given by God to the human race." While sacrifice was known in Israel as a practice of the Gentiles, "given by God to the human race" probably has a particular reference to Israelite sacrifice and is not meant to endorse the sacrifices of others. In S, "he was greatly desirous to find those who desired the sacrifices" means that the high priest wanted to locate those in the people who would agree with him. It may also imply that he desired to convince the whole people to continue the sacrifices. That sacrifice and baptism is the first topic of the debate indicates its primary importance in the *AJ*.

he contested the baptism of our Jesus as recently introduced contrary to this (L). After defending sacrifice, Caiaphas attacks baptism. S offers none of Caiaphas' reasoning against baptism, but L gives two reasons: baptism is "recently introduced," as contrasted with the antiquity of sacrifice, and it is "contrary to" the divinely ordered sacrifices.

4. *Matthew . . . [said] that not only will he who is not baptized be rejected from the kingdom of heaven, but also will be in danger in the resurrection of the dead; even if he is good in manner of life and upright in mind, he will not have eternal life* (S). Matthew, one of the Twelve, defends the necessity of baptism, but does not directly attack the sacrifices. It would appear that "the kingdom of heaven" is a this-worldly possession of believers. Not only will an unbaptized person not enter the kingdom of heaven, but will be in "danger" at the resurrection. This is so even if one has led a "good life" and has an "upright mind," i.e., is righteous in deed and thought. S specifies this "danger" by including, "he will not have eternal life."

1.55-65. General Note on the Order of the Twelve.

The names of the Twelve in 1.55-65 raise the question of the order of their names in the *AJ* and its relationship, if any, to lists in the NT. These lists are found in Mark 3:16-19, Matt 10:2-4, Luke 6:14-16, and Acts 1:13. A table of these lists and the order of the Twelve in the *AJ* would facilitate comparison. In the table, "b." means "son of."

Table 2

NT Lists of the Twelve and Their Order in the *AJ*

Mark	Matthew	Luke	Acts	*AJ*
Simon Peter	Simon Peter	Simon Peter	Peter	Matthew
James b. Zebedee	Andrew	Andrew	John	Andrew
John b. Zebedee	James b. Zebede	James	James	James b. Zebedee
Andrew	John b. Zebedee	John	Andrew	John b. Zebedee
Philip	Philip	Philip	Philip	Philip
Barthol.	Barthol.	Barthol.	Thomas	Barthol.
Matthew	Thomas	Matthew	Barthol.	James b. Alphaeus
Thomas	Matthew	Thomas	Matthew	Lebbaeus
James b. Alphaeus	James b. Alphaeus	James b. Alphaeus	James b. Alphaeus	Simon the Cananean
Thaddaeus/ Lebbaeus	Thaddaeus/ Lebbaeus	Simon the Zealot	Simon the Zealot	Barnabas/ Barabbas
Simon the Cananean	Simon the Cananean	Judas b. James	Judas b. James	Thomas
Judas Isc.	Judas Isc.	Judas Isc.		Peter

Comparison of these lists yields the following results. In general, the order of the Twelve in the *AJ* agrees with both Matthew and Luke against Mark and Acts, in the relative order of Andrew, James, John, Philip and Bartholomew. One point of contact with Acts 1 is the lack of Peter's other name, Simon. But two factors point to Matthew as the origin of the order of the Twelve in the *AJ*. First, while the *AJ* agrees with Matthew and Luke in putting James and John in the third and fourth positions, it agrees with Matthew against Luke in adding that they are the sons of Zebedee. Second, the name "Lebbaeus" is found as a textual variant of "Thaddaeus" in Matt 10:3 and Mark 3:18, but the attestation of Lebbaeus in Matthew is much stronger than in Mark.[47] Thus, it is more likely that the *AJ* drew upon Matthew than Mark for its knowledge of the name "Lebbaeus."

The tenth name in the *AJ*'s order is particularly striking. L has it as *Barnabas, qui et Mathias*. The MSS of L show two variants for "Barnabas," "Barsabas" and "Barsabbas." "Barnabas" is rightly preferred by Rehm, as it is the more difficult and well-attested reading. It is easier to explain how corrections of "Barnabas" would have been made by copyists than how "Barsabbas" would have been changed. S reads "Barabbas" twice, in 1.60.5 and 1.61.1.

How did this confusion arise? Both versions of the *AJ* have misunderstood Acts 1:23-26. L's "Barnabas" confuses one of the names of the unsuccessful candidate for Judas' position, Barsabbas (Acts 1:23), with the Barnabas of Acts 4:36. L adds to the confusion by identifying this "Barnabas" with Matthias, who in Acts is Judas' successor. In S, "Barabbas" is only one letter different from "Barsabbas," and thus may be a confusion stemming from the similarity of the names. Nevertheless, both "Barnabas" and "Barabbas" are (to the modern reader, at least) astounding mistakes. Barnabas is the name of the partner of Paul, who is "the enemy" in the *AJ*. Barabbas is the name of the criminal who was released in place of Jesus (Mark 15:7-15; Matt 27:16-26; Luke 23:18; John 18:40). Since both L and S show confusion

---

47 In the textual apparatus of the *SBSGNT*, "Thaddaeus" in Mark is given an "A" rating by the editorial committee. This rating indicates that it is "virtually certain" that Thaddaeus is the original reading, thus throwing grave doubt on "Lebbaeus." But in Matthew, "Thaddaeus" has only a "B" rating, indicating that the attestation of "Lebbaeus" is stronger than in Mark. The witness of *R* 1.59.7 to "Lebbaeus" should be mentioned in the *UBSGNT* textual apparatus as an evidence from a "church father," even as "seventy-two" of *R* 1.40.4 is given as a witness in Luke 10:1.

on "Barsabbas," there probably was also some confusion on this name in the Greek MSS from which they were translated.

Peter is put last because he will speak at the climax of the debate of 1.55-65; he is last, but certainly not least. But why does the *AJ* lead off its order of the Twelve with Matthew? It is obviously not because of dependence on the NT lists, as Matthew's name is never in the first group of four, much less ever first. One possibility is that the mention of baptism in Matthew's remarks in *R* 1.55.4 can be related to Matt 28:16-20. But in Matthew 28 the triadic formula is used, and the emphasis is on the baptism of all the nations,[48] not on the necessity of the baptism of the Jews, as in *R* 1.55.4. Another possibility is that, in Matthew's Gospel, Matthew is called Levi. With a name with priestly associations, he would thus be able to speak against the high priest, as he does in 1.55. Against this possibility is the consistent use of "Matthew," not "Levi," in the *AJ*. A third and more likely possibility is that Matthew's Gospel is the one most favored by the community of the *AJ*, as evidenced by the many dependencies of the *AJ* on it. The community of the *AJ*, Jews who believed in Jesus as Messiah, held a special place of honor for that Gospel which is closest to Jewish Christianity.[49] But due to the slimness of the evidence, this explanation of Matthew's place in the *AJ* must remain a conjecture.

1.55-62. General Note on the Form of the Temple Debate.

The units of the temple debate in 1.55-62 are framed in a fixed literary form, and it would be well to consider this form before moving further into the exegesis of these chapters. For each unit, we will give an example, followed by references to all other occurrences.

Each unit begins with the identification of the group from whom a spokesman speaks (in each pair, L is first, then S):

... first the high priest began to exhort the people ...
... first the high priest began to appease the people ...

---

48 For a complete treatment of the origin and meaning of the triadic formula in Matt 28:19, see J. Schaberg, *The Father, the Son and the Holy Spirit: The Triadic Phrase in Matthew 28:19b* (SBLDS 61; Chico, CA: Scholars, 1984).

49 It is interesting that one list of Jesus' disciples that we have in Jewish tradition also lists "Matthai" (Matthew) as first; cf. *b. Sanh.* 43a. See also J. Maier, *Jesus von Nazareth in der talmudischen Überlieferung* (Darmstadt: Wissenschaftliche Buchgesellschaft, 1978) 232-5. On the widespread priority of the Gospel of Matthew in Jewish Christianity, see Koch, "Investigation," 239-44, 420-3.

(1.55.2; cf. 1.56.1, 1.57.1, 1.58.1, 1.59.1, 1.60.1, 1.61.1, and 1.62.1).
The next part of each unit is the argument made by these spokesmen
against the believers in Jesus:

> Next, extolling with many praises . . . contrary to this.
>
> But as he was greatly desirous . . . us.

(1.55.3; cf. 1.56.1, 1.57.1, 1.58.1, 1.59.1, 1.61.1-2, 1.62.1-2).
Immediately following the objection is the name of the apostle(s) and
his (their) argument against the charge:

> But Matthew, opposing his arguments, clearly showed . . . mind.
>
> But Matthew refuted this one . . . life.

(1.55.4; cf. 1.56.2-3, 1.57.2-5, 1.58.2-3, 1.59.2-3, 1.60.3-4, 1.61.3,
1.62.3-7).
Because there are only six different parties represented at the debate,
and the author wishes all the Twelve to contribute to the defense of the
faith, some of the Twelve must "double up" before a new opposing
spokesman arises:

> After him James the son of Alphaeus made a speech . . . inferiors.
>
> After him James the son of Alphaeus spoke and taught . . . known.

(1.59.4-6; cf. 1.59.7, 1.60.5-7).
Finally, the ending of each apostle's remarks is cast in a literary form
with very similar wording:

> After having continued with these and similar things, Matthew was
> silent.
>
> . . . when he had said those things and witnessed others like them,
> he then was silent.

(1.55.4; cf. 1.56.3, 1.57.5, 1.58.3, 1.59.3, 1.59.6, 1.59.7, 1.60.4, 1.60.7,
1.61.3, 1.62.7 [S]).

These highly stereotyped endings are the most similar of any unit
of the temple debate. In L, each ending begins with *haec*, "these."
Second is a conjunction, usually *et*, "and," but *auten* and *atque* ("and")
occur once each, probably for stylistic variation. Third comes *his
similia*, "things similar to these." Fourth is a verb of speaking, either
protestor ("proclaim, declare, bear witness") or *prosequor* ("go on with,
continue"). Finally comes the verb *sileo*, "be silent," usually with the
name of the apostle. The only departure from *sileo* is in 1.60.7, *dicendi
finem fecit*, "he made an end of speaking," again probably a stylistic
variation.

In S, this formulaic ending is even more stereotyped. Almost every occurrence reads, "When he had said these things and witnessed others like them, he then was silent." First in S comes a demonstrative pronoun, usually *hnyn*, "those," but sometimes *hlyn*, "these." Second comes the temporal conjunction *hkyl*, "when, then, thus." The verb *'mr* ("to say") is third. Next comes the phrase *whlyn* (or *whnyn*) *dlhyn nqpn 'shd*, "and witnessed others [or "other things"] like them." The only exception is in 1.61.3, where an alternate word for "like, similar to" is used (*d'kwthyn*). This phrase, and its equivalent in L, serve to give the impression of a lengthier speech by each of the Twelve than their brief recorded comments would indicate. Fifth comes *whydyn*, "and then." Finally, the sentence is ended with the verb *štq*, "be silent." The entire sentence has a notable alliterative beauty: *hnyn hkyl 'mr whlyn dlhyn nqpn 'shd whydyn štq*.

In conclusion, the temple debate of 1.55-62 is cast in a highly stylized form. Each spokesman among the crowd begins the unit with an objection, and a member of the Twelve responds with a refutation. When the opponent's argument is refuted, the member of the Twelve ends his remarks. The implications of this rigid structure for the historicity of this debate will be considered in Chapter Five.

* * * * * *

1.56.1 *But the party of the Sadducees, which denies that there is a resurrection of the dead* (L). A Sadducee objects to Matthew's remarks on the resurrection, and the *AJ* explains that the Sadducees do not believe in the resurrection of the dead. This is well-attested in the NT (Matt 22:23; Mark 12:18; Luke 20:27; Acts 4:1-2, 23:8) and in Josephus (on resurrection and / or eternal life, *J.W.* 2.18.14 §165; *Ant.* 13.5.9. §173; 18.1.4 §16-7). The Sadducee asserts that those who think "that the dead ever arise" are mistaken. In the Sadducee's view, if there is no resurrection, there can be no final judgment with reward and punishment, and thus the necessity of baptism is removed. "By denying resurrection and immortality in general, the Sadducees rejected simultaneously the entire messianic hope, in the form at least in which later Judaism, built on Pharisaic foundations, expressed it."[50] This judgment can be extended to the *AJ* - Sadducaic teaching would surely reject its

---

50 Schürer, *History*, 2.392.

kind of messianic hope as well. See the Note on 1.61.3 for more on the Sadducees.

1.56.2 Andrew my brother. "My brother" signifies that Andrew is Peter's (the speaker) literal brother. He is not merely his "fellow-believer," as in 1.55.2 (L) and 1.65.2, and commonly in the NT.

It is not an error . . . that the dead are raised. Andrew counters the Sadducee's charge by pointing to the teaching of the Prophet like Moses. No elaboration is given here to the teaching of Jesus on the resurrection. 1.41.2 states that the Prophet "preached eternal life," and 1.57.4 (S) will refer again to Jesus' teaching on the resurrection. In the NT, Jesus teaches about the resurrection in Mark 12:18-27 and its parallels in Matt 22:23-33 and Luke 20:27-40. In these passages, as in *R* 1.56.2, Jesus teaches the Sadducees about the resurrection. Because the *AJ*'s wording is so general, it is impossible to discern from which Gospel it may be drawing.

The *AJ* could have made an argument here not just from the teaching of Jesus about the resurrection, but from his resurrection itself. But this is not done, perhaps because the Mosaic Prophet is to be heard "in all that he *tells* you" (cf. Deut 18:15, 18 and *R* 1.36.2). Thus the emphasis falls on Jesus' teaching alone.

.3 But if one does not believe that he is the prophet foretold by Moses, who was to come, it first ought to be inquired into, if this one is he. And when we know that it is he, it ought to be easy to learn everything in his teaching (S). The status of Jesus as Prophet like Moses is again urged as the prior question. If the people do not recognize Jesus as the Prophet - and at this point they still do not - this "first" should be addressed. Then Jesus' teachings should be "easy to learn" (S) or have "no further doubt" about them (L). Strecker, *Judenchristentum*, 240, points to a similar argument in *R* 1.16.4, par. *H* 1.19.4-6, and to less similar arguments in *R* 2.34.5; 3.26.7; and *H* 2.5.3, 10-11.

he said (L). *Inquit* ("he said"), a defective verb, is usually found one or two words after the beginning of the direct quotation which it introduces. See also the first-person *inquam* of 1.64.1. In S, all of 1.56.2-3 is in indirect discourse. S usually introduces direct discourse by a verb of speaking, which is missing here; but the content is substantially the same.

1.57.1 But one Samaritan, who thought and considered against the people and God, said that the dead are not raised, and Mount Gerizim instead of the holy place of Jerusalem is the house of worship. As an enemy he said against Jesus that he is not the one foretold by Moses, the prophet who was to come (S). A Samaritan speaks up to oppose

Andrew's remarks on the resurrection. He adds two other charges, one against Jerusalem and the other against Jesus as the Prophet like Moses. Although this Samaritan - with a companion (1.57.2) - is present in the temple and stands among the crowd, the *AJ* is careful to distinguish him from "the people." His remarks are "against the people" because he speaks against the holy city of the Jews, Jerusalem. They are also "against . . . God" because he speaks against the Prophet like Moses and his teaching of the resurrection of the dead. Given the Samaritans' opposition to the Temple, the plausibility of their presence at a temple debate may be questioned.[51]

Did the Samaritans of this era in fact deny the resurrection? One body of scholarly opinion holds that they affirmed it from earliest Christian times.[52] However, after a study of Samaritan eschatology, S. J. Isser concludes that the Samaritans generally denied the doctrine of resurrection.[53] J. Bowman also argues that Samaritan eschatology of this time denied the resurrection.[54] Jewish sources of the Tannaitic period testify that the Samaritans did not believe in the resurrection (e.g., *b. Sanh.* 90b), and Epiphanius says likewise (*Pan.* 9.2; 14.2). The *AJ* is another valuable witness to the Samaritan denial of the resurrection of the dead.

1.57.2 *James and John, the sons of Zebedee.* Because two apostles answer these charges of the Samaritan, the *AJ* adds as an afterthought that "another" Samaritan had also spoken.

---

51 Josephus, *Ant.* 18.2.2 §30, tells of some Samaritans "who had secretly entered Jerusalem" and "began to scatter human bones in the porticoes and throughout the temple" in order to defile it. This expresses well the Samaritan hatred for the Jerusalem temple.

52 E.g., J. MacDonald, *Theology of the Samaritans* (London: SCM, 1964), 375-6; M. Gaster, *Samaritan Eschatology* (n.p.: Search, 1932), *passim.*

53 Isser, *The Dositheans: A Samaritan Sect in Late Antiquity* (SJLA 17; Leiden: Brill, 1976) 143.

54 "Early Samaritan Eschatology," *JJS* 6 (1955) 68-9.

1.57.3 (L) *Although they had a command not to enter their cities nor bring the word of preaching to them, yet so that the speech of these people, if not refuted, would not harm the faith of others, they responded so wisely and strongly that they put them to permanent silence.*

(S) *For even though they had a command not to enter their city nor speak with them, they continued even though they were not to speak with them, and were silent no more, lest they think they attained victory and revile the true faith of the many. Wisely, as though from silence, they spoke with them.*

This "command" is drawn from Matt 10:5, where Jesus instructs the Twelve to enter no town of the Samaritans. Here the one making this command is not specified. It is widened to include the present situation: "nor bring the word of preaching to them" (L) / "nor speak with them" (S). But lest they "harm" or "revile" the true faith, the sons of Zebedee spoke up, and silenced them. Such a silencing is seen as a vindication of the decision to speak up against the Samaritans.

Four times in 1.57.1-4, S uses "the holy place" to describe the temple. This expression, not found in L, serves to defend against the Samaritans' rejection of Jerusalem. "The holy place" is a remarkable description of the temple for the *AJ*. Elsewhere the temple is neither holy nor deserving of honor, but is rejected by God. As L is more consistent with the *AJ*'s attitude to the temple in other passages, and as "the holy place" is lacking in L, this was probably added by the S translator.

1.58.1 *one of the scribes*. A scribe speaks up to dispute the assertion of John in 1.57.5 that the likeness of Jesus' signs and wonders to Moses' shows Jesus to be the Prophet like Moses. The scribe does not dispute Jesus' signs and wonders, or their relationship to Moses' miracles, but rather claims that Jesus worked his signs and wonders "as a magician." In a Note on 1.42.4, we saw that Jewish tradition charged that Jesus was a magician, and here the *AJ* reflects that charge once more. "[A]s a magician, not as a prophet," suggests that the opposite of "prophet" is not "false prophet," but "magician." The *AJ* contains no explicit charge that Jesus was a false prophet.

1.58.2 (L) *Philip vehemently opposed him, showing that by this reasoning he accused Moses also.* (3) *Since Moses worked signs and wonders in Egypt similar to those of Jesus in Judea, it cannot be doubted that whatever was said about Jesus may also be said about Moses.*

(S) *Against this one Philip spoke, and said,"By this saying you accuse Moses also,* (3) *because he did signs and wonders in Egypt in the way that Jesus did here." He said these things so that he might understand that what he said about Jesus could also be said about Moses.*

Philip tries to turn the scribe's charge back upon him with an argument based on the Mosaic Prophet. His charge accuses Moses because it implicitly calls him a magician. The reasoning supporting this counter-charge is found in section three, the similarity of the signs and wonders of Moses and Jesus. L has Jesus working these signs "in Judea," probably to be understood as the whole of Israel. S places them "here," and since this "here" is opposite to "Egypt," it probably means "this nation." On the signs and wonders worked by Moses, see the Note on 1.41.1.

"Whatever was said about Jesus may also be said about Moses" (L) means whatever was said in accusation. 1.59 will show that not everything said about Jesus applies to Moses. S puts it more carefully: "And he [Philip] said these things so that he [the scribe] might understand that what he said about Jesus could also be said about Moses."

.3 *in the way* (S). *bhw 'skym'* is literally "in that way, in that manner." This phrase points to the manner in which the miracles were worked, not to their similarity in type. As all other references in L and S to the similarity of Jesus' and Moses' miracles refer to similarity of type, not much weight should be placed on "in the way."

1.59.1 *Then a certain Pharisee . . . accused Philip, because he said that Jesus was equal to Moses* (L). Philip did not explicitly say that Jesus is "equal to Moses," but the Pharisee draws out this implication and the debate continues. That a Pharisee follows the scribe of 1.58.1 reflects the common order of these two groups in the NT.

.2-3 *Bartholomew firmly taught* (L) / *Bartholomew spoke against him* (S). Bartholomew answers the Pharisee's objection by taking it one step farther. It is not the confession of the church ("we do not say") that Jesus is equal to Moses, but that he is greater. Section three gives the reason for this claim: while both Moses and Jesus were prophets, Jesus is also the Messiah, and therefore greater. That both Moses and Jesus were prophets is based on Deut 18:15, which states that the one

whom Moses predicted will be "a prophet like me." The identification
of Moses as a prophet, and as the greatest of the line of prophets to
follow him, is well established in the OT (e.g., "there has not arisen a
prophet since in Israel like Moses," Deut 34:10) and in Jewish tradition
(see the many passages cited by Ginzberg, *Legends*, 6.324).

Bartholomew does not argue that the Messiah is greater than
Moses. Rather, he contends that he who has the two offices of prophet
and Messiah (Jesus) is necessarily greater than is he with only one
(Moses). Granted the premises that Jesus is the Messiah and that two
offices are better than one, it is logical to conclude that Jesus is greater
than Moses. Heb 3:1-6 also argues that Jesus is greater than Moses,
but the reasons adduced are not related to those here in the *AJ*, so no
dependence can be argued.

1.59.4 *One should not believe in Jesus because the prophets predicted
him. Rather, one should believe the prophets, that they truly were
prophets, because the Christ bears witness to them* (L). James' speech,
which is not provoked by a member of the crowd, might seem to be
related to the speech of Bartholomew in 1.59.1-3 by means of the
catchword "prophet." But there is a more substantive connection. As
Bartholomew tried to reverse the people's understanding of the
relationship of Jesus and Moses, so James reverses their understanding
of Jesus and the prophets. Jesus takes precedence, and it is not the
predictions of the prophets that show Jesus to be the Messiah, but it is
the Messiah who confirms their status as prophets. In fulfilling their
predictions of a Messiah, Jesus shows them to have been true prophets
(cf. Deut 18:22). Jesus' precedence is only a relative devaluation of the
prophets; the *AJ* has an overall positive attitude toward them.

.5 *For the presence and coming of the Christ show them truly to have
been prophets* (L). This section is lacking in S, where Frankenberg's
text skips from 1.59.4 to 1.59.6. It draws out the implication of 1.59.4 -
one should believe the prophets because the Messiah witnesses to
them.

.6 *For the testimony of faith ought to be given, not by the inferiors to
the superior, but by the superior to the inferiors* (L). It is not fitting that
Jesus receive testimony or witness from his inferiors, the prophets.
Rather, the greater should testify about the lesser. Rehm, *Pseudoklementinen*, 42, points to Heb 7:7: "It is beyond doubt that the inferior
is blessed by the superior." Rehm rightly suggests that *R* 1.59.6 only
parallels Hebrews, but does not draw on it.

1.59.7 *Lebbaeus.* Lebbaeus' speech is unlike that of the other apostles, because he "accused" (L) / "condemned" (S) the people for not believing in Jesus. The other eleven seek to persuade the people, but Lebbaeus seeks to shame them. He lists the activities of Jesus which should have led them to believe, which can be portrayed as follows:

L	S
teaching the things of God	exhortation
comforting the afflicted	
healing the sick	healing
relieving the poor	consolatory addresses

"Teaching the things of God" and "exhortation" is the main mission of the Prophet like Moses, who will speak God's word to the people (Deut 18:18). "Comforting the afflicted" could refer to the words and/or deeds of Jesus. The S expression "in his consolatory addresses" (*bwy'why*) could also be translated, "in his exhortations, in his consolations," but as J. Payne Smith notes, the plural often means "hortatory or consolatory discourses." [55] Because the earlier *mrtynwth* is "exhortation, admonition," *bwy'why* here likely has the aspect of consolation.

Despite these "good things," the people had "returned hatred and death" (L) to Jesus. The order of S, "they killed him and hated him," would appear to be reversed, but it does make a certain amount of sense in the light of 1.60.5, which charges that the people still hate Jesus. In the NT, hatred of Jesus is to be found in John 7:7 and 15:18, 23-25. However, the *AJ* shows no literary dependence on these passages, only a general characterization of the people's attitude to Jesus.

1.60.1 *the disciples of John ["the Baptist"].* The phrase "disciples of John" is found in Matt 9:14; Mark 2:18; Luke 5:33, 7:18; and John 1:35, 3:25. We have added "the Baptist" to our translation, as it may not be immediately apparent that the reference is to John the Baptist. One notes, however, that the *AJ* nowhere calls John "the Baptist," or mentions his ministry of baptism. Instead, it traces the institution of baptism solely to Jesus.

---

55 *A Compendious Syriac Dictionary* (Oxford: Clarendon, 1903) 37.

1.60.1 (L) . . . *John was the Christ, and not Jesus: "Inasmuch," he said, "as Jesus himself declared that John was greater than all men and prophets. (2) If therefore," he said, "he is greater than all men, he must without doubt be held to be greater than both Moses and Jesus himself. (3) But if he is greater than all, he himself is the Christ."*

(S) . . . *he was the Messiah, and Jesus was not, "For Jesus himself said about him that he was greater than the prophets who were beforetime. (2) If then he is greater than Moses, it is evident that he is also [greater] than Jesus, because Jesus arose as Moses did. Thus John, who is fittingly greater than these, is the Messiah."*

The disciple of John uses the words of Jesus in Matt 11:7-11 or Luke 7:24-8 to argue that John is the Messiah: "Jesus himself declared that John was greater than all men and prophets" (L) / "Jesus himself said about him that he was greater than the prophets who were beforetime" (S). In L, "greater than all men and prophets" is drawn from Matt 11:9, 11 or Luke 7:26, 28. There John is the greatest "among those born of women" and is "more than a prophet." The S version is taken from Matt 11:9 or Luke 7:26, as it refers not to "men," but only to the prophets. Because of the general wording, we cannot determine if the *AJ* draws on Matthew or Luke. The evidence of the *AJ* is the main testimony we have outside the NT to a second-century sect of the disciples of the Baptist who proclaimed John as the Messiah.[56]

The NT contains some evidence for this claim of John's disciples that John was the Messiah. According to Luke 3:15, there was a popular expectation during the ministry of the Baptist that he might be the Messiah. The Prologue of John's Gospel has a strong apologetic against an enlarged role of John vis-a-vis Jesus (John 1:8-9, 30). John 1:20 and 3:38 explicitly assert that John is not the Messiah, and John 3:30 has the Baptist saying to his disciples that Jesus must increase and

---

56 H. Lichtenberger ("Taufergemeinde und früchristliche Tauferpolemik in letzten Drittel des 1. Jahrhunderts," *TZK* 81 [1987] 36-57) provides evidence from NT and extra-NT sources that circles of John's disciples existed in Rome and Ephesus at the end of the first century. One other much later witness is the fourth-century Syriac father Ephraem, but as C. H. H. Scobie (*John the Baptist* [Philadelphia: Fortress, 1964] 195) remarks, Ephraem seems to be dependent on the same source as PsCl, and adds no new information.

"I must decrease." After discussing these Johannine passages, R. E. Brown concludes, "It is reasonable to suspect that *some* of the negations about John the Baptist in the Fourth Gospel were intended as refutations of claims that the sectarians of John the Baptist made about their master."[57] Finally, Acts 19:1-7 mentions some "disciples," probably of John, who have received the baptism of John but were not yet baptized "in the name of the Lord Jesus" (v 5). They accept Paul's explanation of John as the forerunner of Jesus (v 4), and receive Christian baptism (v 5).

1.60.3 *Simon the Cananaean.* Simon answers the argument by returning to the same NT passage introduced by the disciple of John. Simon admits that John is greater than all prophets who are "the sons of women" (L) / "born of women" (S), but John is not greater than "the Son of Man." While this term has not yet occurred in the *AJ*, Jesus is meant. S makes this clear by using a spelling of "Son of Man" (*brh d'nš'*) which is generally used as a title of Jesus (Payne-Smith, *Dictionary*, 53). This argument over the meaning of the words of Jesus about John culminates in the conclusion stated at the beginning of 1.60.4: Jesus is Messiah in addition to being a prophet, but John is "only a prophet."

.4 (L) *There is as much difference between him and Jesus as between a forerunner and him whose forerunner he is, even as there is a difference between him who gives the law and him who observes the law.*

(S) *But all of these things about Jesus are as distant from comparison with these things about John, as he who is sent as a forerunner is distant from him whose forerunner he is, and he who does the work of the law from him who lays down the law.*

The *AJ* gives two comparisons to illustrate the difference between Jesus and John. In the first, the difference is that between a "forerunner" and him whose forerunner he is. This comparison draws on the Gospel description of John as the one who came to prepare the way for Jesus (Mark 1:7; par. Matt 3:11; Luke 3:16; John 1:26-7). In the second, the difference between John and Jesus is that between "him who observes [S: "does the work of"] the law" and "him who gives [S: "lays down] the law". Note that S has the lesser and greater member in that order in

---

57 R. E. Brown, *The Gospel according to John* (AB 29, 29A; 2 vols.; Garden City: Doubleday, 1966, 1970) 1.LXVIII; emphasis Brown's.

both comparisons; L reverses the expected order of law giver and law observer. An important implication about the *AJ* community can be drawn from this statement. The positive attitude to giving and keeping the law indicates that the community of the *AJ* is law-observant. If it were otherwise, such a statement of law-giving and law-keeping would be a meaningless illustration of the difference between Jesus and John.

1.60.5 (L) *Barnabas... began to admonish the people not to have hatred toward Jesus nor blaspheme him.* (6) *For it is much more proper, even for one who does not know or is doubtful about Jesus, to love him rather than hate him. For God has put a reward on love, a punishment on hatred.* (7) *"Even this," he said, "that he assumed a Jewish body and was born among the Jews, how has this not been an incentive for all of us to love him?"*

(S) *Barabbas . . . advised the people that they neither hate Jesus nor reproach him.* (6) *For it is more virtuous, since they do not know that Jesus is the Messiah, that they not hate him, since God has appointed a reward for love and not for hatred.* (7) *For since he has taken a body from the people of the Jews and became a Jew, God brings not a little loss of death upon him who hates him.*

The speaker addresses the hatred of the people toward Jesus, as Lebbaeus in 1.59, but with a more irenic approach. He urges the people not to hate Jesus nor "blaspheme" (L) / "reproach" (S) him. Blasphemy against Jesus is found in the charge that Jesus was a glutton and demon-possessed (1.40.2). The charge that Jesus was a magician is probably also to be included as blasphemy (1.42.4; 1.58.1; 1.70.2).

Barnabas / Barabbas argues that since they do not know (L includes: "or are doubtful") that Jesus is the Messiah, it would be better to love Jesus rather than to continue hating him. This is so because God has established a reward for love, but a punishment for hatred. While there is no one scriptural origin of the idea that love is better than hate, the *AJ* could be drawing on the command of Jesus to return love and not hatred to one's enemies (Matt 5:43-48; Luke 7:27-31). Because the Matthean form of this command speaks of "reward" for love (v 46), if the *AJ* draws on the love command it likely is once again dependent upon Matthew.

A second reason for loving Jesus rather than hating him is the incarnation of the Prophet. He "assumed a body" (*corpus adsumpsit*)

/ "has taken a body" (*pgr . . . nsb*) from the Jews and became a Jew, and therefore he should be loved by all Jews. The emphasis is not on becoming human, but on becoming Jewish, in accordance with Deut 18:15's "from among you, from your brethren." This is a valuable witness to the *AJ*'s belief in the incarnation of Jesus, and, by implication, his pre-existence.

S includes a solemn warning at the end of section seven. God will bring "not a little loss of death upon him who hates" Jesus. Such a threat stems from Deut 18:19: "Anyone who does not obey him shall surely die" (cf. 1.36.2).

1.61.1 (L) *Then Caiaphas attempted to find fault with the teaching of Jesus, claiming that he said vain things. (2) "For he said that the poor are blessed, and promised earthly rewards, and placed the highest gift in an earthly inheritance, and promised that those who observe righteousness will be satisfied with food and drink."*

(S) *Caiaphas condemned the teaching of Jesus, (2) "Because he said many vain things in his coming, that he gives blessing to the poor and promised earthly reards, that those of virtue will inherit the earth and that they will be satisfied by eating and drinking."*

Caiaphas began the debate in 1.55 with a defense of sacrifice and an attack on baptism. In this chapter he will be the last challenger to speak against the believers. 1.61 thus forms a neat *inclusio* with 1.55.

The scriptural allusions in Caiaphas' remarks are drawn from the Matthean beatitudes, with one allusion to the Lukan beatitudes. "The poor are blessed" (L) / "he gives blessing to the poor" (S) is closer to Luke 6:20-1 than to Matthew 5:3-6, as it lacks the Matthean "in spirit." "Promised earthly rewards" is adapted from Matt 5:5, "they [the meek] will inherit the earth." "Placed the highest gift in an earthly inheritance" (L) / "Those of virtue will inherit the earth" (S) is also drawn from Matt 5:5, as both "inherit" and "earth" are present. The last clause of 1.61.2 stands closer to Matt 5:6 than Luke 6:21, as "righteousness" is peculiar to Matthew. "[F]ood and drink" (L) / "eating and drinking" (S) draws on Matthew, as Luke has only "hunger."

1.61.3 *Thomas argued that his charge is mistaken. He showed that the prophets, in whom he too believes, taught more things, but did not show how these things would be or how they were to be understood* (L). Thomas refuted the charge of Caiaphas, not by denying that Jesus taught such things, but by arguing that the prophets also taught them. L refers to the prophets as those "in whom he too [Caiaphas] believes." S calls them "those who believed beforehand" in Jesus. The L clause "taught more things" probably means "taught these things and more."

Is Caiaphas a Sadducee in the *AJ*? Acts 5:17 presents him as a Sadducee, as Josephus probably does also (*Ant.* 20.9.1 § 199). Because the *AJ* treats Caiaphas and the Sadducees in different sections of the debate, it probably sees them as different. If he were a Sadducee, it is doubtful if he could be said to believe in the prophets in the same sense as the Twelve, as "it is quite possible that the Sadducees considered only the Pentateuch as canonical in the strict sense of the word" (Schürer, *History*, 2.409). However, against Schürer, they may have seen the prophets as interpreters of the law, as in *R* 1.70. But because the *AJ* may not know that Caiaphas is a Sadducee, it can argue from this hope to Jesus. The implication of this ignorance will be discussed again in Chapter Five.

1.62.1 *After this Caiaphas looked at me, in part as if counseling me, in part as if condemning me. He said, "Be silent, and do not proclaim Jesus as the Messiah, because you are bringing destruction upon your soul, as you yourself are going astray after him, and you are leading others astray"* (S). The literary form of 1.62 is at first glance similar to that of the preceding chapters of the debate. The name of an opponent is given and his complaint is reported. But a closer examination of 1.62 shows some dissimilarities to the usual format. First, Caiaphas speaks again, even though he has just spoken in 1.61. Second, he does not address the issue of the debate, but directly attacks the one apostle who has not yet spoken, Peter.

What accounts for these similarities and dissimilarities? Martyn has argued that in 1.62 the *AJ* author (a) begins a strong literary dependence on Acts 4, the trial of Peter and John before the Sanhedrin, and (b) draws some elements from a situation reflected in John 9, that of Jewish Christians being tried in a Jewish court as *mesithim*, religious seducers.[58] Several elements in 1.62.1-3 are drawn from Acts 4: the

---

58 Martyn, "Recognitions," 280-91. Martyn gives this aspect of 1.65.1-3 more detailed treatment than can be offered here.

name Caiaphas (v 4); the warning to the apostle(s) (v 17); the order not to preach Jesus (v 18); and a threat (vv 21, 29, specified in the *AJ* as a threat of death). Elements drawn from the tradition reflected in John include the important "lead others astray" (John 7:12, 47).

In the *AJ*, the S verb for "lead astray" is *t"*. Its first use, "you are going astray [*t'yt*] after him," is in the Pe'al conjugation, and means "to wander, go astray, fall into error." Its second use, "you are leading others astray [*mt"*]" is in the Aph'el conjugation, and has a causative sense: "lead astray, deceive, seduce." Peter is "leading others astray" by bringing them to believe in Jesus as the Messiah, and alienating them from the divinely-ordered sacrifices. *t"* is the S equivalent of the Hebrew verb *yst*, which is found in the treatment of *mesithim* prescribed in m. Sanh. 7:10. In both the Mishnah and the *AJ*, the punishment for *mesithim* is death.

1.62.2 *Then he further charged me with arrogance, because although I myself was ignorant, a fisherman and a rustic, I dared to assume the office of teacher* (L). Caiaphas charges further that Peter was "arrogant" because he was teaching with no qualification to do so. Peter, Caiaphas says in L, is *imperitus*, "ignorant, unskilled, inexperienced." The parallel in S is *hdywt'*, a loan word from the Greek ιδιοτης (cf. this word in Acts 4:13). Both these words for "ignorant" connote "untrained in religious lore." This is the estimation of Peter and John by the Jerusalem authorities in Acts 4, and here the *AJ* is again dependent upon Acts. That Peter is a fisherman implies that his trade does not qualify him for teaching, and betrays his humble status. Such a denigration is plausible from the aristocratic high priest and his circle; but among the equally learned Pharisees a humble trade was no source of embarrassment. L also describes Peter as *rusticus*, "rustic, countrified, provincial." In sum, Caiaphas denigrates Peter by disparaging his lack of formal learning, his trade and (in L) his place of origin.

.3 *I also said words such as these to him: "My danger is less if, as you say, this one is not the Messiah, for I accept him as a teacher of the law. But there is not a little danger, but great danger for you, if he is the Messiah, which he in truth is"* (S). Peter answers by returning to Caiaphas his warning of danger and destruction. If Jesus is not the Messiah, those who accept him as Messiah are in small danger. If he truly is the Messiah, those who deny him are "in great danger." This danger is not specified here, but in 1.55.4 the *AJ* describes it as exclusion from eternal life. The expression "teacher of the law" (νομοδιδασκαλος) is found in Luke 5:17, Acts 5:34 and I Tim 1:7, but never applied to Jesus. Its use here signifies that the *AJ* looks on Jesus as a teacher of the law to his people, and that what he taught is in agreement with the law. Its acceptance of Jesus as a "teacher of the law" is another evidence that the community of the *AJ* was law-observant.

1.62.4 *"For I believe in him who has appeared."* Peter replies that there is more certainty in believing someone to be Messiah who has appeared and whose words and deeds can be judged, rather than refusing to believe and reserving one's faith for a Messiah who has not yet come.

.5 *"But that even I, as you say, an uneducated and ignorant man, a fisherman and a rustic, have more understanding than the wise elders, this,"* I said, *"ought even more to strike terror in you. (6) For if in disputing I overcame you wise and erudite men by some kind of erudition, it would be seen that this knowledge came to me over a long time, and was not granted by the grace of divine power. (7) But now when, as I have said, we ignorant men convince and overcome you wise men, is it not apparent to anyone who has sense that this is not the work of human cleverness, but of divine will and gift?"* (L). 1.62.5-7 introduces another argument to rebuff Caiaphas' warning from 1.62.1. Peter argues from the fact that the Twelve, although unlearned, have refuted the wise religious experts in the present debate. This fact is a sign of divine power in the Twelve and (by extension) of the truth of Jesus' status as Messiah.

In 1.62.6, Peter uses a condition which is contrary to fact: If the Twelve had "gone out for instruction" in religious studies and rhetoric, and then "by . . . erudition" (L) defeated their opponents in debate, such a victory would be "a work of time and diligence" (S). That is, it would be a merely human accomplishment not granted by God and not implying divine approval. It is not only Peter who claims to know more than the experts, as Caiaphas implies, but also the Twelve who have been debating their learned opponents in 1.55-61 ("we," 1.62.7 [L], 1.62.6-7 [S]).

Other passages in *R* also point to a low opinion of learning, and especially of the art of rhetoric; see 1.3.1 and 1.7.14-5. An interesting parallel to 1.62.5-7 is found in 1.9.4-5, where Clement rebukes the "learned and philosophic" for attempting to silence Barnabas' proc- lamation with foolish rhetorical ploys. In spite of this low view of skilled speech, *R* 1 also presents a more balanced in 1.25.2: "If we use learning in asserting the errors of antiquity, we ruin ourselves by gracefulness and smoothness of speech. But if we apply learning and grace of speech to the assertion of the truth, I think that not a little advantage is gained thereby." This quotation is from L; S is similar.

1.64.1 *"For we know that He is very angry because of your sacrificing,
because the time of sacrifices is now complete"* (S). God has shown
opposition to sacrifice by destroying the temple (1.37) and by the words
of the Prophet like Moses, who warned them to cease the sacrifices and
gave baptism to replace it (1.39.1-2, 1.55.3-4). Now God's anger is even
greater since "the time of sacrifices," the period from Moses to the
Prophet in which sacrifice was permitted (1.36), is now complete.

.2 *"the temple will be destroyed and the abomination of desolation*
[will be set up] *in the holy place."* God's anger at sacrifice will once
again result in the destruction of the temple. After this destruction,
"the abomination of desolation" (drawn from Dan 9:27 via Matt 24:15)
will be set up in "the holy place." With such a brief mention, it is difficult
to know how the *AJ* views this "abomination." Probably it refers to the
temple of Jupiter Capitolinus that Hadrian erected on the temple site
after the Bar Cochba revolt, because the *AJ* views this abomination as
erected after the temple is destroyed. "The holy place" is so called
because of the dependence on Matt 24.15, not because the *AJ* now sees
this place as holy.

(L) *"Then the Gospel will be preached to the Gentiles as a witness against you, so that by their faith your unfaithfulness may be judged."*	(S) *"Then the Gospel will be made known to the Genitles as a witness, for the healing of the divisions which exist, and your divisions as well."*

In Matthew 24, the end of the temple and the "abomination of
desolation" are signs of the "great tribulation" at the end of the world.
In the *AJ*, after the temple's destruction the Gospel will be preached
to the Gentiles. Here the time of the Gentile mission is future, but in
1.42.1 (L) the Gospel already "has been sent" into the world. Like
1.42.1-2, the Gospel goes out to the Gentiles because of the unbelief of
Israel in the Prophet. Both L and S of 1.64.2 use the technical term for
"Gospel" (*evangelium, sbrt'*), and this makes it likely that the Greek of
the *AJ* read ευαγγελιον. Rehm, *Pseudoklementinen*, 44, suggests that
this section is to be compared with Mark 6:11 and Luke 9:5. However,
these passages refer to neither the Gospel nor the Gentiles.

While both L and S agree that the Gospel will be preached to the
Gentiles "as a witness," they disagree on the nature of this witness. In
L, it is "against you" (*vestri*, "you" plural). "You" are the unbelieving
Jews. The belief of the Gentiles in Jesus will accentuate the unbelief
of the Jews. In S, the witness will lead to the "healing of the divisions

which exist." That this refers to the healing of division among the Gentiles is made clear by the next clause: "and your divisions as well." Thus, L implies that the Jews will remain unbelieving, but S that the healing of the Gentiles will lead to the healing of the Jews. S seems to fit more carefully into the context, which will turn in section three to talk of the health of the whole world; therefore S is probably more nearly original. Yet the hope that S holds out for the healing (conversion?) of the Jews is uncharacteristic of the rest of the *AJ*. Justin can also cite the faith of the Gentiles as an example for the Jews, employing Mal 1:10-2 and Ps 18:45-6 as proof-texts (*Dial.* 28.5-6).

1.64.3 *"For because the whole world in each generation is sick with evil desire either secretly or openly, that physician who was sought visited for its health* (S). The author adds another reason for the preaching of the Gospel to the Gentiles - to heal their diseases. The entire world is ill, and S correctly interprets this metaphorically, as a spiritual sickness ("evil desire").[59] Both L and S develop the extent of sickness with an either-or contrast: "either generally through all, or through an individual one especially" (L) / "either secretly or openly" (S).

Because this world is sick, it needs a "physician" to visit "for its health." The Gospel tradition calls Jesus a "physician" ($\iota\alpha\tau\rho\sigma$) in Mark 2:17, 5:26; Matt 9:12; and Luke 4:23, 5:31. Later Christian literature echoes this description in Ignatius' *Eph.* 7.2, Clement of Alexandria's *Quis Div. Salv.* 29, and Origin's *Against Celsus* 2.67. In these passages and in the *AJ* the use is metaphorical - the "physician" who visits the world brings salvation as his treatment. Although the *AJ* elsewhere implies that Jesus' ministry was solely to the Jewish people, in the preaching of the Gospel to the Gentiles his "visit" is extended to the whole sick world.

.4 (L) *"We therefore witness to you and we announce that which has been hidden from every one of you. Yours is to consider what is advantageous to you."*

(S) *Behold, we thus witness to each one of you about all that you lack. Yours is now to decide what is helpful for you to do."*

1.64.4 closes the apostles' remarks at the temple debate. L has "we announce that which has been hidden from every one of you." This

---

59 This "evil desire" in S is probably not a reference to the "evil impulse." S has "desire" as *zbyn'*, different altogether than the usual Syriac rendering of "impulse," *yzr'*.

"hidden" thing is the theme of the apostles' remarks, that Jesus is the Messiah. S reads instead, "about all that you lack." This "lack" is faith in Jesus and its expression in baptism.

Peter ends his remarks with a call to decision. It would be more "advantageous" (L) / "helpful" (S) for the Jewish people to believe in Jesus than to continue in disbelief. Such a decision to believe in Jesus will be made later in 1.70, but not yet.

1.65.1 *multitude of priests.* The body of priests is called a "multitude," a term otherwise used in the *AJ* to describe the whole body of the people (1.41.4 [L], 1.56.1 [S]), and once to describe the church (1.55.2 [S]). In Acts, "multitude" ($\pi\lambda\eta\theta os$) is used to describe the church as a whole (4:32, 5:14, and 6:2, 5). The use of this word to describe the priests is designed to emphasize the great uproar that threatened violence against the believers.

.2 *Gamaliel.* The *AJ* calls Gamaliel "a leader [*princeps, ryš*] of the people." In the Talmud, Gamaliel is known as *nasi*, "prince" of Israel, a title which indicates his high standing in the tradition. He is the first in a line of six Gamaliels to bear the title *nasi* (*Shab.* 15a *Baraita*). But there is some controversy over when the actual usage of this term began. Some trace it to Rabbi Judah ha-Nasi (fl. ca. 190), others to pre-Maccabean times as in the Mishnaic dating, and many others to a time between these two poles.[60] Whether Gamaliel was in fact called *nasi* in his lifetime is therefore in doubt. We may safely say that he was not in fact the president of the Sanhedrin, as is claimed in *Shab.* 15a, for "Diese Würde hat, solange der Tempel stand, ausschliesslich in der Hand der Hohenpriester geruht."[61]

In the NT Gamaliel appears only in Acts. He is "a teacher of the law honored by all the people" (5:34), and a respected member of the Sanhedrin who counsels moderation toward the new messianic movement (5:34-9).[62] He is also said to be a teacher of Paul (22:3). This latter statement has occasioned much scholarly debate, but does not come into play in the *AJ*.

An important part of the *AJ*'s portrait of Gamaliel is that he is a secret believer. He is "secretly our brother," and to make sure the reader gets the point, the author adds "in the faith." He remains "among

---

60 For a summary discusssion, see G. J. Blidstein, "Nasi," *EncJud* 12.834-5.

61 Str-B 2.637.

62 Note that the NT does not present him as its president; see Mark 14:53 and Acts 24:1, where the High Priest is assumed to be president.

them," among those who do not believe in Jesus, "by our plan" (L) and "for our advantage" (S). This "plan" and "advantage" will be specified later in 1.66.4.

How did Gamaliel become known to the *AJ* as a secret believer? This motif is not drawn from Acts, where despite his words of caution toward persecuting the church there is no hint that Gamaliel believes in Jesus. Nor is there anything in Jewish tradition to support this. Recent scholarship has seen it as a post-NT Christian development. Schoeps, *Theologie*, 405, agrees with Schürer and Zahn that this passage contains the earliest appearance of the legend that Gamaliel was a crypto-Christian.[63] Martyn, "Recognitions," 283-4, argues that the *AJ* combines Acts 5 with the motif of Nicodemus as a secret believer, a conflation also found in the *Acts of Pilate,* as he points out.

1.65.2 *[M]any were gnashing their teeth in the great rage with which they were filled against us* (S). The anger of the priests which leads Gamaliel to speak up is described in L as "monstrous furor." The more vivid expression of S, "gnashing their teeth," has an illuminating biblical background. Used in the OT as a sign of rage, it is most often found in the NT in the phrase "weeping and gnashing of teeth," in which the gnashing of teeth is a sign of deep sorrow. Only in Acts 7:54 is it done in "rage" and "against" someone (Stephen), as in *R* 1.65.2 (S). In the *AJ*, gnashing of teeth is a sign of murderous intent. If Gamaliel had not intervened, the apostles would have been physically attacked. This is a foreshadowing of what is to come later in the *AJ*.

---

63 One other text sees Gamaliel as a secret believer, the *Expositio* on Acts 5 by Bede (ca. 673-735): "This Gamaliel, as Clement indicates, was a brother in the faith of the apostles, but by their plan remained as a Jew, in order to be able to calm any kind of trouble against them" (*PL* 92.956, translation mine). This is explicitly drawn from *R* 1.62.2-3, and adds nothing to our knowledge of this legend. That the "father of English history" should know the *Recognitions* and quote from it to illustrate Acts 5 is an indication of its standing in early medieval times.

1.65.3 (L) *"Be quiet for a little while, O men of Israel; for you do not perceive the trial which is hanging over us. Therefore leave these men alone. If what they are doing is of a human plan, it will quickly end; but if it is of God, why do you sin without a cause and not gain anything? For who is able to overcome the will of God? (4) Now therefore, as the day is already turning toward evening, I myself will dispute with these men tomorrow in this same place as you listen, so that I may openly oppose and clearly refute every error."*

(S) *"Be quiet and keep silence, O men, sons of Israel, for we do not know what sort of trial this is that stands over us. Therefore leave these men alone. If this thing is of the sons of men, it will fail; but if it is of God, why would you sin uselessly when you are not able to accomplish it? For the will of God always fittingly conquers in everything. (4) Now because this day is passing away, I desire to speak with them tomorrow here in your presence in order to refute their word of error."*

"The trial . . . over us" refers to the necessity of deciding the truth of the believer's faith. The priests have become so enraged that they have lost sight of this "trial," and Gamaliel calls them back to it by posing the alternatives. If the new faith in Jesus is only human, i.e., false, it will fail. But if it is "of God," it cannot be defeated; those who resist it will be resisting God to no avail. This need not be read as the advice of a secret believer. Rather, it is good Pharisaic teaching, and is echoed in the saying of a second-century rabbi, Johanan the Sandalmaker: "Every assembling together that is for the sake of Heaven shall in the end be established, but any that is not for the sake of Heaven shall not in the end be established" (*m. 'Abot* 4:11). The *AJ* author has drawn upon Acts 5:35-39 for this advice of Gamaliel.

In section four, Gamaliel proposes a plan to delay the debate so that a riot can be averted and the issue at hand can be decided later. He urges that they adjourn because of the lateness of the day until tomorrow, when he will debate with the believers. In S, Gamaliel clearly presents himself as against the church as he says that he will "refute their word of error." In L, his remarks are skillfully ambiguous. This is enough to still the uproar, which according to 1.65.5 continued until Gamaliel finished his remarks. Then Gamaliel, in a demonstration of his authority, dismisses the people.

Comment on R *1.55 - 1.65*

In the comment on this section of the *AJ*, we will examine three topics: (1) the theme of the debate, and how it is worked out in 1.55-65; (2) the christology of this debate; and (3) the relation of this center section of the *AJ* with the preceding and following sections.

The theme of 1.55-65 is clear and consistent: Jesus is the Prophet like Moses and Messiah. The theme of the debate is stated even before it begins, in the invitation of the priests (1.43.2, 1.44.2). In 1.55, the debate about Jesus begins with a discussion of the appropriateness of Jesus' establishment of baptism. Chapter 56 starts on the topic of the resurrection, but the debate is redirected to the teaching of Jesus and his status as Mosaic Prophet, a status which secures his teachings. 1.57 continues the discussion of resurrection, but most of this chapter defends Jesus as the Mosaic Prophet against the Samaritans. In 1.58, Jesus is defended against the charge of magic by a reiteration of the Prophet-like-Moses expectation. Jesus is greater than Moses, and is the confirmation of the prophets, in 1.59. In 1.60, Jesus is greater than John, and therefore Messiah. That he was incarnate as a Jew should stir up his people to love him. 1.61 may not seem to be directly associated with the theme of the debate, but its defense of Jesus' teachings is related to the main task of the Mosaic Prophet, to teach. In 1.62, Peter's defense is based on his claim that Jesus is Messiah. 1.64 threatens punishment on those who do not heed the Prophet, and challenges them to decide on Jesus. 1.65 follows the debate proper, and introduces the figure of Gamaliel.

As this debate has a christological focus, it would be well to look at its key christological terms. We have seen that the leading terms are the "Prophet like Moses" and "Messiah." These are interchangeable in 1.55-65, so the *AJ* can and does shift back and forth between them. It need never be argued that the Mosaic Prophet is the Messiah, or *vice-versa*. The equivalence of these terms is seen in 1.43.1, the invitation to debate whether Jesus is "he whom Moses foretold, who is the eternal Christ." The beginning of the debate focuses on Jesus as the Prophet like Moses (1.55-58); "Messiah" is in the background. This title of Mosaic Prophet is explicitly related to the term "Messiah" in 1.59-60. Jesus is both Prophet and Messiah, and therefore greater than Moses (1.59) and John the Baptist (1.60). Chap. 61 shifts back to prophetic terms only - Jesus is greater than the prophets because he interprets their teachings. Another shift is made in 1.62, where the discussion is about Jesus as Messiah, and the Mosaic Prophet fades into the background.

The *AJ* has a rudimentary incarnational christology in 1.60.7, where it is said that Jesus took on a Jewish body and was born a Jew. This incarnational christology is used to urge the Jews to love Jesus rather than hate him, as he decided to come as one of them. An incarnation implies some sort of pre-existence, but this is left completely undeveloped. The *AJ* has no hint of creation through the pre-existent Jesus, nor is pre-existence used as an argument for Jesus' priority over John the Baptist, as in John 1:15, 30. Rather, in accord with the purpose of this debate, incarnation is applied to the Messianic status of Jesus, and is used to persuade the Jewish people to see him as Messiah.

The debate of 1.55-65 continues the treatment of the Mosaic Prophet in 1.33-44. The role of the prophet is developed in terms of his teaching: that sacrifice is replaced by baptism; that the dead are raised to final judgment; that Jesus is the greatest of all prophets. This section of the *AJ* also develops what is said in 1.42 about the preaching of the gospel to the whole world.

1.55-65 also relates well to what follows in 1.66-71. A smooth transition between the two sections is provided by the figure and words of Gamaliel, who ends the first debate and begins the second. The second debate has the same topic as James' speech in 1.69: "Is Jesus the Messiah?" The first debate has foreshadowed the violent ending of the second debate, and has hinted that the Jewish people will not in the end come to faith in Jesus. But the real climax of the *AJ* is yet to come, the speech of James and its aftermath.

Notes to R 1.66-71

1.66.1 *But we, when we had come to our James, explained everything that was said and done. When we had eaten, we stayed with him, making supplication to Almighty God through the whole night, that the discourse of the coming disputation may show the undoubtable truth of our faith* (L). 1.66.1 is a transition from the debate of the Twelve to the speech of James. The Twelve ("we") return to James and give him a report on what transpired in the temple. (Cf. 1.44.3, where the Twelve also give an oral report to James.) They then spend "the whole night" in prayer that the coming debate may show the truth of their faith.

1.66.2 Therefore, on the next day James the bishop went up together with us and with the whole church to the temple, where we found a large multitude that had been waiting for us since the middle of the night (L). Here begins the second debate of the *AJ*. James is mentioned first to indicate his pre-eminence in the church. When he accompanied the whole church to the temple, they found a crowd "waiting for us," and L remarks, "from the middle of the night." Usually the temple was closed during the night, and this is reflected in the *AJ* at 1.71.2. But Josephus says that during Passover, "The priests were accustomed to open the gates of the temple after the middle of the night" (*Ant*. 18.2.2 § 29). *M. Yom.* 1:8 says that "on the feast" the temple was opened "at the first watch" of the night, for on these days, "before the cock-crow drew near the Temple Court was filled with Israelites."

But does the debate of 1.66-71 take place on the Passover? The evidence, while not fully conclusive, points to a negative answer. 1.43-44 mentions the Passover, but much time passes as the priests constantly request a debate. This seems to indicate that the debate takes place after the Passover, perhaps shortly after it. Moreover, nothing in 1.55-71 itself indicates that it is the time of the Passover. Thus, the balance of the evidence suggests that a midnight opening of the temple with its implied time of Passover is not a part of the *AJ*, but was likely added by L.

.3 the place where we were before (L) / *the places of the preceding day* (S). This refers back to the locale of the debate of 1.55-65. No "steps" are explicitly mentioned here, but they do appear at 1.70.8. There it is apparent that James and the church have been standing at the top of these steps through all the events of 1.66-71.

.4 (L) *Then, when there was perfect silence, Gamaliel, who as we said above was of our faith, but by permission remained among them, so that if they should ever attempt anything wicked or impious against us, either would restrain them by a wisely adopted plan, or would warn us so that we would be able either to take care or to deflect it.*

(S) *When there was a great quiet, Gamaliel, who as I said before was secretly among them for our assistance although he was our brother, so that when they in one mind were plotting against us, he would be able to know it and keep it from us, or in fitting counsel would change it by his intercession against those who opposed us.*

Gamaliel appears again, and his role as a secret believer and protector of the church is reiterated in a fashion consistent with 1.65. Both L and S specify two options Gamaliel had when faced with a threat to the church. In L, he would "either restrain them by wisely adopted plan" or "would warn us." In S, he would either "keep it from us" or "in fitting counsel would change it by his intercession against those who were against us."

Despite their differences in wording, these two options are the same in L and S, but reversed. L's "restrain them by plan" (*consilium*, "plan, counsel") corresponds to S's "in fitting counsel . . . us," and L's "warn us . . . it" is roughly equivalent to S's "keep it from us." The first of these two options is illustrated in 1.65, where Gamaliel intercedes for the believers and restrains the fury of the priests. The second is illustrated in 1.71.3, where Gamaliel warns the church of impending persecution.

1.66.5 (L) *He, therefore, as if he were acting against us, first while looking at James the bishop addressed him in this way.*

(S) *. . . nevertheless first wisely spoke as our enemy, and he proclaimed in such a way that he might persuade the people, and that they would hear in love the true words which were spoken. Looking at James the bishop, he began his discourse thus.*

As in 1.65, Gamaliel is said to pretend in his speech to be "acting against us" (L) / "our enemy" (S). He does this by repeating the disparaging words of Caiaphas, calling the believers "children" and "unlearned" (1.67.1). The rest of his speech is far from inimical to the church. Indeed, it is so even-handed that Caiaphas became suspicious of Gamaliel (1.68.1).

L reads that Gamaliel addressed James in his remarks; this is lacking in S. Actually, Gamaliel's remarks are addressed to the whole church (1.67.1-7a) and the crowd in the temple (1.67.7b). We may conclude, therefore, that "him" is an addition by L. "[A]nd he proclaimed . . . spoken," not in L, is likely an addition by S. It explains Gamaliel's motives, which have already been amply stated.

1.67.1 (L) *"If I, Gamaliel, consider it a disgrace to neither my learning nor advanced age to learn something from children and the unlearned, if perhaps there may be something of usefulness or salvation to acquire (for he who lives according to reason knows that there is nothing of more value than the soul), should not this be prized and desired by all, to learn what one does not know, and teach what one has learned?"*

(S) *"I, Gamaliel, who am old, and who have honor among teachers of the truth, am not ashamed to learn from children and unlearned ones something about salvation and helpful for my life, for to those who have a discerning mind there is nothing more excellent than their soul."*

The speech of Gamaliel comprises chap. 67. Although the believers are "children" and "unlearned," they deserve a hearing from the multitude. Gamaliel himself, although learned and old, will be open to anything the believers might teach, and so should all the people in the temple.

The parenthesis in L and its equivalent in S is an aphoristic wisdom saying, and its philosophic orientation is more pronounced in L. "He who lives according to reason" and the emphasis on the value of the soul seem to fit better than S into the context of 1.67.2. L expands this aphorism with "should not . . . learned," which is lacking in S. Despite the differences in wording, the basic meaning of this aphorism is the same in L and S: reason dictates that the soul and its eternal destiny is most important, and therefore all should listen to even "children and the unlearned" if they may know something of value to the soul.

1.67.2 (L) *"For it is very certain that neither friendship nor kindred relationship nor lofty royal power ought to be of more value to one than truth. (3) And so, brothers, if you know anything further, do not hesitate to bring it before all the people of God, that is, to your brothers, as the whole people is listening willingly and in complete silence to what you say."*

(S) *And he declared that neither kings nor friends nor kindred nor fathers nor anything else is more excellent than the truth. (3) As if enticing and coaxing us, he said, "If you know anything, do not be reluctant to give it to your people, because you are brothers in the matter of the worship of God."*

While the wording of section two varies, Gamaliel's point in both L and S is that no human allegiance ought to stand in the way of acknowledging the truth. Neither friendship, kindred, nor political ties should prevent one from confessing Jesus as Messiah.

Gamaliel then encourages the believers to speak freely, and also listen to the counsel of others. "Brothers" is used here as "fellow Jews," but there is a hidden irony in Gamaliel's use of it for the believers, as they are secretly brothers in the faith with him. In these public remarks, Gamaliel clearly aligns himself with those who do not believe in Jesus. He includes himself in the "us" of 1.67.5 (L), 1.67.4-5 (S), and he addresses the believers as "you."

1.67.6 *I swear to you.* Gamaliel knows that some in the crowd are "prejudiced" against the believers, and are planning evil against them. Therefore, he acts in his secret role of protector of the church as he swears by the life of God to permit no one "to lay hands on" the believers. An oath upon the life of God is, according to M. H. Pope, the most common form of oath in the OT.[64] Gamaliel will later fail to perform his oath, when the church is attacked in the temple (1.70).

.7 *"Since, therefore, you have all these people as a witness of this my oath, and hold our sealed covenant as an appropriate pledge, let each one of you without any delay declare what he has learned; and let us, brothers, listen earnestly and in silence."* (L). Gamaliel says to all the people that they are witnesses to his promise, and (by implication) should act accordingly. "Our sealed covenant" (L), the agreement to debate

---

64 "Oath," *IDB* 3.577.

peaceably, is a "pledge" (*sacramentum*) to the church. In early Latin Christian writings, *sacramentum* was the translation for the Greek μυστηριον, "mystery," and was associated with the Eucharist. Here it is used in its nontechnical sense of "pledge, oath, solemn promise." This is confirmed by the word for "pledge" in S, *'rb'*, "security, bail, pledge," which has no overtones of μυστηριον.

Gamaliel ends his remarks by urging "each one of you," the believers in Jesus, to speak what he has learned. He also urges that "we," the priests and multitude, listen. As the debate is about to start, Gamaliel seems to withdraw his insistence on the mutual nature of speaking and learning, which leads to the suspicion of Caiaphas.

1.68.1 (L) *In saying these things, Gamaliel did not greatly please Caiaphas. Seemingly holding him suspect, he began to insert himself subtly into the disputations.* (2) *For smiling at what Gamaliel had said, the chief of the priests asked James, the chief of the bishops, that the conversation about the Christ be drawn from no other place but the Scriptures.*	(S) *When Gamaliel said these things, Caiaphas was not much pleased. I thought he supposed something in his mind against him, and took it upon himself to probe and question.* (2) *As if quietly mocking Gamaliel and James the head bishop, the chief of the priests asked that the debate and disputation about the Messiah be drawn only from Scripture.*

The remarks of Gamaliel called upon the church to begin the debate. But Caiaphas, suspicious of Gamaliel, "began to insert himself into the disputations" (L) / "took it upon himself to probe and question" (S). He redirects the course of the discussion by asking about its scriptural sources. Caiaphas draws James into the discussion, and James will be from this point on the sole spokesman for the church.

A striking expression is found in "the chief of the bishops" (*episcoporum princeps*) / "the head bishop" (*ryš 'psqwp'*). Elsewhere throughout the *AJ*, James is the only leader in the only church, that of Jerusalem, and no other "bishops" have been mentioned. Thus, we should not interpret this expression in the light of the later "archbishop." "Archbishop" was first given in the fourth century to the prelates of important sees, one of which was Jerusalem, and then was given to a bishop set over other bishops.[65] The *AJ* uses "chief / head bishop" in a non-technical sense to put James on an even standing with Caiaphas, "the chief of the priests." L shows this more clearly, by using *princeps* of both James and Caiaphas. In S, James is the *ryš*, "head," bishop, and Caiaphas is the *rb*, "chief," priest.

1.68.3-4 *Then James said, "First we must inquire from what Scriptures we are principally to have the disputation." (4) Then, after he was with difficulty finally overcome by reason, he answered that it must be had from the law; and after this he also made mention of the prophets.* (L). This passage follows up consistently on 1.68.2. There, it is decided that the debate on Jesus be from the Scriptures. Here in 1.68.3-4, the topic is "from what Scripture" it is to be held. "He" in 1.68.4 is Caiaphas.

1.69.1. *James likewise spoke in his speech about the prophets, and showed that everything they said was taken from the law, and is truly in agreement with the law* (S). 1.69.1 continues the topic of 1.68.4. While the law is to be the focus of the debate, the prophets' testimony about Jesus is also to be considered, because what they said is "taken from the law" and agrees with it. No text from the law is cited explicitly here, nor will any from the prophets and writings be cited. Perhaps Deut 18:15-19 is in view, given its role as the key messianic text earlier in the *AJ*, but this can only be a conjecture.

.2 *He also made some comments about the Books of Kingdoms, how and when and by whom they were written, and how they ought to be used.* (L). The beginning of 1.69.2 indicates that a new topic is being introduced. This topic is "the Books of Kingdoms" (*libris regnorum, ktb' dmlkwt'*). "The Books of Kingdoms" is the LXX title of the four books known in the MT as First and Second Samuel and First and Second Kings. In the MT, these are the third through sixth books of the (Former) Prophets. In the LXX, on which the *AJ* draws here, the Books of Kingdoms are "history"; that is, they are Writings, not Prophets. That the *AJ* draws on the LXX is a firm piece of evidence

---

65 See the references under *episcopus* and *archiepiscopus* in the *Latin Dictionary* and the *Oxford Latin Dictionary*. See also A. Souter, *A Glossary of Later Latin* (Oxford: Clarendon, 1949) 22, and the many references in the *Thesaurus Linguae Latinae* (Leipzig: Tuebner, 1906) 1.461.

that the community of the *AJ* was Greek-speaking, and that the *AJ* was written in Greek.

James has said about the prophets that they are in accord with the law (1.69.1). Of the Books of Kingdoms, he now argues about "how and why and by whom they were written," and how they ought to be "used" (interpreted). This is not a bit of early higher criticism of Scripture. Rather, in the light of the context, it is an effort to point the Books of Kingdoms to Jesus as Messiah. They "ought to be used" to establish this point. Thus, James has now argued that the Law, the Prophets and the Writings, i.e., the whole Scripture, testifies to Jesus as Messiah.

1.69.3 *And when he had discoursed fully about the law ... he showed by most abundant arguments that Jesus is the Christ* (L). James returns to the law, and shows how it points to Jesus as Messiah. "Most abundant arguments" (L) / "great arguments without measure" (S) indicates that this was the main part of his speech and its culmination. The point of James' remarks is that Jesus is the Messiah, the same point argued in the debate of 1.55-65.

.4 *For there are two comings of him: one in humbleness, in which he has come; but the second in glory, in which he will come and rule over those who believe in him, who do all these things that he commanded* (S). At the end of 1.69.3 and through 1.69.4, a new point is introduced: Jesus has two comings.[66] The first is characterized by humility, the second by glory. In L, the "glory" of the second coming is Jesus' bringing of the kingdom of heaven and giving it to believers. In S, Jesus is said to "rule over those who believe in him."

Although Rehm and Strecker do not mention it, "observe everything that he commanded" (L) / "do all those things that he commanded" (S) is drawn from Matt 28:20, "observe all that I have commanded." This verse immediately follows the triadic formula of baptism in 28:19. The *AJ* must have been familiar with the ending of Matthew to draw on 28:20, yet it can ignore the triadic formula in favor of baptism "in the name of Jesus."

1.69.5-7, as we have shown above (p. 38), does not belong to the *AJ* source, which resumes in section eight.

---

66 The idea that Jesus has two comings is also shared by Justin (*Dial.* 37, 52, 110-1), who is generally credited with being the first to introduce it.

1.69.8 He also said many things about the Paraclete and baptism, and persuaded all the people with the chief priest through seven complete days that they should immediately hasten and come now for baptism (S). The mention of "the Paraclete" in S is an interpolation that goes with 1.69.7, in which L mentions "the Paraclete." The *AJ* does not mention the Holy Spirit or this Johannine term for the Spirit.

James speaks for seven successive days, which is symbolic of the fullness of his speech. In these seven days, he convinced the high priest and the people of the truth of the believer's faith in Jesus, and brought them to the point of baptism. James has now done what the Twelve could not do.

The brevity of James' speech is notable. It has no development of its themes, and no attack on sacrifice or the temple. While baptism is not explicitly urged as the replacement of sacrifice, the understanding of baptism in James' speech is consonant with 1.33-65. James' speech shares the main theme of the rest of the *AJ*: Jesus is the Messiah.

1.70.1 (L) *When the matter was at the point that they would come and be baptized, a certain hostile man, entering the temple at that time with a few men, began to shout and say, (2) "What are you doing, O men of Israel? Why are you so easily led away? Why are you led headlong by men who are most miserable and deceived by a magician?"*	(S) *Then a certain man who was an enemy came into the temple and toward the altar, while shouting and saying, (2) "What are you doing, O men of Israel, that you are so quickly carried off by miserable men who go astray after a magician?"*

Just as the high priest and people were about to be baptized, someone enters the temple shouting protests. This man is described in L as *homo quidam inimicus*, "a certain hostile man," and in S as *hd 'nš d'ytwhy hw' b'ldbb'*, "a certain man who was an enemy." The enemy evidently has heard about the debate and the success of James, and has come in at the crucial moment to disrupt James' efforts.

The wording of the enemy's shout is given as three questions by L, and one in S, but the content is the same. He charges that the "men of Israel" are being too easily persuaded by those who are "deceived by" (L) / "go astray after" (S) a "magician." This magician is not Simon, but Jesus.[67] The expressions "deceived" and "go astray" are the same encountered earlier in the *AJ* at 1.62.1, and they are similarly used here.

The striking term "enemy" will recur in 1.70.8 and 1.71.3. Outside the *AJ*, it is found in *R* 1.73.4, and in a most important passage in *EpPet* 2.3, where Peter speaks of the "lawless and absurd preaching of the man who is my enemy." In all PsCl, this enemy is never named. (Some see a veiled reference to this enemy in Matt 13:28.) Strecker, *Judenchristentum*, 249, argues from its presence in 1.73.4 that "the enemy" has been planted in *R* 1.70-71 by *G*, who obtained it from the *KerygmataP*. This is corroborated by the *AJ*'s other (nontechnical) use of "enemy" earlier in 1.57.1 (S), where a Samaritan is called an enemy of the Jews. The rest of the treatment of this man in 1.70-71 is peculiar to the *AJ*.

1.70.3 *he was overcome by James* (L) / *he heard James ... overcoming them* (S). Even as the enemy shouts his charge, James effectively refutes it. Realizing that he is losing his argument with James, the enemy disrupts the proceedings by "dissensions" (L) / a "great tumult" (S). Thus the people could not hear or examine James' reply.

.4 (L) *At the same time he accused the priests, and inflamed them by revilings and reproaches, and like a madman incited everyone to murder.*	(S) *Then he shouted even more about the foolishness and feebleness of the priests, and reviled them.*

Unable to disturb James, the enemy reviles the priests. L does not give the content of these insults, while S says that the enemy calls the priests foolish and feeble. His aim is to "incite everyone [of the priests] to murder" (L).

---

67 Other strata of PsCl consistently portray Simon, not Jesus, as the magician who opposed the church. On the history of the Simon tradition, including PsCl, see especially G. Lüdemann, *Untersuchung zur simonianischen Gnosis* (GTA 1; Göttingen: Vandenhoeck & Ruprecht, 1975). See also K. Beyschlag, *Simon Magus und die christliche Gnosis* (WUNT 16; Tübingen: Mohr, 1974).

1.70.5 (L) *"What are you doing? Why are you stopping? O sluggish and idle ones, why do we not lay our hands on them, and dismember them all?"*

(S) *"Why do you delay? Why do you not immediately seize all of them who are with him?"*

"You" is the priests, whom the enemy urges to attack the believers. In S, "him" has no antecedent, but from what follows James is apparently meant. The L form of section five is more developed than S. The priests are urged by the enemy to "lay our hands on them and dismember them all." The expression "lay our hands on them" recalls the promise of Gamaliel in 1.67.3 to prevent just such an attack.

.6 *When he had said these things, he first jumped up and seized a brand from the altar, and began to strike with it* (S). After his shouts to the priests, the enemy goes into action. He seizes "a brand from the altar" and uses it in striking the believers. In the MSS of L, several different words for "brand" appear (*fustis, torris ustor, reustor*), of which the last is the best-attested. The S assists in fixing the meaning of this word: *'wd'* is "a brand, fire-stirrer, oven rake." This brand was, therefore, an instrument for tending the altar fire.[68] It is implied to be of such a weight and size that it could be used by the enemy as a deadly weapon. In the L of 1.70.6, the evil nature of the enemy's lethal action is underlined by "murder."

---

68 Cf. Exod 27:3, 38:3; Num 4:4; I Kings 7:40, 45; II Chron 4:11, 16. In these passages the altar instruments are described as bronze.

1.70.7 (L) *Others also, when they saw him, were carried away by a similar madness. (8) There was loud shouting by all, by the murderers and the murdered alike. Much blood flowed. There was a confused flight, during which that hostile man attacked James, and threw him down headlong from the top of the steps. As he believed him to be dead, he did not care to beat him further.*

(S) When the rest of the priests saw him they did likewise. (8) Many were in flight, and some were falling by the sword. Some of them were consumed, and many died. Much blood of those killed was shed. That enemy threw James from the top of the stairs, and when he fell he was as dead, so he did not strike him a second time.

The priests follow the enemy's example, and a riot ensues. The order of the events of this riot vary from L to S, but they are the same in content: a violent attack on the believers, in which some of them died; a great amount of bloodshed; a flight from the temple by some; and an attack upon James by the enemy. To judge from the last clause in 1.70.8, the enemy first struck James with the brand, then threw him down the stairs.[69] Because he believed that James was dead, he did not strike him again. His intent was to kill James, and in this he wrongly supposed himself successful. He certainly *was* successful in preventing the whole people and the priests from coming for baptism.

---

69 For reasons of space, we cannot enter here into the complex question of the literary relationship of this passage with other traditions of the death of James. On this question, see especially D. H. Little, "The Death of James, the Brother of Jesus" (Ph.D. dissertation, Rice University; Ann Arbor: University Microfilms, 1971) and G. Lüdemann, *Paulus*, 2.99-102, 231-7. I hope in a subsequent work to give a full treatment of James in the history and tradition of early Christianity.

1.71.1 (L) *But our colleagues lifted him up, for they were both more in number and greater in strength than the others. But because of their fear of God, they allowed themselves to be slain by the few father than slay others.*

(S) *When they saw what had happened to James, they came up and rescued him. For although they were more numerous than them, because of their fear of God they would much rather endure killing than kill [others]. Although they were greater and stronger than them, because of their fear of God they were seen as fewer.*

The believers, seeing what happened to James, pick him off the temple floor and in 1.71.2 will carry him out of the temple. This "rescued him" (S) from further danger. At this point the riot ends.

But why, if the believers were "more in number and greater in strength" (L) / "more numerous" (S) than the other Jews, could they be so thoroughly beaten in this riot? The *AJ* answers this in the next part of 1.71.1. "Because of their fear of God," i.e., their faith, they would rather be killed than fight back and kill others. Therefore, they submitted to the violence led by the enemy, until they could flee the temple with James. The *AJ* does not offer any detail on what in their "fear of God" would lead to this. Perhaps it is related to the teaching of Jesus on non-retaliation toward violence (Matt 5:38-42; Luke 6:29-30), but no evidence can be adduced to demonstrate this. S adds that this willingness to submit to violence resulted in the believers being wrongly seen as "fewer" than the other Jews, even though "they were greater and stronger than them."

1.71.2 *But when evening came, the priests closed the temple. We returned to the house of James, and after passing the night there in prayer, we went down before the light to Jericho, about five thousand persons* (L). When the priests closed the temple for the evening, the believers return to the house of James and pray there during the night. This is the same location and activity which preceded the speech of James (1.66.1). In both instances, prayer through the night intimates a major event to follow on the next day. In 1.71.2, this event is a mass movement of the church from Jerusalem to Jericho. That "we" means the whole church rather than just the Twelve is shown by the number "about five thousand," a number probably drawn from Acts 4:4. In both the *AJ* and Acts it is an approximate number of the whole church.

1.71.3 (L) *Then after three days one of the brothers came to us from Gamaliel, of whom we spoke before. He brought secret news to us, that the hostile man had received authority from Caiaphas the high priest (4) to pursue all who believe in Jesus and travel to Damascus with his letters, so that there also by using the help of unbelievers he might bring ruin to the faithful.*

(S) *After three days, one of the brothers came and reported to us ... Those priests who were with him were convinced that he should be as a priest in all their plans, because they did not know that he was a fellow-believer with us. He told us, therefore, that the hostile man had gone before the priests and asked Caiaphas the high priest to destroy all those who believe in Jesus. (4) He had gone to Damascus taking letters from them, so that there the unbelievers would help him destroy those who believe.*

Gamaliel appears once again as the protector of the church. Here he warns the believers of more danger from "the enemy." The wording and meaning of L and S differs here. In L, Gamaliel is mentioned by name. He sends a "brother" with the secret news of the enemy's plans. In S, Gamaliel is not mentioned by name, although the reader can easily understand that he is meant. (It is not necessary to suppose with Rehm, *Pseudoklementinen,* 48, that "Gamaliel" must have fallen out of S.) Also, Gamaliel himself brings this news to the church. S includes a curious explanation of how Gamaliel knew of the enemy's plans - although he was not a priest, the priests took him into their confidence.

The content of this secret information, that the enemy had gone to the high priest and obtained letters authorizing him to arrest the believers in Damascus, is drawn from Acts 9:12. The *AJ* adds three items. (1) The enemy is not just to arrest the believers, but "ruin" (L) / "destroy" (S) them. (2) The letters obtained would authorize the help of "unbelievers," i.e., Jews who did not believe in Jesus, to persecute the church. (3) He particularly wanted to go to Damascus because he believed Peter was there.[70] In this section it becomes plain to the reader who knows canonical Acts that "the enemy" is Saul / Paul.

1.71.5 (L) *About thirty days later he stopped while passing through Jericho to Damascus, when at that time we had gone out to the tombs of two of our brothers.* (6) *Each year these were whitewashed by themselves, a miracle by which the fury of many against us was held back, as they saw that we were held in memory by God.*

(S) *But after thirty days he passed by us there in Jericho < ... > to two of our brothers in the night in the place we had buried them, whose tombs were every year suddenly whitened.* (6) *And the anger of many was suppressed, as they knew that the sons of our faith were worthy of divine remembrance.*

Thirty days later, the enemy stopped in Jericho on his way to Damascus. The S MSS have a lacuna which can easily be filled from the context and from L. S probably read with words such as, "on his way to Damascus, when we had gone." When the enemy passed through Jericho, "we" the church (all five thousand?) had gone out to visit the tombs of two "brothers." These tombs were every year miraculously whitewashed, which showed divine approval on the life of these two believers, and by extension on the church. This miracle restrained those who would otherwise have vented their rage against the believers.

The practice of whitewashing tombs derives, not from a desire to remember the deceased, but from a desire to prevent the impurity that results when one steps on a grave (Num 6:6, 19:16). Whitewashing is not found in the OT, but is referred to in rabbinic law, to which Str-B 1.936-7 gives references. To judge from this passage, the *AJ* community observed this law of purity. Such observance is all the more remarkable for the NT usage of whitewashing, which employs this term in a strongly derogatory way (Matt 23:27-28; Luke 11:44; Acts 23:3).

---

70 Peter's name is in the third person although he is the speaker. This shows that the *G* redactor of the *AJ*, and the Recognitionist after him, failed to change "Peter "to "I," a firm evidence that the *AJ* source was not a first-person account by Peter.

Comment on R *1.66-71*

The final part of the *AJ* begins in 1.66.1-3 with the setting for a debate. While at the house of James, the church prays through the night for victory in the debate. In the morning the believers go up to the temple and stand in the same place as the debate of 1.55-65, on the steps. Next, in chap. 67, Gamaliel sets the terms of the debate, but does not mention its topic. In remarks that are lengthier than the speech of James in 1.69, he urges both sides to speak freely and listen willingly, and invites James to begin. Suspicious of Gamaliel, Caiaphas speaks next. An argument ensues in 1.68 between Caiaphas and James which sets the discussion's topic ("Is Jesus the Messiah?") and terms (from the Scriptures). 1.69 is the speech of James. He convinces all his hearers that Jesus is the Messiah, arguing from the law, prophets and writings, and brings them to baptism.

At that crucial point "the enemy" appears, and undoes all of James' hard-won gains (1.70). After his argument against James fails, he resorts to violence. The believers are attacked; James is assaulted by the enemy, and left for dead. The church then flees the temple, carrying James with them. In 1.71, the church leaves Jerusalem for Jericho. It avoids the enemy, who is travelling to Damascus to persecute the believers there. The *AJ* (as we have it in *R* 1) ends on a note of divine protection: by the miracle of the whitewashed tombs, the anger of the unbelievers was suppressed.

This ending raises the question of whether there was more in the *AJ* source that the redactor did not use. The *AJ* that we have isolated in *R* 1 runs smoothly and consistently from Abraham to the church's move to Jericho, and the redactor has likely used most, if not all, of this part of our source. The *AJ* probably did in fact begin with Abraham, but did it end with whitewashing? One could conjecture further material beyond the content of 1.71: a (false?) conversion of the enemy as he goes to Damascus; a move of the church back to Jerusalem; the further activity of James. These conjectures may pique the modern reader's curiosity, but no evidence can be adduced to demonstrate them. We must be content with the *AJ* source as we have it in *R* 1.

The content of 1.66-71 is in large measure summed up in two themes: the place of James, and anti-Paulinism. These two themes will be taken up again in the next chapter, but it would be well to sketch them briefly here in commenting on 1.66-71.

James is mentioned earlier in the *AJ*, in 1.43.3, where he is said to have been ordained bishop of the church by Jesus. His righteous administration causes the church to grow quickly. In 1.44, James receives oral reports from the Twelve about their activities. But the real emphasis on the pre-eminence of James comes in 1.66-71. His house seems to be the headquarters of the church (1.66.1, 1.71.2). In the temple proceedings of this section, James has the leading role and is the sole spokesman for the church. His office of "bishop" is restated in 1.66.2 and 1.70.3 (L). He is called, somewhat incongruously, the "head / chief" bishop (1.68.2). His is the primacy over the whole church, including the Twelve.

Anti-Paulinism is a new and major feature of this section of the *AJ*. "The enemy" is never named, but the *AJ* has so thinly veiled him that no name is needed. Everyone in the *AJ* community would know who the would-be murderer of James was. He is also charged with calling Jesus a magician and *mesith*, and he implies that the believers are also *mesithim*. The anti-Paulinism of the *AJ* is focused on the loss of the Jewish nation to the church. Paul is charged with sabotaging the believers' mission to their Jewish kin. It would have succeeded, and the Jewish nation been turned from sacrifice to baptism, were it not for this enemy. Therefore, Paul is by implication responsible for the continued disbelief of the Jews, which led to the tragic events of war, captivity and exile. Behind this story is the charge that by preaching his law-free Gospel, Paul prevented the conversion of the Jewish nation to Jesus.

CHAPTER FIVE

MAJOR ISSUES IN THE INTERPRETATION OF
THE ASCENTS OF JAMES

Drawing upon the commentary in Chapter Four, we now offer a synthetic treatment of the most important issues in the interpretation of the *AJ*: its christology, history, and community. In the course of this chapter we will also attempt to locate the *AJ* in the history of Christianity in the first and second centuries.

The Christology of The Ascents of James

Even the most casual reader of the *AJ* knows that its christology is paramount. The Prophet like Moses is the main topic in 1.33-44 and is central to the presentation of Israel's history. The two debates of 1.55-71 feature the status of Jesus as Messiah as the main question of discussion. In our treatment of the theology of the *AJ*, we will first examine several aspects of its christology, beginning with the titles of Jesus and their meaning.

Jesus is the Mosaic Prophet for three reasons. First, and most important for the *AJ*, he is the one who has come to complete the ministry of Moses. He came to abolish the rite of sacrifice, a concession considered never to have been a part of the law, substituting baptism in its place (1.36.1-2, 1.39.2).[1] Second, Jesus modelled his choice of first twelve and then seventy-two disciples after the action of Moses in choosing his "disciples" (1.40.4). Third, Jesus is the Prophet like Moses

---

1 Jesus is not said in the *AJ* to complete or fulfill the law, or give a new law. In fact, he does not alter the law in any way.

in that he performs miracles which are like those of Moses (1.41.4, 1.58.3). The Mosaic-Prophet christology is especially suited to a Jewish-Christian community like the *AJ*, as it stresses Jesus' ties to the OT and the Mosaic law. We noted, indeed, in Chapter Four that the *AJ* has the most highly developed use of the Mosaic Prophet in early Christian literature.

Two other christological titles also appear in the *AJ*. Jesus is called "Lord" twice in 1.43.3. Both uses of this term are absolute, and express Jesus' authority over the church. "Lord" for the *AJ*, to judge from these uses, means "Lord of the church." Another term, "the Son of Man," appears in 1.60.3. Used in the argument with the Baptist's disciples, this title seems to have no particularly eschatological aspect, as it does in the NT.

The *AJ* also mentions the pre-existence and incarnation of the Messiah. We have seen in the Commentary that "the eternal Messiah" (1.43.1) probably refers to the pre-existence of the Messiah from eternity past. In 1.60.7 it is said that Jesus "assumed a Jewish body" and "was born as a Jew." Here incarnation is emphasized, but pre-existence is implied. The *AJ* does not develop the motifs of pre-existence and incarnation beyond this. The pre-existent Messiah is not said to have had a role in creation, and the *AJ* does not attempt to relate the Messiah to God. The vocabulary used (the general term "eternal Messiah," "assume a body") does not seem to be drawn from the NT. The *AJ*'s doctrines of pre-existence and incarnation, undeveloped though they be, are used to argue for the Messianic status of Jesus, and thus have been integrated into the theme of the *AJ*. Given Jewish Christianity's generally "low" christology in the second and third centuries (where there is no belief in the pre-existence of Jesus), the belief of the *AJ* community in the pre-existence and incarnation of the Messiah is remarkable indeed.[2]

In conclusion, the *AJ* is a christological document. It affirms that "Jesus is the Messiah." Jesus is the Messiah because he is also the Mosaic Prophet, who comes to abolish sacrifice and put baptism in its

---

2 Other aspects of the *AJ*'s theology should be stated here. The *AJ* does not mention the Holy Spirit. This is surprising, if only because it draws so heavily on Acts, where the Spirit is prominent. Also, the doctrine of God is undeveloped, perhaps because the *AJ* focuses on Jesus as Messiah. But we should not expect the *AJ* to touch upon or develop every item of the belief of its community.

place. In 1.33-44 and 1.55-65, the Mosaic Prophet is in the foreground as the *AJ* argues that Jesus is the Messiah. In 1.66-71, the Mosaic Prophet drops from view, but Jesus as Messiah is still prominent. The emphasis throughout is on the *fact* of Jesus' messiahship, rather than on its *nature*. Those who believe in Jesus as Messiah and the rest of the Jewish nation are said to be agreed on the nature of messiahship - the Messiah will be the Mosaic Prophet. As the evidence indicates that the Prophet like Moses was not a major figure in Jewish messianic expectation,[3] it is unlikely that the *AJ* community and the greater Jewish community agreed on this point. Rather, it is more likely that this "agreement" reflects the (unfulfilled) wish of the *AJ* community that the greater Jewish community would accept its view of the Mosaic Prophet as the Messiah, and especially of Jesus as that Messiah.

While the *AJ* contains comparatively few references to baptism, these few are important. In 1.39.2-3, proof that baptism is the replacement of sacrifice is said to lie in the salvation from war of those who have believed and been baptized. Baptism is attacked in 1.55.3-4 by the high priest as against sacrifice. Finally, in 1.69.8 - 1.70.1, James persuades all the priests and people to believe in Jesus as Messiah, and brings them to baptism, which will complete the process of conversion. Baptism now conveys in reality what sacrifice formerly was believed to convey: the forgiveness of sins. It is done "in the name of Jesus" because Jesus, the Mosaic Prophet, gave it to complete Moses' work. While this witness to baptism in Jesus' name is preserved only in L, we saw that it likely lies behind S as well. Baptism as the replacement of sacrifice is, for early Christianity, unique to the *AJ*.

However, the *AJ*'s witness to baptism also has strong similarities to the practice of baptism in the Great Church. First, as A. Harnack noted, by the end of the second century baptism in the Great Church was primarily related to the forgiveness of sins.[4] Second, as in the Great Church, baptism is a once-for-all rite. Unlike the rest of the PsCl and other forms of Jewish Christianity, the *AJ* does not speak of baptism as repeated or followed through in daily washings.[5]

---

3 See the Note on 1.36.1, "A prophet like me."

4 Harnack, *History of Dogma* (7 vols.; New York: Scribners, 1961) 2.140.

5 In PsCl, ritual washing (sometimes called *baptismos* in *H*) was done before meals (*R* 1.19, 2.71, 4.3; *H* 8.2 9.23, 10.26), before praying (*R* 6.1; *H* 10.1, 11.1), and after sexual intercourse (*H* 11.30). In general, these ritual washings resemble those in Judaism. Epiphanius says of the Ebionites, "They also receive baptism, apart from their baptisms daily" (*Pan.* 30.16.1).

The *AJ*'s understanding of baptism leads us to consider its view of sacrifice. Passages with an anti-sacrificial animus abound in the *AJ*. Most of them are found in 1.35-39, where Moses is unable to abolish the ingrained sin of sacrifice, and so leaves it to his successor, the Mosaic Prophet. But this prophet was rejected, and like Moses was unable to end the sacrifices. The continuance of sacrifice led to the final and irrevocable destruction of the temple, the culmination of Israel's long history of disobedience.

But why, in the second half of the second century, should there be an argument about sacrifice? Did not the destruction of Jerusalem and the temple in AD 70 remove any possibility of sacrifice?[6] While sacrifice was indeed impossible at the time of the *AJ*, it was, to judge from the *AJ*'s polemic, still valued by the Jews with whom the *AJ* community was in contact. These Jews may even have argued that the temple was to be rebuilt and the sacrifices reinstituted. For example, the *Shemoneh Esreh* (Eighteen Benedictions) an early Jewish prayer which was recited daily, contains a petition in the thirteenth benediction for the rebuilding of the temple and the restoration of the temple service and sacrifice.[7] That the Jewish community as a whole continued to value the temple long after its destruction is evidenced in abundance in the Mishnah and Talmuds. They describe the temple and its sacrifices in great detail, at times with no more recognition of the cessation of sacrifice than the occasional use of the past tense.[8] Even today, the most sacred site in Judaism is the only portion of the temple that remains, the Western ("Wailing") Wall.

---

6 While most historians hold that the temple cultus was swept away in AD 70, K. W. Clark ("Worship in the Jerusalem Temple after A.D. 70," *NTS* 6 [1959-60] 269-80) has argued that some sacrifice may have continued beyond 70. This has not met with much approval, and Clark himself admitted that the cult could not have continued much after 135, when the Jews were banished from Jerusalem and a temple to Jupiter was erected on the site of the Jewish temple. The *AJ* clearly was written in a time when sacrifice had ended.

7 See especially the thirteenth benediction. On the Benedictions as a whole, see K. G. Kuhn, *Achtzehngebet und Vaterunser und der Reim* (Tübingen: Mohr, 1950).

8 E.g., see the Mishnaic tractate *Zebahim*, "Animal Offerings." Cf. also the statement of G. W. E. Nicklesburg (*Faith and Piety in Early Judaism* [Philadelphia: Fortress, 1983] 86): The collectors of the Mishna, the Tosephta and the Talmuds devoted a whole division in each of these works to *Kodashim*, or 'hallowed things,' in which they preserved laws about the temple, its measurement, and the operation of its cult ... They transmitted this material not simply as a remembrance of the past, but also in the hope of a future restoration of the temple and its cult."

Moreover, the *AJ* is not alone in describing the temple cult as still existing. Several other early Christian documents that were written after AD 70 describe the sacrificial cultus as continuing (e.g., Hebrews, *I Clem.* 32.1-2). In Jewish literature, Josephus can describe the temple and its sacrifices as if they still existed (*Ant.* 3.9.1-4 §224-36), although in his *Jewish War* he chronicles in detail the complete destruction of the temple.

Where did the anti-sacrificial animus of the *AJ* originate? Schoeps has argued that it grew along a path through Israelite history. It began with the Rechabites, was continued by some key prophets (Amos, Jeremiah), passed into Essenism, was shared by Jesus and the earliest church, and thence came to the *AJ*.[9]

But the evidence tends to indicate that the *AJ*'s anti-sacrificial animus did not come by this route. First, the *AJ* looks negatively on the wilderness experience of Israel (1.35.3-6), and thus does not agree with the Rechabites' idealization of Israel's wilderness experience (Jeremiah 35). Second, the Essenes of Qumran did not reject sacrifice in principle; they organized themselves along a sacerdotal model. Their quarrel was not so much with temple or sacrifice as with the particular priests who administered the temple, and the way they ran it.[10] Third, the Synoptic tradition does not portray Jesus as inimical in principle to sacrifice and temple. Even Jesus' driving out of the money-changers from the temple is more a "cleansing" of the temple than an attack on it.[11] The Fourth Gospel is more negative toward the temple, stating that Jesus will replace it with his own body and spiritual worship, but it does not imply that the temple was condemned from the start.[12] Finally, the earliest church, as depicted in Acts, seems to have been

---

9 Schoeps, *Jewish Christianity*, 118-21.

10 B Gärtner (*The Temple and the Community in Qumran and the New Testament* [SNTSMS 1; Cambridge: University Press, 1965] 18-21) points to many passages in the Qumran literature that both sharply criticize and are appreciative of the temple and its offerings. Fitzmyer, "Scrolls," 362, concludes on the relationship of Qumran and the Jewish-Christianity of PsCl, "The radical difference of outlook here between the two sects prevents us from saying that the Ebionite attitude developed out of that of Qumran." All the evidence Fitzmyer adduces for the "Ebionite" attitude to sacrifice comes from the *AJ*.

11 See the accounts in Matt 21:12-3; Mark 11:15-7; and Luke 19:45-6, noting the phrase "my [i.e., God's] house."

12 See John 2:13-22; 4:19-24.

positive toward the temple. It worshipped and gathered there, and probably participated in the sacrifices.[13] Thus, Schoeps's explanation of the anti-sacrificial animus of the *AJ* is not convincing.

Other early Christian documents and one Jewish document have a type of anti-sacrificial animus that can arguably be related to the *AJ*. We will briefly examine Hebrews, the *Epistle of Barnabas*, the *Epistle to Diognetus*, and Book Four of the *Sibylline Oracles* to test this claim.

The theology of the Epistle to the Hebrews has often been related to Stephen and the Hellenists, most notably by W. Manson.[14] Hebrews endeavors to show the superiority of Christianity over Judaism to those who are tempted to return to Jewish beliefs and practices, or perhaps to some mixture of Christianity and Judaism. It opposes the cult of sacrifice (9:11 - 10:18), especially by saying that the death of Jesus is the sacrifice to end all sacrifices (7:27). Hebrews accepts the tabernacle as a copy of the heavenly pattern shown to Moses (8:5), and the sacrifices of the Old Covenant are accepted as a type of the death of Jesus, the real High Priest. All this is absent from the *AJ*. The characteristic radicalism of Stephen and the *AJ* about the temple and its sacrifices is not to be found in Hebrews. It may have been influenced by traditions from Stephen and the Hellenists, but Hebrews is not in a line of development between Stephen and the *AJ*.

The Epistle of Barnabas dates from the first half of the second century, and is usually said to have been written in Alexandria. *Barnabas* has some similarities to Acts 7, especially an anti-temple animus. L. W. Bernard uses this to argue that it is a successor of Stephen.[15] *Barnabas* uses allegory to deny all the peculiar institutions of Judaism; they were meant allegorically, but the Jews mistakenly took them literally. Moreover, a false angel deceived them to accept a literal law of circumcision, which is now abolished (9:4-9). *Barnabas* rejects the whole law as "their [i.e., the Jews'] law." It urges rejection of those who say, "The covenant is both theirs and ours," because the Jews never received it (4:6-8; cf. 13:14). Those Christians who keep the law are "shipwrecked" (3:6). Like Hebrews, *Barnabas* can also call the death

---

13 See Acts 2:46, 3:1, 5:2; cf. also Luke 24:53.
14 Manson, *Epistle to the Hebrews* (London: Hodder & Stoughton, 1951) 25-36.
15 Bernard, "St. Stephen and Early Alexandrian Christianity," *NTS* 7 (1960) 31-45.

of Jesus a sacrifice (7:3). Its anti-temple polemic results from its overwhelming anti-Judaism. *Barnabas* rejects all forms of Jewish Christianity, whether that of Stephen or the *AJ*. It most probably is not a successor of Stephen[16] or a direct precursor of the *AJ*.

The Epistle to Diognetus is an anonymous apologetic work of uncertain provenance usually dated in the late second century. It argues that Christianity is superior to Greco-Roman paganism and Judaism. In its argument against Judaism, *Diognetus* rejects sacrifices, saying that they are no better than idol-worship (3:5). It also rejects food laws, Sabbath observance and circumcision (4:1-6). While it shows no knowledge of Jewish Christianity, *Diognetus* would surely have rejected its combination of Judaism and Christianity, especially the close association of the two faiths that we have in the *AJ*.

The Fourth Book of the *Sibylline Oracles* is a Jewish work generally dated at the end of the first century AD and placed by some in Egypt and others in lower Syria.[17] Like the *AJ*, the *Fourth Sibyl* is anti-temple and anti-sacrifice (vv 27-30). It advocates a baptism of repentance: "Ah, wretched mortals . . . do not lead the great God to all sorts of anger, but abandon daggers and groanings, murders and outrages, and wash your whole bodies in perennial rivers" (162-5). J. J. Collins remarks that "Baptism and repentance functionally replace the temple cult in Sib IV,"[18] but this is never explicit. While baptism in the *Fourth Sibyl* is expressly for repentance, the *AJ*'s is for belief and forgiveness, but with no explicit mention of forgiveness. Still, the parallels between these two documents are remarkable. Collins's suggested provenance of the *Fourth Sibyl*, from a Jewish baptist sect in the Jordan Valley, is a provenace close to the *AJ*'s. Moreover, the *Fourth Sibyl* provides a crucial evidence that the strong anti-sacrifice, pro-baptism teaching of

---

16 J. Bihler (*Die Stephanusgeschichte* [MTS 16; Munich: Huebner, 1963] 245) states, "Man kann deshalb auch nicht behaupten, dass die Haltung gegenüber den Tempel in Apg 7 und in Barn 16 identisch sei. Vor allem fehlt in Apg 7 jeder Ansatz zu einer Spiritualisierung der Kultusbegriffe."

17 For text and introduction, see J. H. Charlesworth, ed., *The Old Testament Pseudepigrapha* (2 vols.; Garden City, N.Y.: Doubleday, 1983) 1.381-9.

18 Collins, "The Place of the Fourth Sibyl in the Development of the Jewish Sibyllina," *JJS* 25 (1974) 378.

the *AJ* has some reflection in the Judaism roughly contemporary with it.

The closest parallel to the thought of the *AJ* is Acts 7, the speech of Stephen.[19] Here we find the origin of the anti-sacrificial animus of the *AJ*. This is demonstrated by the many parallels between the Stephen speech and *R* 1.33-44, as noted in the Comment on that section in Chapter Four. Like Acts 7 alone, the *AJ* has a most radical attitude to sacrifice - it was never promulgated or approved by God, but is a remnant of idolatry. The *AJ* develops the Mosaic-Prophet christology of Acts 7 by integrating it with opposition to sacrifice: the Mosaic Prophet comes to abolish sacrifices.

What is the relationship of the anti-sacrifice and anti-temple polemic of the *AJ*? The reader of the *AJ* notes many more statements against sacrifice than statements against the temple. Moreover, most anti-temple statements do not appear alone, but are associated with anti-sacrificial polemic. The *AJ* demands an end of sacrifice, but does not demand that the temple be dismantled. When the temple was destroyed, it was to end sacrifice. Another key indication that the *AJ* is not anti-temple *per se* is the church's going to the temple to debate. That the *AJ* portrays the early church as unwilling to sacrifice, but willing to enter the temple, confirms that the *AJ*'s anti-temple feeling is probably derived from its anti-sacrifical animus.

The Historicity of The Ascents of James

The *AJ* has a strong interest in history. It presents a historical narrative of the life of the people of God from Abraham through the early church. Yet its version of early church history differs markedly from those presented in the NT. In regard to the historicity of the *AJ*, three main topics call for discussion: the temple debates; anti-Paulinism; and the pre-eminence of James.[20]

Many factors weigh against the historicity of the temple debates in 1.55-71. First, the debate of 1.55-65 has a very stereotyped format, as

---

19 Cf. the judgment of L. Gaston (*No Stone on Another* [NovTSup 23; Leiden: Brill, 1970] 160-1): "The only real parallel to Stephen's thought is the Ebionites of the pseudo-Clementines. Apart from Stephen, the Ebionites do not seem to have inherited much from the Jerusalem church."

20 Schoeps, *Jewish Christianity*, 39-46, has argued that these three elements of the *AJ*'s portrayal of the early church are accurate, despite that fact that the *AJ* is on the whole a "false narrative."

we noted in Chapter Three. This format would be highly improbable in such an emotionally charged atmosphere as we have in these chapters. Second, the *AJ* says that the whole church goes up to the temple for debate. However, it would be physically impossible for the church (a majority of the Jews!) to fit in the temple sanctuary where the debate takes place. Third, the place in which the *AJ* locates the debates is reserved for priests and Levites, but the *AJ* seems to understand that the general public has access to it. Fourth, the Samaritans are said to take part in the debate of 1.55-65; but they would not be admitted to the temple, even if they tried (which is itself doubtful). Fifth, only with great difficulty, if at all, could the normal worship of the temple be maintained during such debates as we have in the *AJ*. Indeed, the impression is given that the high priest and the other priests devote all their attention to the debates. Finally, in a Note on 1.66.1 we saw as improbable the assertion that the temple was open to the public "from the middle of the night." The cumulative effect of these factors indicates that the temple debates of 1.55-71 have no good claim to historicity.

Next, we will consider the *AJ*'s attack on Paul. Paul is blamed with causing the failure of the mission to the Jewish nation. Is this accusation accurate?

The *AJ* community's effort to convert Jews may indeed have been hindered by the law-free gospel of the Great Church, a gospel which Paul likely symbolized to the *AJ* community. But the main portrait of Paul in 1.70 is most probably not historical. No other early Christian text speaks of Paul's attack on the church in the temple. Aside from this, the NT offers two witnesses that bear upon the question of Paul's responsibility for the failure of the mission to the Jews: Acts 21 and Romans 9-11.

In Acts 21:17-26, James and the elders report to Paul that "many thousands . . . among the Jews" have believed in Jesus. They are "all zealous for the law," and have heard that Paul's mission has taught Jews in the Diaspora to neglect law observance (vv 20-1). This has caused distress among law-observant believers in Jerusalem. But it is also apparent that Paul's activity has not done any substantial harm to the mission among the Jews, as James and the elders can speak proudly to Paul of "how many thousands" of the Jews have believed. In Acts 21, James does not blame Paul for the difficulty or failure of the mission to the Jews.

In Romans 9-11, Paul gives his view of the overwhelming failure of the mission to Israel. Rather than blaming it on himself, or on the law-free mission to the Gentiles, Paul attributes it to the mysterious purposes of God (9:6-33). "Israel's unbelief is not just a matter of human disobedience, but a divine hardening is involved."[21] Though zealous for the law, the Jewish nation as a whole has not come to faith (10:1-4). Yet God has not rejected Israel. A remnant has attained salvation (11:3-10), and the "stumbling" of the rest has brought salvation to the Gentiles. When "the fullness of the Gentiles comes in," "all Israel will be saved" (11:25-6). Remarkably, Paul and the *AJ* both relate the Gentile mission to the unbelief of Israel, but in other regards they are far apart.

In the *AJ*, the dominant explanation for the failure of the mission to the Jews is that only a few understand God's purposes in history for Israel, an explanation not found in Romans 9-11. The people did not turn from sacrifice in Moses' time, nor in the time of the Prophet like Moses. Moreover, even before Paul appears on the scene in 1.70 a Gentile mission is envisioned. It has a theological cause: the unbelief of the Jews necessitates a mission to the Gentiles to fill up the number shown to Abraham. This unbelief must be large, since to compensate for it the Gospel is to go "into all the world" (1.42.1 [L]; cf. 1.64.2). We may conclude, then, that while the end of the *AJ* wishes to blame Paul for the loss of the Jewish nation, this is inconsistent with other parts of the *AJ*, and is not supported by the NT.

Regarding the *AJ*'s portrait of the pre-eminence of James in the earliest church, three pieces of evidence show that this is not historical. First, the *AJ* contradicts itself by saying that James is the "head bishop" (1.68.2), when elsewhere in the *AJ* he is the *only* bishop mentioned. Second, the *AJ* states that James was ordained bishop of the earliest church by Jesus (1.43.3). However, no evidence from any other first or second century text indicates that Jesus ordained bishops.[22] Third, it follows from his ordination by Jesus that James is the leader of the church from the first. However, evidence from other early Christian sources indicates that James, when he appeared on the scene, shared

---

21 C. E. B. Cranfield, *Epistle to the Romans* (ICC; 2 vols.; Edinburgh: Clark, 1979) 574.
22 The usual pattern, which became a common understanding in the Great Church, was that Jesus chose the Twelve, and the Twelve ordained the first bishops (cf. *I Clem.* 42, 44.1-2). Irenaeus testifies to the apostolic ordination of the bishops of Rome and Smyrna (*Against Heresies* 3.3.2-4).

authority with the Twelve, who were the first leaders. This evidence comes not only from Gentile-Christian sources (Acts of the Apostles, Paul), but also from a key Jewish-Christian source, Hegesippus. As related in Eusebius' *Hist. eccl.* 2.22.1, Hegesippus says that it is the Twelve who make James bishop of Jerusalem.

Judged by modern standards of historicity, then, the *AJ* is indeed "false narrative," not (as Schoeps claims) in part, but in large measure. Its portrait of the life of the earliest church contradicts what is known from the NT and other early Christian literature. Indeed, that portrait is at some points internally inconsistent. Any claim to historicity, whether by Schoeps or others, must also be weighed against the late date of the *AJ* - at least one hundred years after the events which it ostensibly narrates - and the *AJ*'s marked dependence on the NT. In this imaginative narrative we can read the theology and history of the *AJ* community, but Schoeps's claim that the *AJ*'s portrait of the earliest church is mostly reliable is untenable.

This is not to say, however, that the *AJ* has no contribution to make to our knowledge of early Christian history. As a second-century text, it gives us several valuable pieces of information about developments in the second century. First, the *AJ* is the only second-century witness we possess to an organized group of disciples of John the Baptist, who proclaim their master as Messiah and are opponents of the church. Second, it is the earliest witness to the Jewish claim that Jesus raised himself from the dead by the power of magic.[23] Third, it offers corroboration for a law-observant mission to the Gentiles in the second century.[24] Fourth, the *AJ* contains the earliest attestation of the tradition that Jesus appointed seventy-two disciples.[25] Finally, it affirms that the Samaritans of the second century did not believe in the resurrection of the dead.[26]

More important than these specific items, the *AJ* offers a view of a particular Jewish-Christian community, to which we now turn.

---

23 See the Note on 1.42.4 for other references to this claim.
24 See Martyn, "Mission," for further references in PsCl to a law-observant mission to Gentiles.
25 See Metzger, "Disciples," for full references in the MS tradition to "seventy-two."
26 See the Note on 1.57.1.

The Community of The Ascents of James

In this section, we will examine three major issues on the community of the *AJ*: its law observance, its Jewish-Christian character, and its relationships with Judaism and other Christian churches.

Our commentary has uncovered numerous passages in the *AJ* where observance of the Mosaic law is viewed positively. By depicting the early church as law-observant, the *AJ* intimates that its community is also a law-observant one. We will now survey these passages, and see what they contribute to our understanding of the community of the *AJ*.

In 1.33.3-5 circumcision is described positively, and hence it is possible that the *AJ* community practiced this rite. This passage also shows an appreciation for the "purity" that circumcision entails. In 1.35.2 the *AJ* speaks positively about the giving of the law to Israel. The Mosaic Prophet who first appears in 1.35 does not at first seem to be related to law observance, but he does have ties to the law because of Moses' role as the lawgiver. In Jesus' teaching the work of Moses is completed, and sacrifice is ended. We have noted that the *AJ* sees nothing lacking in the law itself, but only in the Mosaic concession of sacrifice. That sacrifice is not in the law is strongly implied but not explicitly stated.

The *AJ*'s approach to sacrifice and the law can be compared with two other somewhat contemporary approaches, the first from Jewish Christianity, the second from Gnosticism. *R* 2.38-46, a passage which Strecker has assigned to the *KerygmataP* but in any event is Jewish-Christian, uses the theory of "false pericopes" to bring the OT into agreement with its understanding of the teaching of Jesus. All that denigrates God - sacrifice, anthropomorphism, etc. - was interpolated into the law after Moses' death. The teaching of Jesus is the criterion for discerning true pericopes from false, and expunging the latter.

Another approach to the law is shown in Ptolemy's *Letter to Flora*.[27] This letter, an example of Valentinian Gnosticism, divides the law into three parts. The first is the legislation of God, "pure and not mixed with inferiority." This is the Decalogue, which was rightly given by Moses, and affirmed and completed by Jesus. The second is the law

---

27 Found in Epiphanius' *Panarion* 33.3-7; English translations in R. Grant, *Gnosticism* (New York: Harper, 1961) 184-90, and in Williams, *Panarion*, 198-204.

which is "a work of injustice," filled with contradictions, which was destroyed by Jesus. This is the Mosaic law outside the Decalogue, in which sacrifices would be included. The third is that law which is "spiritual and transcendant, which the Savior transferred from the perceptible and phenomenal to the spiritual and invisible"; these are largely Jewish customs and feasts.

These two documents are similar to the *AJ* in their approach to sacrifice and law. The *KerygmataP*, like the *AJ*, argues that the teaching of Jesus is the key to correct what is wrong in Judaism. The *KerygmataP* holds that these faults are in the (falsified) law, while the *AJ* sees a lack (but no fault) in the dispensation of Moses after the law. The *Letter to Flora* also makes divisions between good and evil in the law, accepting the Decalogue and rejecting all else.[28] But the *AJ* makes no such divisions within the law. Instead, it argues a division between God's law and the concession granted by Moses. Thus, while the *AJ* does have certain remarkable parallels with these two documents, its understanding of the relationship of law and sacrifice marks it as distinctly different from them.

Other evidence that the *AJ* community was law-observant is found in 1.43.2. Here the only point of disagreement between those Jews who believe in Jesus and those who do not is said to be the messianic status of Jesus. This implies that the *AJ* community sensed no disagreement

---

28 This acceptance of the Decalogue and rejection of the rest of the Mosaic code was, independently of the struggle with Gnosticism, to become the characteristic position of the Great Church toward the Mosaic law. For example, according to Irenaeus the Decalogue is a part of the natural law; it was affirmed by Jesus, and is binding on all Christians (*Against Heresies* 4.8-16).

on keeping Torah, and sees itself as fully law-observant. The *AJ* community keeps the Passover (1.44.1). The *AJ* probably sees a "good life" and "an upright disposition" (1.55.4) as a law-observant life, even if this, apart from baptism, cannot bring salvation. In 1.60.4 giving and keeping the law is positively viewed; the people of God keep God's law. Jesus is received as "a teacher of the law" by the *AJ* community in 1.62.3. According to 1.68.4, the kingdom of heaven is given to those who believe in Jesus as Messiah and who observe his commandments. Here again Jesus is a teacher of the law, and his commandments are in accordance with the law. Finally, in the whitening of tombs, the *AJ* shows a concern for ritual purity according to the law of Moses (1.71.5-6). In conclusion, the evidence is clear and convincing that the *AJ* community was law-observant.[29]

Is it proper to call the community of the *AJ* "Jewish-Christian"? Here we encounter the problem of defining this term, a vexing issue in the history of research.[30] For our purposes in this study, "Jewish Christianity" is that part of early Christianity which was predominantly Jewish in membership, practice and belief.

As we saw in Chapter One, almost all researchers into PsCl, regardless of their understanding of the nature of Jewish Christianity,

---

29 *Pace* Lüdemann, *Paulus,* 2.243-4, who argues that the community of the *AJ* did not practice circumcision nor follow any laws of purity. We have argued that, even though the *AJ* does not explictly promote these, it has a positive view of them that makes their denial most unlikely. Moreover, it must be emphasized that the *AJ* never attacks any part of the law other than sacrifice. Unlike Justin, *Barnabas,* and other early Christian literature, it has no anti-circumcision or anti-sabbath polemic.

30 See the various attempts at definition, among many others, by Schoeps, *Theologie,* 1-14; J. Danielou, *Theology of Jewish Christianity* (Philadelphia: Westminster, 1984) 7-10; B. J. Malina, "Jewish Christianity or Christian Judaism," *JSJ* 7 (1970) 46-57; R. A. Kraft, "In Search of 'Jewish Christianity' and its 'Theology'," *RSR* 60 (1972) 81-92; A. F. J. Klijn, "The Study of Jewish Christianity," *NTS* 20 (1974) 419-31; and S. K. Riegel, "Jewish Christianity: Definitions and Terminology," *NTS* 24 (1978) 410-5. See also, most recently, R. E. Brown, "Not Jewish Christianity and Gentile Christianity but Types of Jewish / Gentile Christianity," *CBQ* 45 (1983) 74-9. Brown holds that the distinction between Jewish and Gentile Christianity, while of dubious validity when applied to NT times, "May be justifiable in the second century" (p. 75).

have seen the special source(s) of *R* 1.33-71 as Jewish-Christian. Only S. K. Brown has argued that the *AJ* is not Jewish-Christian (see above, pp. 21-22). Brown based his argument on his rejection of 1.43.2, which we have included in the *AJ*. But the evidence of the *entire AJ* shows that it does indeed witness to a Jewish-Christian community as we have defined it. In its membership, the church of the *AJ* is Jewish in ethnic origin; it promotes an identification with the Jewish people as "our people." In practice, the community of the *AJ* is composed of law-observant Jews. They keep Jewish feasts and customs; they may practice circumcision. In belief, they are Jewish-Christian as well. Their christology, that of the Mosaic Prophet, is rooted in Jewish belief. Moreover, the *AJ* has a knowledge of Jewish sects and rabbinic traditions not obtainable from the NT, but probably gained from close contact with Judaism. In conclusion, aside from its acceptance of Jesus as Messiah and what follows from it, the community of the *AJ* is one with Judaism. We can affirm, therefore, the judgment of J. L. Martyn on the *AJ*: "There is, in fact, no section of the Clementine literature about whose origin in Jewish Christianity one may be more certain."[31]

The relationship of the *AJ* community with Judaism is only partly revealed in its Jewish-Christian nature. While it has similarities with other Jews, it also has notable differences. First, the community of the *AJ* has been separated from other strands of Judaism. This is most apparent in the "we"/"they" distinction that surfaces in 1.40.3 and continues to the end of the *AJ*. Second, it is evident from 1.44.2, 1.62 and 1.70-71 that the community of the *AJ* has undergone persecution at the hands of Jewish authorities.

Why are the Essenes not mentioned in *R* 1 (or, for that matter, anywhere else in PsCl)? Schoeps has argued that the *AJ* draws on Essene tradition, especially its opposition to the temple. He sees a veiled reference to the Essenes in 1.37.5, "right opinion with liberty is the prerogative of the few" (L),[32] which we have identified in a Note on 1.37.5 as a wisdom saying. A simpler explanation accounts for the

---

31 Martyn, "Recognitions," 271. Martyn has suggested that, for such a community as that of the *AJ*, the term "Christian Jews" might be more appropriate than "Jewish Christians." "Christian Jews" would likely be in accord with the self-understanding of the *AJ* community, and one could also suggest that the term "Messianic Jews" would be appropriate. While there is value in questioning the adequacy of the general term "Jewish Christianity" in studying the *AJ*, we will adhere to the more common scholarly term.

32 Schoeps, *Jewish Christianity*, 119-20.

lack of mention of the Essenes. The Essene sect had been destroyed in the events of AD 66-70, a century before the writing of the *AJ*, and the *AJ* community therefore had no contact with it. Also, the NT has no explicit mention of the Essenes upon which the *AJ* could draw.

Next, we will consider briefly the relationship of the community of the *AJ* with other Christian churches. In varying degrees, leading Great Church authorities of the second century stigmatized Jewish Christianity as an intolerable diversity within the Christian movement. Ignatius of Antioch, in his *Epistles to the Magnesians* and *Philadelphians* (ca. 110), ruled out any possibility of combining faith in Christ and the practice of Judaism (*Magn.* 8-9, 10.3; *Phil.* 8.2). Although he did not use the term "heretical," he did approximate it by calling the combination of Judaism and Christianity "heterodoxy" (*Magn.* 8.1). Justin, in his *Dialogue* (ca. 150-160), distinguished two types of Jewish Christians. The first type urges law observance as necessary for all Christians, i.e., they hold that the only true Christianity is Jewish Christianity. The second type of Jewish Christians does not see universal law-observance as necessary; they affirm, at least in principle, the legitimacy of the Great Church. The former type of Jewish Christians will not see salvation, but the latter may (*Dial.* 47:1). By the end of the second century, Irenaeus brands all Jewish Christians as heretics (*Against Heresies* 1.26.2; 3.15.1; 5.1.3).

Would the *AJ* be considered unacceptable by the rigid approach to Jewish Christianity of Ignatius, or by the more tolerant approach of Justin?[33] Its christology probably would not be considered heterodox by late second-century theologians, as it features a rudimentary pre-existence christology and does not deny the Virgin Birth. But the *AJ*'s strong insistence on universal law-observance would put its community outside salvation, even by the standard of Justin.[34]

The *AJ* neither contains traces of Gnosticism nor betrays any contact with it. This is rather remarkable, since the second century saw the climactic battle between the church and gnosis. In his treatment

---

33 We say "would be considered" because there is no evidence that second-century Great Church fathers knew of the *AJ* community or its particular type of Jewish Christianity.

34 It was the rigid approach of Ignatius which became the norm in the Great Church of the third and fourth centuries, as the more tolerant standard of Justin was forgotten. Therefore, all forms of Christianity that were law-observant or bore the name "Jewish" or "Ebionite" were deemed *ipso facto* heretical. Epiphanius' *Panarion* 30 is the most notable example of this.

of Gnosis in Palestine and Syria, H. Koester claims that "the history of Jewish Christianity indicates how viable Gnosticism . . . was as a possibility of interpretation within the Christian tradition," especially in the christology of Jewish Christianity. He points to the *Gospel of the Ebionites* and to the *KerygmataP*'s gnostic concept of a True Prophet in suggesting that "a suitable milieu for the development of Jewish Gnosticism may have been the area of Syria and Palestine." Regardless of how one accepts Koester's claim that Gnosticism is a viable interpretation of earliest Christianity, the *AJ* is a testimony that Gnosticism may not have reached into every part of Jewish Christianity in Palestine and Syria.

What is the relationship of the theology of the *AJ* to later Jewish Christianity in PsCl? The differences between the type of Jewish Christianity in the *AJ* and that of other strata of PsCl were dealt with in Chapter Two, and there is no need to restate them here. But there must be some key similiarities as well, if only to explain why the *AJ* found its way into the *Recognitions*. Like the *AJ*, much of the rest of PsCl is anti-sacrificial and anti-Pauline. An insistence on law-observance is shared by the *AJ* and the rest of PsCl. While the Mosaic Prophet is not found outside the *AJ*, much of the christology of PsCl is a prophetic christology, featuring the True Prophet.

We have argued above that the *AJ* can properly be called a Jewish-Christian document. Is it Ebionite as well? Epiphanius describes it as an Ebionite book, but as Klijn and Reinink remark, "Epiphanius starts from the mistaken assumption that everything Jewish-Christian must be called Ebionite." [35] Many researchers from Hilgenfeld to Schoeps have applied this name to *R* 1.33-71. Here again we encounter a problem of definition. Like Epiphanius, Schoeps seems to call all Jewish Christianity "Ebionite." However, most modern researchers reserve this term for the more extreme forms of Jewish Christianity, especially those holding an adoptionist christology opposed to any form of pre-existence. An ideal of poverty is also characteristic of Ebionism. As the *AJ* has a form of pre-existence christology and shows

---

35 Klijn and Reinink, *Evidence*, 43. This tendency among heresiologists to label all Jewish Christianity "Ebionite" can be traced to Irenaeus' influential *Against Heresies* 1.26.2.

no evidence of adoptionism or an ideal of poverty, its community probably should not be considered Ebionite.

Finally, our conclusions on the community of the *AJ* have a bearing on the positions of J. Munck and S. G. F. Brandon on Jewish Christianity. They have argued that authentic Jewish Christianity did not survive the fall of Jerusalem in AD 70.[36] As Munck put it, "The Jewish Christianity to be found later in Palestine and Syria, including Pella, is of a new type, having no connexion with primitive Christianity."[37] We have shown in this study that one form of second-century Jewish Christianity does indeed have a strong connection with the primitive church, especially to the theology of Stephen and the Hellenist Jewish Christians depicted in Acts. While there is not enough evidence to conclude that the community of the *AJ* is the lineal *physical* descendant of the Hellenist Jewish Christians of Acts, it is certainly a *spiritual* descendant of Stephen and his circle. The position of Munck and Brandon, therefore, is in need of correction.

Summary and Conclusion

In this study, we have isolated a hypothetical source in *R* 1.33-71, and identified it as *The Ascents of James*. The *AJ* stems from a Greek-speaking Jewish-Christian community living probably in Transjordan, and can be dated in the second half of the second century. This community practices baptism in the name of Jesus and observes the law of Moses, of which circumcision is possibly a part. It exalts James as leader of the Jerusalem church, and denigrates Paul as the one who prevented the conversion of the whole Jewish nation to faith in Jesus as Messiah. It has been separated from the main body of Judaism by its belief in Jesus and from the Great Church by its insistence on law-observance. But the community of the *AJ* clings faithfully to its main belief, the one around which the *AJ* revolves: Jesus is the Prophet like Moses and Messiah.

---

36 Munck, "Jewish Christianity in Post-Apostolic Times," *NTS* 6 (1960) 103-16; Brandon, *Fall, passim.*

37 Munck, "Jewish Christianity," 104.

BIBLIOGRAPHY

Arnold, G. *Das heiligen Clementis von Rom Recognitiones. Nunmehr ins Teusche übersetzt mit einem Vorbericht.* Berlin: Rudiger, 1702.

Baronio, C. *Annales Ecclesiastici.* Frankfurt: Schonwetter, 1614.

Baur, F. C. *The Church History of the First Three Centuries.* London: Williams & Norgate, 1878.

--------. "Die Christuspartei in der Korinthischen Gemeinde, der Gegensatz des petrinischen und paulinischen Christentums in der ältesten Kirche, der Apostel Petrus in Rom." *Tübinger Zeitschrift für Theologie*, 1831, 61-206.

--------. "Über den Ursprung des Episcopats in der christlichen Kirche." *Tübinger Zeitschrift für Theologie*, 1838, 117-56.

Beyschlag, K. *Simon Magus und die christliche Gnosis.* WUNT 16. Tübingen: Mohr, 1974.

Bienaimé, G. *Moïse et le don l'eau dan la tradition juive ancienne.* AnBib 98. Rome: Biblical Institute, 1984.

Bigg, C. "The Clementine Homilies." *Studia Biblica et Ecclesiastica.* 2 vols. Oxford: Clarendon, 1890, 2.157-93.

Bihler, J. *Die Stephanusgeschichte.* MTS 16. Munich: Huebner, 1963.

Blidstein, G. J. "Nasi." *EncJud* 12.834-35.

Bousset, W. "Die pseudoklementinen Homilien und Rekognitionen." *Göttingische gelehrte Anzeigen* 167 (1905) 425- 47.

Bowman, J. "Early Samaritan Eschatology." *JJS* 6 (1955) 63-72.

Bright, J. *A History of Israel.* 3rd ed. Philadelphia: Westminster, 1981.

Brown, R. E. *The Gospel according to John.* 2 vols. AB 29, 29A. Garden City, N.Y.: Doubleday, 1966, 1970.

----------. "Not Jewish Christianity and Gentile Christianity But Types of Jewish/Gentile Christianity." *CBQ* 45 (1983) 74-9.

Brown, S. K. "James: A Religio-historical Study of the Relations between Jewish, Gnostic, and Catholic Christianity in the Early Period through an Investigation of the Traditions about James the Lord's brother." Ph.D. dissertation, Brown University. Ann Arbor: University Microfilms, 1972.

Bruce, F. F. *Peter, Stephen, James, and John.* Grand Rapids: Eerdmans, 1980.

Calvin, J. *The Acts of the Apostles.* 2 vols. Edinburgh: Oliver & Boyd, 1965.

Chapman, J. "On the Date of the Clementines." *ZNW* 7 (1908) 21-34, 147-59.

Clark, K. W. "Worship in the Jerusalem Temple after A.D. 70." *NTS* 6 (1959-60) 269-80.

Collins, J. J. "The Place of the Fourth Sibyl in the Development of the Jewish Sibyllina." *JJS* 25 (1974) 365-80.

Cotelier, J. B. *Ss. Patrum qui Temporibus Apostolicis Floruerunt.* 2 vols. Paris: Petri le petit, 1672.

Cranfield, C. E. B. *Epistle to the Romans.* 2 vols. ICC. Edinburgh: Clark, 1976, 1979.

Cullmann, O. *Christology of the New Testament.* Rev. ed. Philadelphia: Westminster, 1963

----------. *Le Probléme littéraire et historique du roman Pseudo-Clémentin.* Etudes d'Histoire et de Philosophe religieuses 23. Paris: Alcan, 1930.

Danielou, J. *Theology of Jewish Christianity*. Philadelphia: Westminster, 1984.

Daube, D. "Concessions to Sinfulness in Jewish Law." *JJS* 10 (1959) 1-13.

Dodwell, H. *Dissertationes in Irenaeum*. Oxford: Sheldonian Theatre, 1689.

Ellis, E. E. *Paul's Use of the Old Testament*. Edinburgh: Oliver & Boyd, 1957.

Enslin, M. S. "James, Ascents of." *IDB* 2.794.

Fitzmyer, J. A. "The Qumran Scrolls, the Ebionites, and their Literature." *TS* 16 (1955) 335-76.

Fortna, R. *The Gospel of Signs*. SNTSMS 11. Cambridge: University Press, 1970.

Frankenberg, W. *Die syrischen Clementinen mit griechischem Paralleltext*. TU 48,3. Leipzig: Hinrichs, 1937.

Gärtner, B. *Temple and the Community in Qumran and the New Testament*. SNTSMS 1. Cambridge: University Press, 1965.

Gaster, M. *Samaritan Eschatology*. N.p.: Search, 1932.

Gersdorf, E. G. *S. Clementis Romani Recognitiones*. Leipzig: Tauchnitz, 1838.

Ginzburg, L. *Legends of the Jews*. 7 vols. Philadelphia: Jewish Publication Society, 1925.

Glare, P. G. W. *Oxford Latin Dictionary*. Oxford: Clarendon, 1980.

Grant, R. *Gnosticism*. New York: Harper, 1961.

Hahn, F. *The Titles of Jesus in Christology.* Philadelphia: Westminster, 1965.

Hahn, J. *Das "Goldene Kalb".* Frankfort: Lang, 1981.

Harris, H. *The Tübingen School.* Oxford: Clarendon, 1975.

Harter, W. "The Causes and Course of the Jewish Revolt against Rome, 66-74 C.E., in Recent Scholarship." Ph.D. dissertation, Union Theological Seminary (New York). Ann Arbor: University Microfilms, 1984.

Headlam, A. C. "The Clementine Literature." *JTS* 3 (1902) 49-58.

Hereford, R. T. *Christianity in Talmud and Midrash.* London: Williams & Norgate, 1903.

Hilgenfeld, A. *Die clementinischen Recognitionen und Homilien.* Jena: Schreiber, 1848

--------. "Uber die Composition den klementinischen Recognitionen." *Theologische Jahrbücher*, 1850, 63-93.

--------. "Der Ursprung der pseudoclementische Recognitionen und Homilien, nach dem neusten Stand den Untersuchung." *Theologische Jahrbücher*, 1854, 483-535.

Hirsch, E. *Das vierte Evangelium.* Tübingen: Mohr, 1936.

Holl, K. *Epiphanius (Anacoratus und Panarion).* GCS 25. Leipzig: Hinrichs, 1915.

Horbury, W. "The Twelve and the Phylarchs." *NTS* 32 (1986) 503-27.

Hort, J. F. A. *Judaistic Christianity.* J. O. F. Murray, ed. London: Macmillan, 1894.

--------. *Notes Introductory to the Study of the Clementine Recognitions.* J. O. F. Murray, ed. London: Macmillan, 1901.

Hull, J. M. *Hellenistic Magic and the Synoptic Tradition.* SBT 28. London: SCM, 1974.

Irmscher, J. "The Pseudo-Clementines." E. Hennecke, *New Testament Apocrypha*, W. Schneemelcher, ed. 2 vols. Philadelphia: Westminster, 1963, 1965, 2.532-70.

Isser, S. J. *The Dositheans: A Samaritan Sect in Late Antiquity.* SJLA 17. Leiden: Brill, 1976.

Johnson, P. *A History of the Jews.* New York: Harper & Row, 1987.

Jones, F. S. "The Pseudo-Clementines: A History of Research." *SecCent* 2 (1982) 1-33, 63-96.

Jonge, M. de. "Het Motief van het gescheurde Voorhangsel van de Tempel in een antal vroegchristelijke Geschriften." *NedTTs* 21 (1967) 257-76.

----------. "Two Interesting Interpretations of the Rending of the Temple-Veil in the Testaments of the Twelve Patriarchs." *Bijdragen* 46 (1985) 350-62.

Klijn, A. F. J. "The Study of Jewish Christianity." *NTS* 20 (1974) 419-31.

Klijn, A. F. J., and Reinink, G. *Patristic Evidence for Jewish-Christian Sects.* NovTSup 36. Leiden: Brill, 1973.

Koch, G. A. "A Critical Investigation of Epiphanius' Knowledge of the Ebionites: A Translation and Critical Discussion of *Panarion* 30." Ph.D. dissertation, University of Pennsylvania. Ann Arbor: University Microfilms, 1987.

Koester, C. R. "The Tabernacle in the New Testament and Intertestamental Jewish Literature." Ph.D. dissertation, Union Theological Seminary (New York). Ann Arbor: University Microfilms, 1987.

Koester, H. *Introduction to the New Testament.* 2 vols. Philadelphia: Fortress, 1982.

Köstlin, R. "Die klementinischen Recognitionen und Homilien." *Allgemeine Literatur-Zeitung* (Halle), Nrs. 73-7, cols. 577-8, 585-608, 612-6.

Kraft, R. A. "The Study of 'Jewish Christianity' and its 'Theology'." *RSR* 60 (1972) 81-92.

Kuhn, K. G. *Achtzehngebet und Vaterunser und der Reim.* Tübingen: Mohr, 1950.

Lagarde, P. de. *Clementis Romani Recognitiones Syriace.* Leipzig: Brockhaus, 1861.

Langen, J. *Die Klemensromane.* Gotha: Perthes, 1890.

Lefevre d'Etaples, J. *Pro piorum recreatione et in hoc opere contenta . . . Epistola Clementis. Recognitiones Petri. Complementum Epistola Clementis. Epistola Anacleti.* Basel: Stephanus, 1504.

Lehmann, *Die clementinischen Schriften mit besonderer Rucksicht auf ihr literarisches Verhältniss.* Gotha: Perthes, 1890.

Lichtenberger, J. "Taufergemeinden und frühchristliche Tauferpolemik in letzten Drittel des 1. Jahrhunderts." *ZTK* 81 (1987) 36-57.

Lightfoot, J. B. *The Epistle of St. Paul to the Galatians.* London: Macmillan, 1865.

Lindemann, A. *Paulus im ältesten Christentum.* BHT 58. Tübingen: Mohr, 1979.

Lipsius, R. A. *Die apokryphen Apostelgeschichten und Apostellegenden.* 2 vols. Braunschweig; Schwetschke, 1887.

--------. *Die Quellen der römischen Petrus-Sage kritisch untersucht.* Kiel: Schwers, 1872.

Little, D. H. "The Death of James, the Brother of Jesus." Ph.D. dissertation, Rice University. Ann Arbor: University Microfilms, 1971.

Lüdemann, G. *Paulus, der Heidenapostel*, vol. 2: *Antipaulinismus im frühen Christentum*. FRLANT 130. Göttingen: Vandenhoeck & Ruprecht, 1983.

----------. "The Successors of Pre-70 Jerusalem Christianity: A Critical Evaluation of the Pella Tradition." *Jewish and Christian Self-Definition*. E. P. Sanders et al., eds. 3 vols. Philadelphia: Fortress, 1980-2, 1.161- 73.

----------. *Untersuchung zur simonianischen Gnosis*. GTA 1. Göttingen: Vandenhoeck & Ruprecht, 1975.

MacDonald, J. *Theology of the Samaritans*. London: SCM, 1974.

Maiberger, P. *Das Manna*. 2 vols. Wiesbaden: Harrassowitz, 1983.

Maier, J. *Jesus von Nazareth in der Talmudischen Überlieferung*. Darmstadt: Wissenschaftliche Buchgesellschaft, 1978.

Malina, B. J. "Jewish Christianity or Christian Judaism." *JSJ* 7 (1970) 46-57.

Manson, W. *The Epistle to the Hebrews*. London: Hodder & Stoughton, 1951.

Martyn, J. L. "Clementine Recognitions 1, 33-71, Jewish Christianity, and the Fourth Gospel." *God's Christ and His People: Studies in Honour of Nils Alstrup Dahl*. J. Jervell and W. Meeks, eds. Oslo: Universitets-forlaget, 1977, 265-95.

--------. *History and Theology in the Fourth Gospel*. Rev. ed. Nashville: Abingdon, 1979.

--------. "A Law-Observant Mission to Gentiles: The Background of Galatians." *SJT* 38 (1986) 307-23.

Metzger, B. M. "Seventy or Seventy-Two Disciples?" *Historical and Literary Studies: Pagan, Jewish and Christian*. NTTS 8. Grand Rapids: Eerdmans, 1968, 67-76.

Meyboom, H. U. *De Clemens-Roman.* 2 vols. Groningen: Wolters, 1902, 1904.

Mosheim, J. L. von. *Dissertatio de turbata per recentiores Platonicos ecclesia.* Published in R. Cudworth, *Systeme Intellectuale huius universi.* Jena: Meyer, 1733.

--------. *Institutes of Ecclesiastical History.* 2nd ed. 2 vols. London: Longmans, 1850.

Neander, J. A. W. *Genetische Entwicklung der vornehmsten gnostischen Systeme.* Berlin: Dummler, 1818.

--------. *A General History of the Christian Religion and Church.* 2 vols. Boston: Crocker & Brewster, 1872.

Nicklesburg, G. W. E. *Faith and Piety in Early Judaism.* Philadelphia: Fortress, 1983.

Payne-Smith, J. *A Compendious Syriac Dictionary.* Oxford: University Press, 1903.

Rehm, B. "Clemens Romanus II (PsClementinen)." *RAC* 3.197-206.

--------. *Die Pseudoklementinen II: Rekognitionen in Rufins Übersetzung.* GCS 51, 2. Berlin: Akadamie, 1965.

---------. "Zur Entstehung der pseudoclementinischen Schriften." *ZNW* 37 (1938) 77-184 .

Riegel, S. K. "Jewish Christianity: Definitions and Terminology." *NTS* 24 (1978) 410-5.

Rius-Camps, J. "Las Pseudoclementinas: Bases Filológicas para una Nueva Interpretación." *Revista Catalana de Theologia* 1 (1976) 79-158.

Ritschl, A. *Die Enstehung der altkatholischen Kirche.* Bonn: Marcus, 1851.

Roberts, A., and Donaldson, J., eds. *The Writings of Tatian and Theophilus; and the Clementine Recognitions.* ANF 3. Edinburgh: Clark, 1868.

Salmon, G. "The Clementine Literature." *Dictionary of Christian Biography.* W. Smith and H. Wace, eds. London: Murray, 1877, 1.567-78.

Schaberg, J. *The Father, the Son and the Holy Spirit: TheTriadic Phrase in Matthew 28:19b.* SBLDS 61. Chico, CA: Scholars, 1984.

Schliemann, A. *Die Clementinen nebst den verwandten Schriften und der Ebionitismus.* Hamburg: Perthes, 1844.

Schoeps, H. J. *Jewish Christianity: Factional Disputes in the Early Church.* Philadelphia: Fortress, 1969.

--------. "Das Judenchristentum in den Pseudoklementinen." *ZRGG* 11 (1959) 72-7.

--------. *Theologie und Geschichte des Judenchristentums.* Tübingen: Mohr, 1949.

Schürer, E. *The History of the Jewish People in the Age of Jesus Christ.* G. Vermes et al., eds. Rev. ed. 3 vols. Edinburgh: Clark, 1973-87.

Schwartz, E. "Unzeitgemässe Beobachtungen zu den Clementinen." *ZNW* 31 (1932) 151-99.

Scobie, C. H. H. *John the Baptist.* Philadelphia: Fortress, 1964.

Short, C. *Latin Dictionary.* Oxford: Clarendon, 1879.

Sichard, J. *Divi Clementis Recognitionum libri X ad Jacobum fratrem Domini Rufino Torano Aquil. interprete.* Basel: Stephanus, 1526.

Simon, M. "La Migration à Pella: Légende ou Réalité?" *RSR* 60 (1972) 40-52.

Simon, M.. *St. Stephen and the Hellenists*. London: Longmans & Green, 1958.

Skarsaune, O. *The Proof from Prophecy: A Study in Justin Martyr's Proof-Text Tradition*. NovTSup 56. Leiden: Brill, 1987.

Stinespring, W. F. "Temple, Jerusalem." *IDB* 4.534-60.

Stötzel, A. "Die Darstellung der ältesten Kirchengeschichte nach den Pseudoklementinen." *VigChr* 36 (1982) 24-37.

Strecker, G. *Das Judenchristentum in den Pseudoklementinen*. TU 70,2. Berlin: Akadamie, 1981.

--------. "On the Problem of Jewish Christianity." W. Bauer, *Orthodoxy and Heresy in Earliest Christianity*. R. A. Kraft and G. Krodel, eds. Philadelphia: Fortress, 1971, 241-85.

Teeple, H. *The Mosaic Eschatological Prophet*. SBLMS 10. Philadelphia: Society of Biblical Literature, 1957.

Thomas, J. *Le Mouvement baptiste en Palestine et Syrie*. Universitas Catholica Lovaniensis Dissertationes, Series 2, 28. Gemboux: Duculot, 1935.

Uhlhorn, G. *Die Homilien und Recognitionen des Clemens Romanus nach ihrem Ursprung und Inhalt dargestellt*. Göttingen: Dieterich, 1854.

Venradius, L. G. *D. Clementis opera omnia orgumentis et pereruditis partim J. Sichardi, partim Lamberti Groteri recens illustrata*. Cologne: Friess, 1563.

--------. *Clementina h.e. Clementis Opera cum nova praefatione de veris falsisque Clementis Scriptis*. Cologne: Friess, 1570.

Waitz, H. *Die Pseudoklementinen Homilien und Rekognitionen: Eine quellenkritische Untersuchung*. Leipzig: Hinrichs, 1904.

Wehnert, J. "Literarkritik und Sprachanalyse: Kritische Anmerkung-
    en zum gegenwärtigen Stand der Pseudoklementinen-
    Forschung." *ZNW* 74 (1983) 268-301.

Williams, F. *The Panarion of Epiphanius of Salamis, Book One.* NHS
    35. Leiden: Brill, 1987.

INDEX OF PASSAGES

This index covers all the chapters of this book except the third, where all passages of the *AJ* can be found *ad loc*. The addition of "n" to the page number indicates that the reference is to a footnote.

I. The Pseudo-Clementines

Recognitions

1.1-3	30
1.3.1	138
1.4-5	30
1.6	31
1.7	31
1.7.14-15	138
1.7-10	31
1.11-13	31
1.11-26	39
1.14-16	31
1.14.1-2	32
1.15-16	32
1.16-18	32, 39
1.16.2	32, 81
1.16.4	126
1.17-19	31
1.17.3	117
1.19	165n
1.21	39
1.21-71	16
1.21.7	31, 32, 81
1.22	31
1.22-74	13
1.25.2	138
1.25.5-7	32
1.26	104
1.27-34	77n
1.27-41	16
1.27-42	15, 25
1.27-43	11, 25

1.27-71	12, 16, 17, 19, 25, 26, 41
1.27-72	9, 10, 11, 12, 16, 17, 25
1.27-74	12, 18, 19, 25
1.27.1	31
1.29-32	32n
1.30	32, 41
1.30.3	31
1.30.4	31
1.30.5	31
1.31.1	31
1.31.2	31
1.32	31
1.32.1	33
1.32.1,4	31
1.32.3	41
1.32n	33
1.33	31, 32, 110
1.33-44	32, 77, 79, 115, 120, 145, 163, 165, 170
1.33-44.2	25
1.33-45	42
1.33-65	23, 42, 43, 153
1.33-71	1, 3, 20, 21, 22, 23, 24, 26, 29, 30,40, 43, 44, 45, 46, 177
1.33.1	32, 41
1.33.1-2	32, 33
1.33.2	33
1.33.3	32, 33, 34, 37, 41, 81, 82n
1.33.3-4	82

Recognitions (cont'd.)

1.33.5	7, 83
1.34.1	81, 83, 84
1.34.2	41, 84, 85, 104, 116
1.34.3	85, 116
1.34.4	31, 85, 97, 115
1.34.4-7	116
1.34.5	85
1.34.6	86
1.34.7	85
1.35	33, 120, 174
1.35.1	85, 86, 97, 98, 117
1.35.1,6	31
1.35.2	86, 87, 116, 174
1.35.2,5-6	31
1.35.3	87
1.35.3-4	89
1.35.3-6	167
1.35.4	88
1.35.5	89, 116, 117
1.35.6	89, 97
1.36	33, 102, 120, 139
1.36-37	39
1.36-39	116
1.36-71	9, 10, 25
1.36.1	31, 40, 89, 90, 91, 99, 117
1.36.1-2	116, 163
1.36.2	86, 90, 91-93, 135
1.37	31, 33, 78, 99, 102, 143
1.37.1	92, 96, 99, 118
1.37.2	93, 94, 100, 101, 102, 104, 118
1.37.2-3	31
1.37.2-5	97
1.37.3	95, 98, 118
1.37.3-4	31, 97
1.37.3-5	118
1.37.4	95, 96
1.37.5	96, 102, 177
1.38	33
1.38.1	31, 96
1.38.1-2	96
1.38.1-3	97
1.38.2	115
1.38.3	97, 116
1.38.4	31, 40, 116
1.38.4-5	97
1.38.5	97, 102
1.39	33, 78, 79, 94, 104, 118
1.39-41	39
1.39-42	116
1.39.1	98, 115
1.39.1-2	31, 139
1.39.2	39, 95, 98, 99, 100, 101, 103, 163
1.39.2-3	165
1.39.3	31, 98, 99, 100, 101, 102, 116
1.40	34, 118
1.40.1	101, 116
1.40.2	102, 103, 138
1.40.3	40, 103, 107, 177
1.40.4	84, 98, 103, 106, 116, 122n, 163
1.41-42	34
1.41.1	104, 132
1.41.1-2	118
1.41.2	98, 105, 126
1.41.3	105, 106, 108
1.41.4	107, 140, 164
1.42	151
1.42-44	116
1.42-71	16
1.42.1	38, 40, 108, 139, 172
1.42.1-2	113, 139
1.42.3	109, 111
1.42.4	40, 42, 105, 111, 115, 118, 134, 138
1.43	16, 113
1.43-44	152
1.43-44.3	34
1.43-53	16

1.43.1	34, 40, 98, 112, 116, 117
	118, 119 ,122, 164
1.43.1-3	122
1.43.2	34, 35, 40, 115, 144, 175
1.43.3	113, 116, 120,
	145, 160, 172
1.44	161
1.44-52	16
1.44-54	9, 14
1.44-71	10, 11, 25
1.44.1	40, 113, 114, 116, 176
1.44.1-3	118
1.44.2	36, 40, 114, 117, 120,
	123, 149, 179
1.44.2-3	118
1.44.3	23, 31, 34, 35, 38, 122, 151
1.44.4	31, 34
1.44.4-1.52	35, 36
1.44.5-6	35
1.44.6	35
1.45.2	35
1.45.3	35
1.45.3-4	40
1.45.4	112n
1.45.5	35
1.46	35
1.46.2-4	40
1.46.4	40
1.48.5	36
1.50.1,6	40
1.50.5	34, 39n, 40
1.50.7	35
1.52	34
1.52.1,6	35
1.53	31, 41
1.53-71	16
1.53.1	40
1.53.3	35, 36
1.53.4	36, 118
1.53.5	40
1.54	31, 36, 38
1.54-65	14, 15
1.54-71	14, 15, 17, 25, 26
1.54-71	77n
1.54.1	41
1.54.2	36
1.54.3	36
1.54.4	36, 41
1.54.5	41
1.54.6-7	37
1.54.7	36
1.54.9	36
1.55	38, 40, 123, 144
1.55-60	38
1.55-65	23, 34, 35, 37, 38, 39, 41,
	42, 46, 77, 95, 113, 115,
	118, 121, 144, 145, 152,
	158, 160, 170, 171
1.55-71	43, 46, 79, 163, 172
1.55.1	34, 36, 113, 122
1.55.1-2	119
1.55.2	45, 119, 120,
	121, 126, 140
1.55.3	120, 124
1.55.3-4	39, 139, 165
1.55.4	41, 120, 123,
	124, 141, 176
1.56	37, 144
1.56-59	39
1.56.1	124, 125, 140
1.56.2	126
1.56.2-3	98, 124, 126
1.56.3	124, 126
1.57	37, 38, 39, 144
1.57.1	98, 124, 126, 160
1.57.1-4	128
1.57.2	127
1.57.3	128
1.57.4	37, 40, 98, 126
1.57.5	124, 128
1.57.6	37

Recognitions (cont'd.)

1.58.1	40, 42, 128, 132, 134, 138
1.58.2	129
1.58.2-3	124, 129
1.58.3	124, 129, 164
1.59	37, 40, 132, 134, 144
1.59.1	124, 129
1.59.1-3	130
1.59.2-3	124, 129
1.59.3	124
1.59.3-5	40
1.59.3-6	42
1.59.4	130
1.59.4-6	42, 124
1.59.5	130
1.59.6	124, 130
1.59.7	124, 130, 131
1.60	37, 38, 144
1.60.1	121, 131, 132, 136
1.60.1-4	37, 40, 41
1.60.3	132, 133, 164
1.60.3-4	124
1.60.4	124, 133, 176
1.60.5	122
1.60.5-6	134
1.60.5-7	124, 134
1.60.7	112, 124, 145, 164
1.61	136, 144
1.61-62	37
1.61.1	124
1.61.1-2	124, 135
1.61.3	42, 124, 125, 136
1.62	136, 177
1.62.1	124, 136, 154
1.62.1-2	124
1.62.2	137
1.62.2-3	147n
1.62.2-8	22
1.62.3	137, 176
1.62.3-4	41
1.62.3-7	124

1.62.4	138
1.62.5-7	138
1.62.6	138
1.62.7	124
1.63	38, 39, 41
1.63.1	37
1.63.2-3	38
1.63.3	38
1.64	38, 39, 144
1.64.1	126, 139
1.64.1-2	39
1.64.2	40, 110, 139, 172
1.64.3	140
1.64.4	140
1.64.4-1.67	39
1.65	38, 39, 42, 144, 147, 153
1.65.1	140
1.65.2	126, 141, 142
1.65.2-5	41
1.65.3-4	143
1.66	44
1.66-70	115
1.66-71	13, 15, 16, 19, 20, 25, 34, 41, 42, 77, 146, 165
1.66-72	26
1.66.1	40, 145, 157, 161
1.66.1-3	39, 160
1.66.2	45, 146, 161
1.66.3	41, 45, 46, 146
1.66.4	140, 142, 146
1.66.4-7	42
1.66.5	147
1.67	42, 148, 160
1.67.1	147
1.67.2	148, 149, 153
1.67.3	155
1.67.5	149
1.67.6	149
1.67.7	149
1.68	39, 160
1.68.1	153

1.68.1-2	123, 150	2.34.5	126
1.68.2	34, 40, 41, 42,	2.52.3	89
	157, 161, 172	2.71	165n
1.68.3	41	2.72	40
1.68.3-4	151	2.8	40
1.68.4	177	2.8-11	36
1.68.8	40	2.8	37n
1.69	18, 38, 43, 145, 160	3.26.7	126
1.69.1	41, 151, 152	3.27.3	32n
1.69.2	151	3.63	40
1.69.3	39, 41, 152	3.68.1	82
1.69.4	43, 152	3.75	12, 14, 17, 18
1.69.5-7	38, 152	3.76	40n
1.69.8	41, 100, 153, 165	4.19-20, 27-30	32
1.70	38, 114, 119, 140, 141,	4.27.2	82
	154, 160, 170	4.29	32, 39
1.70-71	45, 177	4.35.5	37
1.70.1	40, 100	4.9.2	32n
1.70.1-2	153	5.20.2-3	89
1.70.2	40, 42, 134	6.1	165n
1.70.3	154, 161	6.11.2	36
1.70.4	154	6.15	39n, 40
1.70.5	155	6.15.2-3	37
1.70.6	155	7.34	39n, 40
1.70.7-8	156	7.35.2-3	37
1.70.8	45, 46, 154	8.59.7	32n
1.71	39, 160	9.3.2	82
1.71.1	157		
1.71.2	142, 157, 161		
1.71.3	160		
1.71.3-4	158	*Homilies*	
1.71.4	79	1.1-20	31
1.71.5-6	159, 176	1.19.4-6	126
1.72-72	12	2.24	36
1.72.7	41, 117	2.42-3.20	16n
1.73.4	100, 154	2.5.3	126
1.74.5	31	2.38.1	103
1.75.2-5	127	3.45-46	90
2	40	3.46	40
2-10	40	3.47.1	104
2.1.2	82	3.53.3	90

Homilies (cont'd.)

8.2	165n
8.10-19	32
8.10.3	32n
9.3	32
9.3-7	32
9.23	165n
10.1	165n
10.16.2	89
11.1	165n
17.13-19	22,25
18.4.3	84
20.2.2-3	114

Epistula Petri

2.1	105, 154
2.3	154

II. BIBLICAL LITERATURE
Genesis

15:2-3	82n
15:2-4	81
15:5	108
15:13	85
15:13-16	85
16:11-15	82
17:15-21	84
17:23-27	83
18:1-15	84
21:1	84
46:26-27	84

Exodus

1:5	84
4:1-9, 17	102
12:42	91n
14:1-29	85
19-20	86
19:16-19	86
20:1-6	86
20:2	87

20:2-6	87
20:3-6	87
27:3	155n
38:3	155n

Numbers

4:4	153n
6:6	159
11	87
11:16	103n
12:7	89
19:16	159
21:17	88

Deuteronomy

4:11	86
5	86
5:22	86
12:5-14	92
17:14-20	97
18:15	90, 91, 105, 126,129, 135
31:7, 23	96
34:6	96
34:10	130

Joshua

13:1	97
14:1-2	97

I Kings

7:40, 45	155n

II Chronicles

4:11, 16	155n
7:12	93

Psalms

105	115
106	115
106:41-43	95

Isaiah
56:7   98

Daniel
9:27   139

Hosea
6:6   93, 98

Malachi
1:10-12   140

Matthew
3:11   133
4:23   105
5:3-6   135
5:38-42   134
9:13   93, 95
9:14   131
10:2   102
10:3   122
10:5   128
11:18-19   102
11:9, 11   132
12:7   93, 95
21:12-13   167n
21:13   98
22:23   125
22:23-33   126
23:27-28   159
24:15   139
24:15   139
2414-22   100n
26:3, 57   114
27:45   106, 108, 109
28:11-15   109
28:13   109
28:16-20   123
28:20   182

Mark
1:7   133
3:16-19   121
3:18   122
3:30   102
5:26   140
6:30   102
11:15-17   167n
11:17   98
12:18   125
12:18-27   126
13:14-20   100n
14:53   114, 141n
15:33   108, 109
15:38   106
17:31   106

Luke
3:2   114
3:15   132
3:16   133
5:5   135
5:7   137
6:13   103
6:14-16   121
6:20-21   135
6:29-30   157
7:18   131
7:23-31   134
10:1,17   103
11:44   159
12:42   89
19:45-46   167n
19:46   98
20:27   125
20:27-40   126
21:20-24   100
23:18   122
23:44-45   106, 108, 109
23:45   106
24:53   167n

John

1:8-9	132
1:15	145
1:20	132
1:35	131
2:13-22	167
3:25	131
3:38	132
4:19-24	167
4:48	104
7:7	131
7:20	102
7:47	137
10:20	102
11:49	114
12:34	112
15:18, 23-25	131
18:13-14, 24	114
18:40	112

Acts

1:23-26	122
2:19, 22	104
2:38	99
2:46	167n
3:1	167n
3:22	90, 91
4:4	157
4:6	114
4:13	137
4:30	104
4:32	199, 141
4:36	122
5:2	167n
5:12	104
5:14	119, 141
5:35-39	143
6:2, 5	119, 141
6:8	105
7	32, 168-169, 155-117
7:6	85, 116

7:8	85, 116
7:14	84
7:17	85, 116
7:20	44, 117
7:36	105, 116
7:37	91, 116
7:38	86, 116
7:41	116
7:41-42	117
7:44	116
7:45	97, 116
7:47	97, 116
7:52	116
7:53	86
7:54	142
8:16	99
9	43
9:12	158
11:26	111
13:17-31	115
14:3	105
15:12	105
19:1-7	133
19:5	99
21:17-26	171
22:3	141
23:3	159
23:8	125
24:1	141n

Romans

6:3	99
9-11	171
9:6-33	171
10:1-4	171
11:3-10	171
11:25-26	171
16:18	103

I Corinthians

1:13-15	99
10:4	88

Galatians

3:27-	99

I Timothy

1:7	137

Hebrews

3:1-6	130
3:3,5	89
7:7	130
10:19,20	106
11	115

Revelation

11:3-13	91
12:3-6, 13-16	100n

III. Other Early Christian Literature

Apostolic Constitutions

5.20	92
6.20	89

Barnabas

3:6	168
4:6-8	168
7:3	168
9:4-9	168
13:14	168
16	168

Clement of Alexandria,
Pedagogue

1.7	92

I Clement

32.1-2	
42, 44.1-2	172n

Didache

7:1	99

Diognetus

3:5	169
4:1-6	169

Epiphanius, *Panarion*

9.2	127
14.2	127
29.7.2	127
29.7.5, 8-9	112n
30	42,79, 177
30.16.1	165n
30.16.6-9	44-46
33.3-7	174

Eusebius, *Historia Ecclesiae*

2.22.1	172
3.53	100
4.6.3	100

Gospel of Peter

5.20	106
6.21	106
8.28-30	107

Ignatius
Ephesians

7:2	140

Philadelphians

8:2	178

Magnesians

8-9	177
8:1	177
10:3	177

Irenaeus, *Against Heresies*
1.26.2	177, 178, 179n
3.3.2-4	172
3.15.11	177
4.8-16	174, 175n
4.26.1	90
5.1.3	171

Justin
Apology
1.61	99

Dialogue
19.6	90
22.1,11	90
28.5-6	140
47.1	177
69	104, 110
113.1	96

Lactantius, *Divine Constitutions*
4.10	89
4.17	92n

Origen, *Against Celsus*
1.28,32,69	110
2.67	140

Tertullian, *Against Marcion*
4.22	92n

IV. Jewish Literature
Talmud and Related Writings
m. Abot
4:11	143

m. Mid.
3:36	129

b. Sanh.
43a	110, 123n
90b	127
106a	110n
107	110

b. Sota
47a	110

t. Sukkah
3:11	88

Mid. Deut. Rab.
3	91

Abot R. Natan
A4	93

Philo
On the Decalogue
5	86
9	86n
12	87

Life of Moses
1.29	86
2.6	86

Migration of Abraham
36	84

Who is the Heir?
1-2, 61-62, 39-40	82

Josephus
Antiquites of the Jews
3.5.5	86, 87
3.9.1-4	167
13.5.9	125
18.1.4	125
18.2.2	127n, 146
18.4.3	114
20.9.1	136

Jewish War
2.18.14	125

Sibylline Oracles, Book IV
27-30	169
162-5	169